「惠」游祠堂

瞿立新　张一
邵映红
张立英 ◎ 著

中国纺织出版社有限公司

内 容 提 要

本书系统梳理惠山祠堂群的历史脉络，深入挖掘其文化内涵，分为"邀你进'群'""惠风祠话""诗画梁溪"三篇，中英文对照，并配有视频、音频，旨在让每一位读者都能在这片古老而又充满生机的土地上找到心灵的共鸣，收获关于历史、文化、艺术的深刻感悟。希望本书能够成为读者游览惠山古镇的良伴，给读者带来别样的文化体验。

图书在版编目（CIP）数据

"惠"游祠堂 / 瞿立新等著. --北京：中国纺织出版社有限公司，2025.7. -- ISBN 978-7-5229-2672-8

I . K928.75

中国国家版本馆CIP数据核字第20255VB377号

责任编辑：沈　靖　　责任校对：高　涵　　责任印制：王艳丽

中国纺织出版社有限公司出版发行
地址：北京市朝阳区百子湾东里 A407 号楼　邮政编码：100124
销售电话：010—67004422　传真：010—87155801
http://www.c-textilep.com
中国纺织出版社天猫旗舰店
官方微博 http://weibo.com/2119887771
北京华联印刷有限公司印刷　各地新华书店经销
2025 年 7 月第 1 版第 1 次印刷
开本：710×1000　1/16　印张：22.75
字数：282 千字　定价：128.00 元　插页：3

凡购本书，如有缺页、倒页、脱页，由本社图书营销中心调换

编委会

主 任：瞿立新

副主任：张 一　邵映红　张立英

顾 问：俞铁军　金石声

编 委：夏 莹　赵 建　肖 慧　陈翊霖

导言

"江南好,真个到无锡!"无锡,太湖明珠、江南盛地。马家浜文化墓葬的考古探源印证了这里有着约7000年的人类生活史;公元前11世纪,泰伯为让王位于三弟季历,偕二弟仲雍,东奔江南,定居梅里,筑城立国,自号"勾吴",这是关于无锡的历史上最早的文字记载,距今已有3100多年;自汉高祖五年(公元前202年)始置无锡县,也已过去2200余年。万里奔腾的长江、千里穿行的大运河、孕育吴越的太湖赋予无锡灵动的气质、开放包容的胸襟;长江文化、大运河文化、江南文化、吴文化、工商文化,这些丰厚的文化积淀赋予无锡厚积薄发的文化张力。李绅的《悯农》传唱千年,钱钟书的《围城》家喻户晓,阿炳的《二泉映月》闻名中外……江南文脉在此生生不息。

惠山,"江南第一山,天下第二泉"。惠山寺,梵音悠远;寄畅园,山色溪光。这里风景佳绝、人文荟萃,被誉为集中展示江南吴地文化的"露天历史博物馆"。陆羽在此品茶,苏轼在此题诗,文徵明在此作画……乾隆皇帝御笔亲题"惟惠山幽雅闲静"。

祠堂是中国人纪念祖先或先贤的场所。祠堂文化是中华宗族文化、纲常文化的集中体现，是中华优秀传统文化的重要组成部分。国家5A级旅游景区——惠山古镇，因祠堂而成，因祠堂而兴，在这片0.3平方千米的土地上，鼎盛时期汇聚了从唐代至民国时期的100余座祠堂，串起千年吴地历史，织就了一幅"家国天下"的壮丽画卷。惠山祠堂群凝聚了无锡人千百年来难以忘怀的乡愁和共同记忆，蕴含着无锡尊贤尚德、崇文重教、忠孝节义、务实创新、开放包容的人文精神。

走进惠山古镇的祠堂群，就像翻开了一部厚重的历史书卷，每一座祠堂都承载着一段独特的历史，每一块石碑都镌刻着一段动人的故事。这些祠堂不仅见证了家族的兴衰更替，更映射出社会的变迁与发展，既是家族荣誉的象征，更是维系宗族情感、传承家国情怀的重要纽带。

本书名为《"惠"游祠堂》，"惠"为"惠山"之"惠"，点明祠堂所处地理位置，同时"惠"与"会"谐音，希望本书能够引领读者穿越时空的隧道，步入这一片充满历史韵味与文化底蕴的胜地，深入了解每一座祠堂背后所承载的家国故事与人物传奇，领略惠山的人文之美，真正"会"游祠堂。

本书系统梳理惠山祠堂群的历史脉络，深入挖掘其文化内涵，分为"邀你进'群'""惠风祠话""诗画梁溪"三篇，中英文对照，并配有视频、音频，还配备了不同时期的三张祠堂分布图，其中最新的一张由本书作者实地探访后绘制而成，是祠堂修复以来最新最全的版本，旨在让每一位读者，无论是远道而来的游客，还是土生土长的市民，都能在这片古老而又富有活力的土地上，找到心灵的共鸣，收获一份关于历史、文化、艺术的深刻感悟。

本书系2023年全国文化艺术职业教育和旅游职业教育提质培优行动计划——学生实践引领计划"精准对接 精进技艺 精益服务——中国特色学徒制下无锡文旅人才培养实践"（项目编号1107001016）成果，由无锡城市职业技术学院与无锡市文化旅游发展集团有限公司校企共建的"文旅特色学徒班"师生共创，参与学生：施雨洁、胡雅玲、章猛、翟芝艺、高洁、李红桃、刘成成、张栓豪、宫艳、谭一楠、张峻豪、梅婷、蔡文婷、王高意、陈振华、陈鸣谦、黄婉婷、杭至妍、袁惠怡、李峻丰等；企业导师：俞铁军、金石声、肖慧、董强、吴娜德、俞争燕、黄景波、董佳琳等；学校教师：瞿立新、夏莹、刘芳、张一、邵映红、张立英、赵建、陈翊霖、贾玎、郭瑞、崔建周、王瑾璟、顾秀玲、沈倩、陈坤芳、邵林涛、潘霞洁、任晨、曹长波、汪徐真意、林武、郑伟、张岩岩、章丹芸、孙春艳、丛哲、沈言蓓、鲍艳利、杨嗣玲、陈皖、陆久龄、陈兰荣、王绪辉、吴培培、樊悦任。本书亦为2024年江苏省高校"高质量公共课教学改革研究"专项课题"高校美育课程与专业课程互动性研究——以旅游类专业为例"（课题编号：2024GZJX017）成果。

本书由当代著名教育家顾明远先生题写书名。顾明远先生是新中国第一代建设者，是伴随着新中国成长起来的第一代教育家，见证了中国教育的发展，又亲历了多次重大教育讨论和变革。顾明远先生的题词不仅体现了他一如既往对家乡教育的关心，更承载着他的浓浓游子意、依依故乡情。

本书在创作过程中参考了诸多文史资料，在此不逐一列出，谨向有关部门和相关作者表示感谢！书中难免存在不足和疏漏之处，恳请广大读者批评指正。

作者

2025年7月

目录

第一篇　邀你进"群"

惠山祠堂群是如何形成的	2
为什么会在惠山出现祠堂群	8
惠山祠堂群里到底有多少祠堂	14
祠堂里有哪些建筑,又有哪些功能	21
惠山祠堂群有多少种祠堂	29
家谱里都写了什么	44
祠堂中的涓涓细流是什么水	49
祠堂里可不可以有花园	53
为什么泥人艺术家出自祠堂	57
"马头墙"在无锡叫什么	62

第二篇　惠风祠话

无锡的皇亲国戚	68
祠堂群里的"海龙王"	73
祠堂群里的抗金英雄	80
三让天下的圣人	86
古人有多孝	94

与陆游齐名的无锡诗人	101
祠堂群里的茶圣是谁	106
无锡最大的清代祠堂建筑	110
"事事关心"的人	116
明代的"千金不受先生"	122
邵宝最珍贵的墨宝	130
祠堂群里的驱虫专家	134
被"送来送去"的惠山寺	136
祠堂群里最美的祠堂	141
冒死反对"花石纲"的斗士	150
哪个家族是无锡民族工商业的先行者	156
把日子过成"朝如青丝暮成雪"的地方	162
"晚到"的祠堂	166
著名画家是位美食博主	170
内相经纶,清风传家	177
祠堂群里最迷你的戏台	183
祠堂群里规格最高的祠堂	192
肚里能撑船的太平良相	196
一位年轻的县官,为何在无锡有三座祠堂	203
祠堂中的忠靖之士	210
出现在《滕王阁序》里面的高士	218
粉身碎骨浑不怕,要留清白在人间	223

祠堂群里最古老的祠堂	227
古代的"慈善机构"	232
祠堂群里的"医国圣手"	238
名泉酿名酒	249
"心与理一"的清正之士	255
从王武愍公祠看祠堂布局	260
宰相祠里大器晚成的宰相	269
祠堂群里最"潮"的祠堂	275
让乾隆皇帝青睐有加的祠堂	279
祠中古树寄情怀	285
谁创办了无锡第一所中学	295
保留下来的三大影壁	303
亭子为什么没有顶	307
回响在祠堂群里的世界名曲	311

第三篇　诗画梁溪

无锡篇	320
惠山篇	328
祠堂篇	339

第一篇 邀你进『群』

邀请您走进惠山祠堂群,从整体上了解惠山祠堂群的分布、成因、数量、种类,祠堂的建筑风格、主要功能以及与祠堂相伴而产生的文化现象等,为您解开祠堂群的秘密。请跟随我们的步伐,一同感受惠山祠堂群的历史底蕴与文化魅力吧!

惠山祠堂群是如何形成的

惠山在无锡人的心中是一处特别的存在。"爬惠山，爬锡山，爬到屁股粉粉碎"在坊间广为传唱，是很多无锡人自幼谙熟的"黑暗童谣"，年轻人选择夜爬惠山，中老年人享受晨练进公园，这里有无锡人放松身心、亲近自然的山野林泉，也有中外游客慕名而来、流连忘归的名胜古迹。这里充满了浓厚的市井生活气息，商铺林立，街巷繁华；这里更被誉为集中展示江南吴地文化的"露天历史博物馆"，文脉绵长，积淀深厚。惠山古镇的人文景观中最具特色的莫过于"惠山祠堂群"文化景观，大量江南民居式祠堂成组成群的独特风景，是无锡极为珍贵的文化遗存。

历经1200多年陆续修建的100余座祠堂及遗址密布在古镇沿河、临街、近泉、靠山之处，这里的祠堂不仅数量多、密度大，而且类型的多样性、设计的独特性、历史的悠久性、内涵

的丰富性都相当出色，是研究中国传统宗族文化的绝佳样本。

那么，惠山的祠堂群是如何形成的呢？

据历代邑志等地方文献记载，祠堂群形成经历了上千年，在惠山0.3平方千米范围内，祠堂呈现着动态的发展过程。总体上，萌芽于唐，发展于明，盛于清中期，延续到民国。

在明代之前惠山的祠堂并不多，且为官设公祠，据无锡现存最早的一部元代《无锡志》记载，元末惠山仅2座祠堂，是春申君祠和三贤祠。明早期，惠山祠堂仍为个位数，以贤孝祠为主，这是因为当时建造祠堂是皇室贵族的特权，民间严禁私自建祠。历史的转机出现在明中期，嘉靖帝允许民间"联宗建祠"，各地兴起建祠的热潮，无锡的大姓望族遂纷纷在惠山择地建祠，惠山祠堂群的基本架构即形成于这一时期。

清代是惠山祠堂建筑的鼎盛时期，乾隆、嘉庆年间，惠山

视频 惠山古镇概览

祠堂数量成倍增加，咸丰七年（1857年）达到79座。此后，惠山祠堂群曾在太平天国军队占领无锡期间遭到损毁，但因着无锡人对祠堂的崇敬和执着，战后迅速得到重建，据光绪七年（1881年）的《无锡金匮县志》记载，惠山祠堂群已恢复到战前的79座左右，并出现了一批纪念这场战争中死难者的祠堂。

民国时期，封建传统虽然受到革命冲击，但祠堂数量仍在增加，民国十九年（1930年）《新无锡》报道了惠山祠堂群调研结果，记载有祠庙118座、平楼房屋935间。从记载还可以看出，惠山祠堂群数量日益增多的同时，惠山祠堂在全无锡祠堂的占比也在不断增加，清嘉庆时期更是高达72%，也就是说无锡大多数祠堂都建在惠山。

The Formation of the Huishan Ancestral Hall Cluster

In the hearts of Wuxi residents, Huishan holds a special place. A popular local rhyme, "Climb Huishan, climb Xishan, climb until you're completely exhausted" is familiar to many Wuxi natives from childhood. Young people often choose to hike up Huishan at night, while middle-aged and elderly residents enjoy morning exercise in its parks. For Wuxi locals, this mountain offers a retreat into nature, a place to relax and unwind. It also attracts visitors from near and far, who are drawn to its historic sites and often find themselves reluctant to leave. The lively atmosphere of everyday life is palpable, with bustling streets lined with shops, and Huishan has even been called an "open-air museum" showcasing the rich and deep cultural heritage of the Jiangnan region. Among the many cultural landscapes in Huishan Ancient Town, the "Huishan Ancestral Hall Cluster" stands out as a unique feature. This cluster of ancestral halls, built in the traditional Jiangnan residential style, is a precious cultural relic of Wuxi.

Over 100 ancestral halls and sites, constructed over the span of 1,200 years, are scattered throughout the ancient town, along rivers, streets, springs, and hills. What makes this collection remarkable is not just the sheer number and density of halls but also the diversity of their types, the uniqueness of their designs, the length of their histories, and the richness of their cultural significance. This makes the Huishan Ancestral Hall Cluster an excellent case study for research on traditional Chinese clan culture.

So, how did the Huishan Ancestral Hall Cluster come to be?

According to local historical documents and county annals, the formation of the Ancestral Hall Cluster was a process spanning over a millennium. Within Huishan's 0.3 square kilometer area, the development of these halls evolved dynamically. The cluster began to take shape in the Tang Dynasty, expanded in the Ming Dynasty, flourished in the mid-Qing period, and continued into the Republican era.

Before the Ming Dynasty, there were relatively few ancestral halls in Huishan, and most of them were official halls. According to the earliest extant local record, *The Wuxi Gazetteer* from the Yuan Dynasty, there were only two ancestral halls in Huishan at the end of the Yuan period: the Chun Shen Jun Hall and the Hall of the Three Sages. In the early Ming period, there were still only a handful of Huishan shrines, mostly consisting of filial piety halls. This was because, at the time, only the royal family and nobility were permitted to build ancestral halls, and commoners were strictly forbidden from doing so. The turning point came in the mid-Ming period when Emperor Jiajing allowed commoners to build clan halls. This policy sparked a wave of hall-building across the country. In Wuxi, prominent families began selecting sites in Huishan to construct their own ancestral halls, and by this time, the basic framework of the

Huishan Ancestral Hall Cluster was established.

The Qing Dynasty marked the peak of ancestral hall construction in Huishan. During the reigns of Emperors Qianlong and Jiaqing, the number of halls in Huishan doubled, reaching 79 by the seventh year of the Xianfeng period. The cluster suffered damage during the Taiping Rebellion when Wuxi was occupied, but due to the deep reverence and dedication of the Wuxi people, the ancestral halls were quickly rebuilt after the war. By the seventh year of Emperor Guangxu's reign, *The Jin Kui County Gazetteer of Wuxi* recorded that the Cluster had been restored to its pre-war size of around 79 halls, and a number of new halls were built to honor those who had perished in the war.

Despite the challenges to feudal traditions during the Republican period, the number of ancestral halls in Huishan continued to grow. A survey conducted in the 19th year of the Republic of China, published in the *New Wuxi*, reported that the Huishan Ancestral Hall Cluster had 118 halls and 935 individual buildings. This survey also showed that, as the number of ancestral halls in Huishan increased, so did their proportion relative to the total number in Wuxi, peaking at 72% during the Jiaqing period of the Qing Dynasty. This means that the majority of Wuxi's ancestral halls were concentrated in Huishan.

为什么会在惠山出现祠堂群

关于惠山祠堂群的成因，可谓是众说纷纭，学者们结合历史传承和民间传说，提出了空间说、风俗说、时世说、衍生说、榜样说等诸多学说。具体到某家祠堂的设立原因，更是一家有一家的理由。

人们有理由相信，无锡的世家望族争相在惠山建祠，是有着多重考量的。在文化、经济、社会等多重因素的作用下，加上惠山的自然山水、林泉胜迹优势，使得无锡的祠堂呈现向惠山集中发展的趋势，并最终在0.3平方千米的范围内，集中分布着100余座各类祠堂，形成了祠堂群落。

明清两朝，无锡所处的江南核心区，被誉为"人文渊薮地，富贵鱼米乡"。这一时期，江南农耕文明臻于完善，经济富裕，文化兴盛，宗族制度走向成熟，宗族组织日益强化，世家望族更是高度重视诗礼传家，再加上嘉靖年间朝廷对于民间建祠的态度转变，使得民间建祠热情高涨，祠堂发展所需的精神和物质条件一应俱全，其结果就是整个明清时期江南祠堂数量快速增长。

中国人常说"祖宗十八代"，这从一个侧面反映出中国宗族文化的悠久与昌盛。宗族文化绵延千年，而祠堂呈现了宗族文化极为具象的一面，在过去，祠堂承载着家族文化、宗族情感和祖先记忆，对于家族传承具有重要意义。

祠堂群所在的无锡城外西郊，位于锡、惠二山之间，依

山面水,自古就是佛、道、儒诸教立足的圣地,至德先贤泰伯、春申君黄歇这些无锡百姓最为尊敬的先贤祠堂均建于此,能在这里安置祖先,彰显了家族的社会地位,意味着家族兴旺,对于无锡人是一份荣耀。尤其难得的是,历史上的惠山在祠堂群建造期正好因各种变故出现了大片空地,再加上过去的惠山古镇与无锡城紧邻,交通便利,有水、陆两条路线通向无锡城。陆路是五里街,连接惠山与无锡西门;水路由寺塘泾出发,向东连接黄埠墩。过去的无锡人去惠山祭祖,举族出行不说,还要携带大量的祭祀用具,甚至会带门窗家具,大多数人家会选择运载能力更强的船只。在诸多有利因素的加持下,山环水绕、交通便利的惠山渐渐成为无锡官方和民间建祠的首选之地。

惠山祠堂群是密集的城市型祠堂建筑群落，宅祠分离，祠堂的主人平时生活在城里，在举行祭祀活动时才去祠堂。而其他地区的祠堂多建在家族聚居的村中，宅祠一体，拥有祠堂的家族就在村中世代聚居，这也是农耕文化时期的典型生活形态。

清晚期江南农村水稻、棉花、蚕桑三大主要作物形成种植分区，专业市镇兴起，商品经济快速发展，无锡出现了著名的米码头、布码头、丝码头和钱码头，原本乡居的人们的生活形态发生变化，基于经济利益，生活重心由乡村转向都市，开启了城里人生活。城居化的人们，把资源财富也转移到无锡城中，阖家共同居住在大宅院里，以围墙封闭起来，无锡民间称为"墙门人家"。墙门人家是共居、共财、共祭的大家庭。这种大家庭的规模，与家族财富的数量基本呈正相关，而当时的无锡可能居住着全国最富有的一些宗族，他们主导着无锡商业活动的上游，推动无锡成为近代工商文化最早萌芽的城市之一。

这些望族渐渐形成城市士绅群体，平时参与地方社会的治理，他们有文化修养，有经济实力，有社会地位，有精神追求，热衷于追溯远祖，修订族谱，并以在惠山古镇争一席之地建祠为荣。此类祠堂多是得到官方认可的公祠，建成之后也不局限于族人的祭祖，而是广泛接受普通百姓的瞻仰。从这层意义上来讲，惠山祠堂群的出现就是工商文化所催生的一种特殊文化现象。

所以，可以说无锡惠山古镇祠堂群是中国几千年的农耕经济或耕读文化，在向近代工商经济或工业文明发展过渡的特殊条件下，形成的与城市化相适应的独特祠堂群落。

Why Did the Huishan Ancestral Hall Cluster Emerge?

The reasons behind the formation of the Huishan Ancestral Hall Cluster are varied and have sparked much scholarly debate. Researchers, drawing on historical records and local folklore, have put forth several theories, including spatial factors, local customs, historical context, offshoot theories, and exemplary influences. Each family had its unique reasons for establishing an ancestral hall.

There is strong reason to believe that the deep motivations attracting Wuxi's prominent families to build ancestral halls in Huishan were multifaceted. Cultural, economic, and social factors, combined with Huishan's natural landscape of scenic mountains and streams, created favorable conditions for ancestral halls to be concentrated in this area. Over time, more than 100 halls, spanning 0.3 square kilometers, were built, forming a distinctive cultural cluster.

During the Ming and Qing Dynasties, Wuxi, located in the core area of the Jiangnan region, was celebrated as a cultural and economic hub, often described as a "cradle of talent" and "land of abundance." In this period, the agrarian civilization of Jiangnan reached its zenith, with an affluent economy, a flourishing culture, and a well-established clan system. The family structure became increasingly solidified, with noble families placing great emphasis on education and cultural heritage. The imperial court's change in attitude toward private ancestral hall construction during the Jiajing Emperor's reign further fueled a wave of hall-building. As a result, all the necessary spiritual and material conditions were in place for the rapid growth of ancestral halls throughout Jiangnan during the Ming and Qing periods.

The Chinese saying "eighteen generations of ancestors" reflects the deep-rooted tradition of clan culture in China. This culture has thrived for millennia. Ancestral halls represent one of the most tangible manifestations of this culture. In the past, they carried the weight of family heritage, clan sentiment, and ancestral memory, playing a vital role in family continuity.

The area where the ancestral halls are located, between Xishan and Huishan, is embraced by mountains and bordered by water, making it a sacred place for Buddhism, Taoism, and Confucianism. The halls of Wuxi's most revered sages, such as Taibo and Huang Xie, were built here. Constructing an ancestral hall in such a prestigious location symbolized a family's social standing and guaranteed its prosperity, making it a source of pride for Wuxi's families. Furthermore, historical events during the hall-building period left large tracts of land available for construction. Huishan was also conveniently located near Wuxi's urban center, with easy access via both land and water routes. In the past, families would travel together to Huishan for ancestor worship, often transporting large amounts of ceremonial items by boat due to their capacity.All of these advantageous factors—its scenic surroundings, convenient transportation, and spiritual significance—gradually made Huishan the preferred site for both official and private ancestral halls in Wuxi.

The Huishan Ancestral Hall Cluster form a densely packed urban cluster, where the halls are separated from their owners' residences. Families lived in the city, only visiting their ancestral halls during sacrificial rituals. In contrast, ancestral halls in other regions were typically located within the family's village, with the halls and homes integrated. This reflected the traditional agrarian lifestyle, where families lived in the same village for generations.

By the late Qing Dynasty, Jiangnan's agricultural economy saw the emergence of specialized towns, and Wuxi experienced rapid commercial development, with its famous rice, cloth, silk, and money markets. The lifestyle of rural families began to change as their economic focus shifted from the countryside to the city. These city-dwelling families brought their wealth into Wuxi's urban areas, residing with their extended families in large, walled compounds, known locally as "walled family homes." These homes were large, enclosed communities where families lived, worked, and worshipped together. The size of such homes was often proportional to the family's wealth, and Wuxi may have been home to some of the wealthiest clans in China at the time, who dominated local commerce and helped Wuxi become one of the earliest cities where industrial and commercial culture emerged.

Over time, these prominent families formed a distinct class of urban gentry, participating in local governance, pursuing cultural refinement, and tracing their ancestral roots with pride. They eagerly revised their genealogies and sought to build ancestral halls in Huishan. These ancestral halls, officially recognized as public halls, were not only for the worship of clan members but also open to the general public. In this sense, the emergence of the Huishan Ancestral Hall Cluster can be seen as a cultural phenomenon spurred by the rise of commerce and industry.

Therefore, the Huishan Ancestral Hall Cluster can be viewed as a unique architectural and cultural entity, formed in the context of China's transition from an agrarian to an industrial society, and shaped by the urbanization process that accompanied the shift from a traditional agrarian economy to a modern industrial one.

惠山祠堂群里到底有多少祠堂

惠山到底有多少祠堂，这是很多人都非常好奇的。惠山祠堂的数量，有118说，有108说，还有120说。这祠堂可是真真切切的物质存在，怎么会忽多忽少？实际上到底是多少呢？

确实，要讲祠堂的数量，一定要明确时间节点。因为祠堂在不同的历史时期，有兴建，有改建，有拆毁，数字可不是不变的。

让我们拨开历史的迷雾，来看看惠山祠堂是怎样慢慢变多的。关于惠山的祠堂，有史料可查最早的是春申君祠，《汉书·地理志》提到"无锡，有历山（即惠山），春申君岁祠以牛"，可以推论，惠山最早的祠堂出现在西汉高祖五年（公元前202年）无锡建县甚至更早。现存惠山祠堂里最古老的是华孝子祠，建祠时间可以追溯到南齐建元三年（481年），《南齐书》里讲述了华宝故宅建祠的故事。此后千年的岁月里，惠山祠堂数量增长缓慢，元代《无锡志》（1341—1368年）记载惠山有祠堂2座，明万历二年（1574年）《无锡县志》记载仍为个位数，7座，其主要的原因在于官方的限制。

惠山祠堂数明显增多始于明代嘉靖皇帝允许民间联宗立庙，到清初，惠山祠堂达20余座，增长一倍有余。第二轮显著增长在清代，康熙皇帝六下江南，七次到惠山，乾隆皇帝六下江南，十二次到惠山，极大激发了民间建祠热情，光绪七年（1881年）《无锡金匮县志》记载惠山有祠堂79座，无锡大半

祠堂都集中在惠山了。此后，无锡民族工商业兴起，民间财富增长，建祠热情不减，1921年《惠山新志》列出祠堂94座，1930年《新无锡》报的惠山祠堂调查达118座，2004年有关调查也认为有118座祠堂，惠山古镇导览馆有一张绘制的惠山古镇祠堂群分布图，上面清清楚楚标注了这118座祠堂的名称和位置，这张图绘制规范，被广泛引用，故而118座成为最常见的版本，流传范围相当广。

新中国成立后，惠山祠堂群建筑再无新增。由于锡山公园（锡惠公园前身）的设立，有30余处祠堂由公园管理，园外的90余处以民宅的形式归地方或部队管理，并保存下来一批宝贵的祠堂平面图、租赁合约等史料。故而很多学者认为，惠山祠堂群在1949年之前祠堂数量肯定是大于120座的。

2000年前后，惠山泥人大师喻湘涟等曾实地勘察，走访古镇原住民，复原绘制了惠山古镇历史上第一张——标注1949年惠山祠堂的地图。对此图精确统计，有祠堂93座。以此为基础，金石声先生又逐片精确核对，补上漏登和未纳入走访区域的祠堂，认为漏登的祠堂至少有21座，加上图上93座，一共是114座，其中5座祠堂当时可能已毁佚，惠山古镇1949年时实际存在祠堂109座。这109座祠堂就是1949年的存量，且大多数在战乱中受损，保留完好的并不多。

此后，从1949—2001年，因道路扩建、绿化种树、景区建设等，祠堂有些被拆毁、改建或者局部拆除，有些则被改名、征用，改作店铺、公司、医院、银行等。实际上，到2001年还存在的祠堂仅49座，其中完好的仅少数几座。

从2001年开始，惠山祠堂进入恢复期，一些祠堂陆续修复。2017年10月的调查统计，惠山古镇实际存在祠堂为99座，规划重建的祠堂9座，共有祠堂108座。基于此，惠山古镇景区官网介绍写道："有自唐以来至民国的108个祠堂及园林"。这108座祠堂，具体分布在秦园街4座、惠山浜11座、上河塘10座、下河塘14座、下河塘—烧香浜7座、惠山直街北16座、惠山直街南20座、惠山寺—观泉街18座、听松坊8座。需要说明的是，惠山第一古祠春申君庙和花园祠堂寄畅园秦氏双孝祠均已湮灭，并未列入108祠中，鉴于其独特性，特收录在本书新版地图中。

据金石声先生研究，如果算上文献记载的祠堂，曾经出现在惠山这片时空的祠堂总量约达160座。大量的祠堂已经湮灭在历史长河中，还有一些祠堂几经改建，易主易名，以不同的名称出现在不同的文献中，比如历史上的三贤祠、七贤祠、十贤祠，都是指今天的尊贤祠；又比如列为市级文保单位的锡金山货公所旧址（惠山花神庙），其实就是今天的二泉园老菜馆，多年来从不曾列入各版本的祠堂名录；细心的游客还会发现有同名的祠堂。种种情况，愈发让我们难识祠堂真数量。

2008年的《中国文物地图集》中称惠山古镇有祠堂38座，这些祠堂原有建筑空间、生态环境基本完整的。这其中，钱武肃王祠、淮军昭忠祠、华孝子祠、尤文简公祠（万卷楼）、至德祠（泰伯殿）、陆宣公祠、留耕草堂（潜庐）、杨藕芳祠、顾洞阳先生祠、王武愍公祠等10座核心祠堂被列为全国重点文物保护单位，光霁祠、张文贞公祠、薛中丞祠、倪云林先生祠、张中丞庙、邵文庄公祠（二泉书院）等6座祠堂被列为江

惠山古镇祠堂群清单

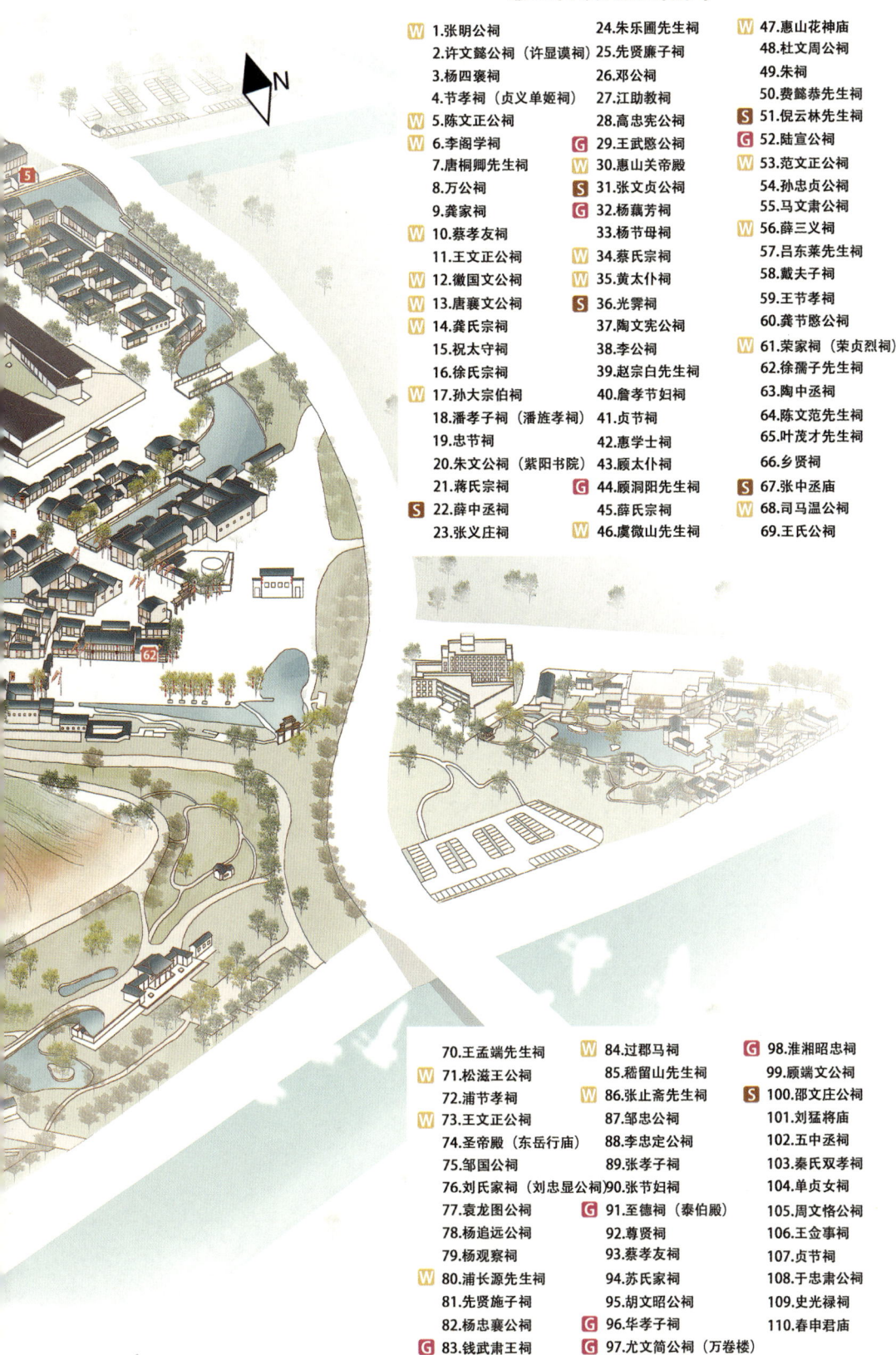

- 1. 张明公祠
- 2. 许文懿公祠（许显谟祠）
- 3. 杨四褒祠
- 4. 节孝祠（贞义单姬祠）
- 5. 陈文正公祠
- 6. 李阁学祠
- 7. 唐桐卿先生祠
- 8. 万公祠
- 9. 龚家祠
- 10. 蔡孝友祠
- 11. 王文正公祠
- 12. 徽国文公祠
- 13. 唐襄文公祠
- 14. 龚氏宗祠
- 15. 祝太守祠
- 16. 徐氏宗祠
- 17. 孙大宗伯祠
- 18. 潘孝子祠（潘旌孝祠）
- 19. 忠节祠
- 20. 朱文公祠（紫阳书院）
- 21. 蒋氏宗祠
- 22. 薛中丞祠
- 23. 张义庄祠
- 24. 朱乐圃先生祠
- 25. 先贤廉子祠
- 26. 邓公祠
- 27. 江助教祠
- 28. 高忠宪公祠
- 29. 王武愍公祠
- 30. 惠山关帝殿
- 31. 张文贞公祠
- 32. 杨藕芳祠
- 33. 杨节母祠
- 34. 蔡氏宗祠
- 35. 黄太仆祠
- 36. 光霁祠
- 37. 陶文宪祠
- 38. 李公祠
- 39. 赵宗白先生祠
- 40. 詹孝节祠
- 41. 贞节祠
- 42. 惠学士祠
- 43. 顾太仆祠
- 44. 顾洞阳先生祠
- 45. 薛氏宗祠
- 46. 虞微山先生祠
- 47. 惠山花神庙
- 48. 杜文周公祠
- 49. 朱祠
- 50. 费鹓恭先生祠
- 51. 倪云林先生祠
- 52. 陆宣公祠
- 53. 范文正公祠
- 54. 孙忠贞公祠
- 55. 马文肃公祠
- 56. 薛三义祠
- 57. 吕东莱先生祠
- 58. 戴夫子祠
- 59. 王节孝祠
- 60. 龚节愍公祠
- 61. 荣云祠（荣贞烈祠）
- 62. 徐孺子先生祠
- 63. 陶中丞祠
- 64. 陈文范先生祠
- 65. 叶茂才先生祠
- 66. 乡贤祠
- 67. 张中丞庙
- 68. 司马温公祠
- 69. 王氏公祠
- 70. 王孟端先生祠
- 71. 松滋王公祠
- 72. 浦节孝祠
- 73. 王文正公祠
- 74. 圣帝殿（东岳行庙）
- 75. 邹国公祠
- 76. 刘氏家祠（刘忠显公祠）
- 77. 袁龙图公祠
- 78. 杨追远公祠
- 79. 杨观察祠
- 80. 浦长源先生祠
- 81. 先贤施子祠
- 82. 杨忠襄公祠
- 83. 钱武肃王祠
- 84. 过郡马祠
- 85. 稽留山先生祠
- 86. 张止斋先生祠
- 87. 邹忠公祠
- 88. 李忠定公祠
- 89. 张孝子祠
- 90. 张节妇祠
- 91. 至德祠（泰伯殿）
- 92. 尊贤祠
- 93. 蔡孝友祠
- 94. 苏氏家祠
- 95. 胡文昭公祠
- 96. 华孝子祠
- 97. 尤文简公祠（万卷楼）
- 98. 淮湘昭忠祠
- 99. 顾端文公祠
- 100. 邵文庄公祠
- 101. 刘猛将庙
- 102. 五中丞祠
- 103. 秦氏双孝祠
- 104. 单贞女祠
- 105. 周文恪公祠
- 106. 王金事祠
- 107. 贞节祠
- 108. 于忠肃公祠
- 109. 史光禄祠
- 110. 春申君庙

惠山古镇祠堂分布图

图例
- 15 祠堂编号
- 13 地标点
- G 全国重点文保单位
- S 江苏省文保单位
- W 无锡市文保单位

惠山 Huishan Hill
锡山 Xishan Hill
映山湖 Yingshan Lake

惠山古镇地标点

1. 惠山寺
2. 寄畅园 (G)
3. 精忠贯日照壁
4. 两朝忠节照壁
5. 隔河照壁
6. 溪山第一楼
7. 阿炳墓
8. 人杰地灵牌坊
9. 天下第二泉 (G)
10. 唐宋石经幢 (G)
11. 留耕草堂 (G)
12. 无锡非物质文化遗产展示馆
13. 宝善桥
14. 龙光塔
15. 绣嶂阁

版权申明：2023年全国文化艺术职业教育和旅游职业教育提质培优行动计划之学生实践引领计划"精准对接 精进技艺 精益服务——中国特色学徒制下无锡文旅人才培养实践"项目组绘制，2025年7月

苏省文物保护单位，薛义士祠、松滋王公祠、范文正公祠、司马温公祠、荣贞烈祠、孙大宗伯祠、锡金山货公所旧址（惠山花神庙）、惠山关帝庙、陈文正公祠、李阁学祠、唐襄文公祠、徽国文公祠（徽州会馆）等12座祠堂被列为无锡市级文保。2021年，过郡马祠、张义士祠、张明公祠、浦长源先生祠、王文正公祠、蔡氏宗祠、黄斗南先生祠、虞薇山先生祠、龚氏宗祠、蔡孝友祠等10座祠堂被公布为无锡市历史建筑。

今天的惠山古镇到底有多少座祠堂？不妨现在就出发，去古镇走一走、数一数。

How Many Ancestral Halls Are There in the Huishan Hall Cluster?

The precise number of ancestral halls in the Huishan area has long intrigued scholars and visitors alike. While some sources cite 118, others claim 108 or even 120. Given that these halls are tangible architectural entities, such discrepancies raise the question: what is the actual number?

To answer this, one must consider the temporal context. The number of ancestral halls has varied across historical periods due to new constructions, renovations, or demolitions. The figure is, therefore, inherently dynamic.

The earliest known ancestral hall in Huishan is the Hall of Lord Chunshen, referenced in *The Book of Han—Geographical Records*, which notes that "in Wuxi, on Mount Li (i.e., Huishan), sacrifices were offered annually to Lord Chunshen using oxen." This suggests the origin of Huishan's ancestral hall tradition dates back to at least 202 BCE, during the reign of Emperor Gaozu of the Western Han. Among the extant halls, the oldest is the Hall of Filial Piety for Hua, built in 481 CE during the Southern Qi Dynasty, as recorded in *the Book of Southern Qi*. For nearly a millennium, the growth in the number of halls was slow, primarily due to governmental restrictions. The *Wuxi Gazetteer* from the Yuan dynasty (1341–1368) records only two halls. By the Wanli era of the Ming dynasty (1574), this number had risen modestly to seven.

A significant expansion occurred during the reign of the Jiajing Emperor of the Ming Dynasty, who permitted commoners to build clan temples. By the early Qing Dynasty, Huishan had over 20 halls. The second wave of expansion took place under the Kangxi and Qianlong emperors, who visited Huishan multiple times, sparking popular enthusiasm for ancestral construction. By 1881, *the Jinkui Gazetteer of Wuxi County* documented 79 halls, marking Huishan as the principal hub for such structures in Wuxi.

With the rise of industry and commerce in the early 20th century, private wealth fueled continued construction. *The New Gazetteer of Huishan* (1921) recorded 94 halls, and a 1930 survey by *Xin Wuxi* newspaper listed

118. A 2004 study also supported this count. Today, a widely circulated and meticulously drawn distribution map in the Huishan Ancient Town Visitor Center identifies all 118 halls by name and location, solidifying this figure as the most widely accepted.

After 1949, no new halls were constructed. Approximately 30 halls within the newly established Xishan (now Xihui) Park came under park management, while over 90 others, located outside the park, were administered as private residences or by military units. Valuable historical records such as floor plans and lease agreements were preserved during this time. Many scholars believe that before 1949, the number of halls in Huishan exceeded 120.

Around 2000, master clay sculptor Yu Xianglian and colleagues conducted a detailed field survey and interviewed long-time residents, producing the first historically grounded map marking the locations of ancestral halls as of 1949. This map lists 93 halls. Based on further verification, scholar Jin Shisheng identified an additional 21 unlisted halls, bringing the total to 114. Of these, five were likely destroyed by that time, leaving 109 still extant, though many were damaged during wartime and only a few remained intact.

Between 1949 and 2001, urban development projects such as road expansion, greening, and scenic reconstruction led to the demolition, repurposing, or modification of many halls. Some were renamed or converted into shops, companies, hospitals, or banks. By 2001, only 49 halls remained, and only a handful were in good condition.

Beginning in 2001, restoration efforts resumed. By October 2017, a survey found 99 standing halls and nine under planned reconstruction, yielding a total of 108. The current Huishan Ancient Town official website reflects this number, describing "108 ancestral halls and gardens dating from the Tang dynasty to the Republic of China."

These 108 halls are distributed as follows: 4 in Qinyuan Street, 11 along Huishan Bang, 10 in Shanghetang, 14 in Xiahetang, 7 from Xiahetang to Shaoxiang Bang, 16 in the northern section of Huishan Straight Street, 20 in its southern section, 18 from Huishan Temple to Guanquan Street, and 8 in Tingsong Lane. It should be noted that both the Chunshen Temple (the most ancient hall on Huishan) and the Qin Family's Double Piety Hall (a garden-style hall at Jichang Garden) have been lost to time and thus excluded from the list of 108 ancestral halls. Given their exceptional significance, however, both sites have been specially included in the updated cartographic documentation of this book.

According to Jin Shisheng's research, including halls mentioned only in historical documents, the total number that once existed in Huishan may approach 160. Numerous ancestral halls have faded into history, while others have undergone repeated alterations, changing ownership and names to appear in historical records under various designations. For instance, the Three Sages Hall, Seven Sages Hall, and Ten Sages Hall referenced in ancient texts all correspond to today's Veneration of Worthies Hall; likewise, the site of the Xijin Native Goods Guild (formerly known as Huishan Flower Deity Temple)—now designated as a municipal-level cultural preservation site—is in fact the current Second Spring Garden Old Restaurant, which has never been included in any catalog of ancestral halls. Additionally, observant visitors may discover identically named halls. These complexities render it increasingly challenging to determine the exact number of ancestral halls.

If one assesses the authenticity of surviving halls, the National Cultural Heritage Administration provides another reference. According to *the Chinese Cultural Relics Atlas* (2008), 38 halls in Huishan maintain their original structures and ecological context. Of these, 10—including the Halls of Prince Qian Wusu, the Huai Army Martyrs, and Hua of Filial Piety—are listed as nationally protected heritage sites. Six others are protected at the provincial level, and 12 more at the municipal level. In 2021, another 10 halls were designated as historic buildings of Wuxi, including those dedicated to figures such as Guo Junma, Zhang Yishi, and Wang Wenzheng.

So, how many ancestral halls does Huishan Ancient Town truly have today? Perhaps the most compelling answer is found not in numbers but in experience—take a walk through the town, and count for yourself.

祠堂里有哪些建筑，又有哪些功能

惠山古镇的祠堂依据不同地形条件，因地制宜、合理布局，借山借水借景，使建筑与环境巧妙地融为一体。祠堂总体上采用传统的中轴对称、纵深布局的方式，其纵向进深及横向路数，随祠堂规格、建造者财力及用地规模形态而变化，主要有以下几种。

一是单进、单路祠堂，即由单座建筑（享堂）构成的祠堂，如刘猛将祠、王孟端先生祠。

二是两进祠堂，即由祠门、享堂构成的祠堂，两侧由两厢或廊道连接，近似民居院落，侧翼有时设置祠丁居住的别院附房，如陶中丞祠、周濂溪祠。

三是三进祠堂，其布局通常分为两类：一类由祠门、享

堂、寝堂（或后楼）构成，如顾可久祠、薛中丞祠、周文恪公祠；另一类由祠门、二门（仪门）、享堂构成，如张中丞祠、陆宣公祠，其侧翼还可能有祠丁居住的别院或附房。

四是四进祠堂，即由祠门、二门、享堂、后堂构成的祠堂，两侧可能有边路，如华孝子祠、春申君祠、杨四褒祠、昭忠祠，此类祠为敕建的官祠。

五是三路四进式或边路三进式，即主轴线保持三进或四进，并有左右两路或一路，一进或二进式。如王武愍公祠，是平面布局最完整的三路四进式；张中丞庙为两路三进式，西路由许远殿、鲁班殿、垂花厅组成；邵文庄公祠为两路三进式，有北路超然堂。

祭祀先祖自然是祠堂最重要的功能。古代祭祀祖先的活动相当频繁，基本上每个月都会有，后来逐渐简化，但仍保留了新年的瞻仰先祖以及春秋两祭。每到举行春秋两祭的日子，提前三天就要洒扫祠堂，铺设洁净，以示诚敬。等到祭祀开始，族人会按辈分排队，至于祭礼的规格，每家祠堂都有自己的规定，对于祭筵的食物、杯筷、香烛等物品数量均有明确详尽的要求。读祭文也是例行的环节，先官祭，后家祭，祭文的内容都是固定的。

祭祀结束，多数宗族会在祠堂中设宴，叫享胙或饮胙。族人按尊卑长幼入席。饭后，族人还会得到胙肉、馒头之类，称作散胙或"散福"，年高德昭或有功于族的男子，以及守节的寡妇等，能得到"增胙"的奖励，而违反家法族规者则会受到"革胙"之罚。

祠堂的另一重要功能是修谱藏谱。家谱（族谱、宗谱）是一类特殊史籍，对于宗族有着特别的意义，形式可以是记传、论志、图表，内容包括家族的方方面面，如家族的起源迁徙、重大事件、杰出人物、世系传承、族产族务、家规家训等情况都会得到记载，由本姓宗亲们负责掌管并作为家族的处事准则。具体说来，范围最小，侧重"家"的血缘传承，详细记录某一支系内族人生卒、嫁娶、职业的称作家谱；范围较广，侧重"族"的发展脉络，强调支系相互关系的称作族谱；范围最广，侧重"宗"的整体秩序，全面阐述祖先起源和宗法制度的称作宗谱。作为一份以血缘关系为纽带的档案，修谱的目的是明世系、序昭穆，维系家族认同，有着教化、敬贤、理政、信史的功用，族人还可据此确定自己在宗族中的地位，并获得相应的权利。有些族务如祭祖、扫墓、认亲等，也需要依据家谱来决定，因此家谱也成为家族的行事指南。按惯例，家谱十年一小修，三十年一大修，印谱、祭谱、供谱、领谱、掌谱，这是全家族的大事。政府还设有谱局，对各家谱进行审查，防止伪谱产生。

祠堂还有着助学育才的重要功能。在惠山，祠田也是祠堂的一部分，收益用于家族子弟的助学教育，家族子弟如外出求学，可得到一定的补助和奖励，在秦氏、邵氏等实力殷厚的私家祠堂内设有私塾，用以教养家族子弟，恪守着吴地"耕读传家"的古训。

祠堂是宣讲学教礼法的课堂。祭祀仪式开始之前，会有专人向族人进行"读谱"，讲祖宗艰难创业的历史，定时读家

法族规，宣讲劝诫训勉之词和先贤语录，是族人的思想教育课堂。

祠堂又是讨论族中事务的会场。凡有关系到家族未来的重大事宜，如推选族长、兴建祠堂、编修家谱、购置族产、同邻族打官司等，都会在祠堂开会讨论。

祠堂还是家族的"法庭"。过去说家法伺候，说的就是族规，是家族的法律。在封建社会时期，家法是国法的补充。族人犯法违规，小则祠堂治以家法，大则送公庭治以官刑。

每当风俗年节或族内重大的喜庆活动，祠堂还是全族欢庆或娱乐的场所，好戏连台、寓教于乐。大一些的祠堂里，戏台建筑可算标配，张中丞祠、陆宣公祠、昭忠祠、范文正公祠内均有戏台，既是祭祀敬祖的场所，也是年节娱乐的中心。

What Are the Architectural Elements and Functions of the Ancestral Hall?

The ancestral halls in Huishan Ancient Town are designed according to the natural terrain, integrating with the surrounding environment through clever use of mountains, water, and scenic views. Architecturally, they adopt a traditional axial symmetry and longitudinal layout, with variations in depth and number of routes depending on the hall's scale, the builder's financial resources, and the land size. The main types of layouts include:

Single-depth, single-route ancestral halls: These consist of a single building (the main hall), such as the Liu Mengjiang Hall and Wang Mengduan Hall.

Two-depth ancestral halls: These are composed of an ancestral gate and a main hall, with side wings or corridors connecting the structures, resembling a courtyard-style residence. Sometimes, side annexes were provided for the residence of caretakers, as seen in the Tao Zhongcheng Hall and Zhou Lianxi Hall.

The "three-section" ancestral hall is a common architectural layout that generally falls into two categories. The first consists of a front gate, a main hall for ritual offerings, and a rear hall or back building—examples include the ancestral halls of Gu Kejiu, Xue Zhongcheng, and Zhou Wenke. The second configuration comprises a front gate, a second gate (ceremonial gate), and a main hall for ancestral rites, such as seen in the ancestral halls of Zhang Zhongcheng and Lu Xuanggong; flanking structures often include side courtyards or annexes that historically accommodated clan retainers.

Four-depth ancestral halls: These consist of an ancestral gate, a second gate, a main hall, and a rear hall, often featuring side pathways. Examples include the Huaxiaoci Hall, Chunshenjun Hall, Yang Sibao Hall, and Zhaozhong Hall, which are official halls built by imperial decree.

Fifth is the tri-axial quad-courtyard layout or lateral tri-courtyard layout, meaning the main axis maintains three or four courtyard sequences, flanked by two or one lateral axis of one or two courtyards. For instance, the Wang Wumin Hall exemplifies the most complete tri-axial quad-courtyard plan layout; while the Zhang Zhongcheng Hall is a two-route three-depth hall with halls such as Xuyuan Hall, Luban Hall, and Chuihua Hall forming the west route. The Shao Wenzhuang Hall also follows a two-route three-depth layout, with the North Route featuring Chaoran Hall.

The most important function of the ancestral hall is ancestor worship. Sacrificial ceremonies were frequent in ancient times, often monthly, though over time they were simplified to annual worship during the New Year and the biannual Spring and Autumn sacrifices. For the Spring and Autumn sacrifices, the hall would be cleaned thoroughly three days in advance as a sign of respect. During the ceremony, participants were arranged in order of seniority. Each hall had its own rules for the ceremony, with specific requirements for the number of offerings, cups, chopsticks, incense, and candles. A fixed sacrificial text was read, starting with an official sacrifice, followed by a family one.

After the sacrifice, most clans would host a banquet in the ancestral hall, known as "Xiangzuo" or "Yinzuo," where participants dined according to rank and seniority. After the meal, food such as meat and buns would be distributed to the clan members as "Sanzuo" or "*Scattered blessings*." Elders of great merit or widows who had remained chaste would receive additional rewards, while those who had violated clan laws faced penalties, such as the reduction of their share.

Another crucial function of ancestral halls is compiling and preserving genealogical records. Genealogies (including clan genealogies and comprehensive ancestral genealogies) represent a unique category of historical documentation that holds profound significance for kinship groups. These records may take the form of biographies, chronicles, commentaries, or charts, comprehensively documenting all aspects of a family—such as its origins, migrations, major events, eminent figures, lineage succession, clan properties, clan affairs, family rules, and instructions. Preserved by members of the same surname kinship group, these records serve as the clan's guiding principles.Specifically: Family genealogies cover the smallest scope, focusing on bloodline continuity within a "household" by meticulously recording births, deaths, marriages, and occupations within a specific branch. Clan genealogies encompass a broader scope, emphasizing the developmental lineage of a "clan" and highlighting interconnections between branches. Comprehensive ancestral genealogies cover the widest scope, prioritizing the collective order of an "ancestral lineage" with thorough accounts of ancestral origins and patriarchal systems. As kinship-based archives, genealogies aim to clarify lineage hierarchies, sequence generational order, and preserve family identity. They serve educational purposes, honor distinguished ancestors, inform governance principles, and provide reliable historical records. Clan members use them to ascertain their status within the kinship structure and claim corresponding rights. Activities like ancestral worship, tomb sweeping, and kinship recognition also rely on genealogical guidance, making these records essential for clan protocols. Traditionally, genealogies undergo minor revisions every decade and major revisions every thirty years. The processes of printing, ritual worship, enshrinement, distribution, and custodianship of genealogies constitute significant events for the entire clan. Government-established Genealogy Bureaus review all genealogies to prevent the creation of falsified records.

In addition to these roles, ancestral halls also played a crucial role in education and scholarship. In Huishan, ancestral hall lands generated income used to fund the education of clan members, providing financial support for those studying elsewhere. Wealthy families, such as the Qin and Shao clans, even established private academies within their ancestral halls to educate their descendants, adhering to the traditional Confucian values of "passing on the family legacy through farming and studying."

Furthermore, ancestral halls were venues for lectures and moral education. Before the start of sacrificial ceremonies, clan members would gather to hear readings from the genealogy, accounts of the clan's history, and lessons on clan rules and laws. These sessions also included exhortations and moral teachings, serving as a platform for reinforcing the clan's values.

Ancestral halls were also used for clan meetings to discuss important family matters, such as the election of clan leaders, the construction of new halls, the compilation of genealogies, or the purchase of clan property. Disputes with neighboring clans were also resolved in these settings.

In terms of legal functions, the ancestral hall acted as a court for the enforcement of family law. Clan members who violated the rules faced family-based penalties, and serious offenders were turned over to official authorities. In this way, clan law complemented state law in traditional society.

Finally, ancestral halls were venues for festivities and celebrations. On important occasions, the hall became the site for clan-wide gatherings and entertainment, including opera performances.

惠山祠堂群有多少种祠堂

惠山祠堂群的规模在国内首屈一指，有确切名称的就有100余座，时间跨度自唐代至民国约1200余年，涉及姓氏70余个，历史名人约180个，是公认类型丰富、形态多样的祠堂文化景观。那么，惠山这小小0.3平方千米的祠堂群里可以划分出多少种不同的祠堂呢？

祭祀，在中国传统社会占有重要地位。《礼记》记载："夫圣王之制祀也，法施于民则祀之，以死勤事则祀之，以劳定国则祀之，能御大灾则祀之，能捍大患则祀之。"也就是说，有功于民众的应祭祀，操劳国事而死的应祭祀，有安邦定国功勋的应祭祀，为大众防御重大灾害的应祭祀，保卫民众、抵御重大外患的应祭祀，明确规定了五类祭祀对象。古代祠堂，按照祭祀对象的不同，分为祭天、祀祖、尊贤三大类。按设立者的不同，总体上分为公祠、私祠两大类。公祠就是官方出资设立的祠堂，祭祀的对象主要是贤烈，行的是官祭大礼，重在治国平天下。私祠则是民间出资设立的祠堂，奉祀的对象是家族的始迁祖或杰出人物，行的是民祭大事，意在宗族之昌盛。还有一些特殊的祠堂，可以算公私兼顾，如华孝子祠、至德祠就兼具公祠和私祠的身份。

1. 尊贤祠类

尊贤祠是惠山祠堂中一类很重要的祠堂，旨在纪念无锡历史上的先贤，属于官祭公祠。惠山尊贤祠，最早由邵宝创立，

以"生游殁葬惠山，名在天下者"为入祠标准，由此惠山祠堂群出现了一个有趣的现象，祠堂里纪念的先贤很多并不是无锡人，而是造福无锡的名人高士，这也从一个侧面反映了无锡人开放的心态。尊贤祠初为三贤祠，后内祀人物渐增至十贤。明清两代，纪念的名贤不断增祀至52位，还有附设的报忠祠、报功祠。

惠山祠堂里还有大量乡贤的专祠。所谓乡贤，特指无锡籍的历代先贤。无锡历代人才辈出，这些先贤的高洁品格为后世所尊崇，此类祠堂有顾端文公祠（明代东林书院首任山长顾宪成）、高忠宪公祠（明代东林党继任领袖高攀龙）、光霁祠（北宋理学鼻祖周敦颐）、顾洞阳先生祠（明代"骨鲠之臣"顾可久）、李忠定公祠（宋代抗金名帅李纲）、倪云林先生祠（元代大画家倪云林）、唐桐卿祠（清代卓著的救赈官唐锡晋）等。乡贤祠中有4座杨姓祠堂都出自无锡的民族工商巨族杨家，分别是杨忠襄公祠（世祖杨邦乂）、杨四褒祠（迁锡八世祖杨延俊，留耕草堂）、杨宗濂祠和杨宗瀚祠。杨氏一门四祠风格迥异，有风格清丽的园林祠，有洋为中用的西式祠，在形式上也颇有新意，有留耕草堂潜庐父子同祠的，有杨宗瀚祠融乡贤祠与行业祠为一体的，默默表达着务实创新、经世致用的精神，成为惠山祠堂群的一道独特风景。

2.墓祠类

墓祠是惠山最原始的祠堂。起初是古人在墓地旁边搭建的小房子，用来守墓和祭拜。东晋孝子华宝、宋代宰相李纲都曾在惠山结庐守墓多年。这些为了守墓而居住的屋子后来慢慢变成祭祀的建筑，无锡人称为"坟堂屋"，是早期的祠堂类型。

典型的惠山墓祠有贞义单姬祠、浦孝节贞烈祠和蔡孝友祠等，受土地限制，明代以后基本停止发展，惠山的墓祠数量不多，却是传统孝义精神的体现。

3.忠孝节义祠类

忠烈祠有点类似今天的烈士纪念堂。纪念的是为国殉职、精忠报国的英烈。惠山祠堂群中此类最大的为昭忠祠，是李鸿章奏请清朝政府批准后，为淮湘战死将士而修建的合祠，李鸿章在全国先后修了多座昭忠祠，无锡的是第一座，祠堂建在被太平军损毁的惠山寺原址上，以徽派建筑风格为主体，精美的砖雕、木雕、石雕为惠山祠堂所罕见。李忠定公祠、杨忠襄公祠、王武愍公祠、嵇留山先生祠等也都属于忠烈祠。

孝子祠在惠山为数众多，自华孝子祠始，张孝子祠、蔡孝友祠、秦氏双孝祠、浦孝节贞烈祠、潘孝子祠等的设立，都以表彰"孝道"为出发点。惠山的孝义文化自孝祖华宝开创，历朝历代都备受尊崇，始终为华氏后人及无锡百姓所珍视。

惠山节妇祠是祠堂中数量较多的一类，是专门建造用于纪念节妇烈女的特殊祠堂。历史上，官府在惠山的五个方向（东、南、西、北、中）都建立了贞节总祠，用来统一纪念各地的贞节女性。此外，还有许多专门纪念特定贞节女性的祠堂、牌坊，因为旧时的女性多无名，常冠以夫姓，如张节妇祠、杨节妇祠、荣贞烈祠、马贞女坊、秦孝贞女坊等。这些祠堂前面通常会立有贞节牌坊，用来表彰这些女子恪守妇道、坚贞不渝。

义士祠主要用来纪念品德高尚、乐善好施的人。惠山有张义士祠、祝太守祠等，直街的薛三义祠也是其中之一，这些祠

堂前立有"乐善""好施"牌坊，以表彰他们的善行。

4. 宗祠类

宗祠是中国人纪念祖先、弘扬家族文化的重要场所，按照规模和范围可以分为总祠、宗祠、支祠和家祠四种，不同级别的宗祠反映了家族的规模、地位和影响力。

总祠的等级最高，纪念的范围超出了地域限制，不仅包括同姓同宗的人，还包括不同支派甚至异姓但有血缘关系的家族，是更大范围内族人的共同精神象征。惠山的紫阳书院、钱武肃王祠、华孝子祠都是总祠的例子。宗祠是地域范围内同姓同宗各支共建合祀的祠堂，规模较大，是宗族文化和精神的象征。如在惠山有一祠之地，在无锡算得上光宗耀祖，是家世显赫的象征。支祠是宗祠下一级的祠堂，由血缘关系更近的家族支派建立，纪念的范围较小，是支派尊祖的地方。家祠是最小的祠堂类型，多设在家庭住所内，用于祭拜祖先，是民间宅祠合一的早期形式。

5. 专祠类

专祠是为表彰特定人物而建的祠堂，在惠山祠堂中占有很大比例。被纪念的人物通常为国为民，建功立业，造福一方，德行显著。专祠经官府批准后才能建立。专祠是一份荣誉，褒奖先人、表率乡里，而且不分前朝当代、活人死者，都可以立祠。例如，惠山浜的唐桐卿先生祠就是为纪念晚清杰出的救赈官吏唐桐卿而建，他一生在全国8省51个县赈灾，惠泽万里。

6. 书院祠

书院祠通常纪念的是该书院山长，生前办书院，死后书院

改成祠堂。书院是古代教育和学术研究的重要场所，主要功能包括藏书、读书、教书、讲学以及编印书籍。无锡历来有尊师重教、诗礼传家的传统，惠山作为无锡历史上的文化高地，曾创办过尚德书院、二泉书院（邵宝书院）、紫阳书院、锡山书院、遂初书院等5处书院，以及拥有500多年历史的民间诗社碧山吟社。这些书院不仅是学习的地方，还是文化传播和学术交流的中心。

邵宝书院是惠山最重要的书院之一，由无锡人邵宝在明正德年间创办。邵宝是无锡历史上一位杰出的文学家、理学家和清官，以清正廉洁著称，被尊称为"千金不受先生"。他创办邵宝书院，在此讲学11年，对无锡的文化教育影响深远。邵宝去世后，书院被改为纪念他的祠堂，但依然保留了书院的功能，成为书院祠堂的典范。邵宝书院也与东林志士顾宪成先生的著名长联"风声雨声读书声声声入耳，家事国事天下事事事关心"有着密切的联系，这副对联正是在邵宝书院的环境中产生的。

7. 园林祠

园林祠是指拥有花园的祠堂，或者原来是园林，后来因为某种原因改园为祠。走进惠山古镇，古朴、清幽、雅致的祠堂花园给很多人留下美好印象。这些大隐于市的古典园林也被叫作园林祠。园林祠既有祠堂的功能，也是精美的园林，可居可赏可玩。因为惠山的风景实在是漂亮，历代有见识有品位的名人争相跑来建园林，如元代的惠麓小隐，明代的愚公谷、寄畅园、王园、黄园，清代的留耕草堂、思园，据考证，到1949年止，惠山先后出现过18处风格各异的祠堂花园。然而不少

园林已无处寻觅，在漫长的岁月里，一旦主人遭遇变故，园林就保不住了。例如，愚公谷就曾是明代江南四大名园之一，规模宏大，因园主身故而废弃，今天的愚公谷仅为旧时一隅。

那么，惠山最著名的园林寄畅园"五百年来不易姓"，有什么奥秘呢？

寄畅园是江南名园，还是一座园林祠，备受清康熙、乾隆二帝喜爱，均曾多次驾临。康熙所题"山色溪光"，乾隆所题"玉戛金摐"，两块牌匾至今并排挂在园内墙上。寄畅园也曾历尽沧桑，却能基本完整地留给后代，这背后的玄机就是它是一座家族守护的祠堂。作为祠产，寄畅园是秦氏宗族的共有资产，从性质上保障了寄畅园不被转卖、不被拆分。

8.行会祠

行会祠是惠山的祠堂群里一类特殊的祠堂，分为会馆祠和行业祠。

会馆祠的设立，既有时代背景因素，也有地缘因素，明清时的惠山浜与北塘米市、布码头相去不远，大运河上商贾云集，各地商团陆续在古镇沿河设立会馆。会馆是以地缘关系为纽带的民间社团组织，多由商贾集资建立，用于同乡集会和祭祀，也是同乡间交流商业信息的场所。其中，徽商众多，惠山浜的徽州会馆规模宏大，设徽国文公祠，纪念朱熹。

行业祠是祭祀特定行业始祖的祠堂，也叫行业公所。惠山的盐业公所、无锡建筑营造业公所均为此类，会定期举行祭祀活动。如惠山的鲁班殿就是无锡建筑行业的行会祠，主祀鲁班。鲁班是能工巧匠的代表，被尊为"百工鼻祖"，泥木工匠均尊鲁班为祖师爷,全国各地都有大小不等的鲁班庙。

　　说了这么多,你可能已经发现,如此密集的祠堂群,如此繁杂的门类,惠山百余所祠堂,并非一成不变,随着朝代更迭,世事变迁,数易其主。民居、别墅、庙堂、道观、书院、园林、会所,百祠百景,时而辉煌,时而衰败,惠山祠堂群始终在动态变化着,不变的是"血脉相连、认祖归宗"的家国情怀。

无锡惠山祠堂群中姓氏一览表

序号	姓氏	序号	姓氏	序号	姓氏	序号	姓氏
1	陈	20	海	39	吕	58	武
2	储	21	侯	40	荣	59	徐
3	蔡	22	季	41	孙	60	许
4	程	23	蒋	42	司马	61	薛
5	戴	24	江	43	苏	62	杨
6	邓	25	嵇	44	施	63	袁
7	杜	26	廉	45	邵	64	尤
8	丁	27	鲁	46	单	65	虞
9	范	28	陆	47	史	66	俞
10	费	29	李	48	谈	67	于
11	过	30	刘	49	陶	68	叶
12	顾	31	孟	50	唐	69	祝
13	高	32	马	51	汤	70	张
14	龚	33	倪	52	魏	71	周
15	黄	34	浦	53	韦	72	朱
16	何	35	潘	54	卫	73	邹
17	华	36	钱	55	王	74	赵
18	胡	37	秦	56	万		
19	惠	38	强	57	吴		

How Many Types of Ancestral Halls Are There in the Cluster?

There are over 100 ancestral halls with known names in the Huishan Ancestral Hall Cluster, covering a time span of over 1,200 years, from the Tang Dynasty to the Republic of China. The cluster represents more than 70 surnames and commemorates approximately 180 historical figures. It is recognized as a diverse and abundant ancestral hall cultural landscapes in China. So, how many types of ancestral halls can be classified within this small 0.3 square kilometer area of Huishan?

In traditional Chinese society, rituals and sacrifices held significant importance. The *Book of Rites* also known as the Liji states: "When the sage king instituted rituals and sacrifices, they were established for those who benefited the people, died while serving the state, contributed to the nation's stability, protected the people from major disasters, and defended against foreign threats." This clearly defines five types of sacrificial objects: those who contributed to the people, died serving the country, had merits in stabilizing the nation, protected the people from major disasters, and defended against significant external threats. In ancient times, ancestral halls were divided into three major categories based on the sacrificial objects: sacrifices to heaven, ancestral worship, and veneration of the virtuous. Based on the identity of the founders, they can be generally divided into public and private halls. Public halls were funded by the government and mainly served to worship deities or revered figures, performing grand official ceremonies aimed at governing the state and ensuring peace. Private halls, funded by families, worshipped the founder of the family lineage or distinguished individuals, focusing on clan prosperity. Some ancestral halls were a mix of both public and private, such as the Huaxiaozi Hall and Zhide Hall.

1. Halls for the Virtuous

Halls dedicated to the virtuous are another important part of

Huishan's Ancestral Hall Cluster, commemorating the historical figures who made significant contributions to Wuxi. These halls were generally public halls sponsored by the government. The first of such halls, the Hall of the Three Worthies, was established by Shao Bao, who set the criterion for inclusion as "those who, though born elsewhere, were buried in Huishan and whose reputations spread across the land." This led to an interesting phenomenon where many of the virtuous figures commemorated in Huishan's ancestral halls were not native to Wuxi but were esteemed figures who contributed to the city's development, reflecting the openness of the Wuxi people. Over time, the number of honorees increased from three to ten. By the Ming and Qing Dynasties, the number of worthies worshipped had expanded to 52, and additional halls like the Hall of Loyalty and the Hall of Merit were established.

Huishan also has numerous ancestral halls dedicated to local worthies, individuals from Wuxi who were renowned for their virtuous qualities across different historical periods. Such figures include Gu Xiancheng, the first head of Donglin Academy in the Ming Dynasty (at the Gu Duanwen Hall), Gao Panlong, a prominent leader of the Donglin Party in the Ming Dynasty (at the Gao Zhongxian Hall), Zhou Dunyi, the founder of Neo-Confucianism in the Northern Song Dynarsty (at the Guangji Hall), and Tang Xijin, a notable relief officer in the Qing Dynasty (at the Tang Tongqing Hall). The Yang family, a distinguished industrial clan from Wuxi, constructed four halls dedicated to their ancestors, each reflecting distinct architectural styles. These include the Yang Zhongxiang Hall, Yang Sibao Hall, Yang Zonglian Hall, and Yang Zonghan Hall, featuring innovative designs and embodying the Yang family's spirit of practicality and innovation.

2. Tomb Halls

Tomb halls represent the most original form of ancestral halls in Huishan. Initially, small houses were built near graves as places for descendants to fulfill their filial duties by guarding and worshipping at the tombs. These houses later evolved into formal sacrificial structures, known in Wuxi as "Fen Tang Wu," or tomb halls, an early type of ancestral hall. Some notable tomb halls include the Zhenyi Danji Hall, Puxiaojie Zhenlie Hall, and Caixiaoyou Hall. Due to land constraints, the development of tomb halls ceased after the Ming Dynasty, but the few that remain stand as testaments to the traditional Chinese virtues of filial piety and loyalty.

3. Halls of Loyalty and Filial Piety

The halls of loyalty and martyrdom are somewhat akin to contemporary martyrs' memorials, honoring heroes who sacrificed their lives for their country. Among the Huishan Hall Cluster, the largest of this type is the Zhaozhong Hall, which was built after Li Hongzhang petitioned the Qing government for its approval in memory of the soldiers who died in the Huai and Xiang campaigns. Li constructed a total of seven Zhaozhong Halls across the country, with the one in Wuxi being the first. This hall was erected on the original site of Huishan Temple, which was destroyed by the Taiping Army. Its architecture primarily features the Hui style, characterized by exquisite brick, wood, and stone carvings, which are rare in Huishan. Other halls of loyalty include the Li Zhongding Hall, Yang Zhongxiang Hall, Wang Wumin Hall, and Ji Liushan Hall.

The Huishan area is also home to numerous halls dedicated to filial piety, beginning with the Huabao Hall and followed by Zhang Xiaozi Hall, Cai Xiaoyou Hall, Qin Family Shuangxiao Hall, Pu Xiaojie Zhenlie Hall, and Pan Xiaozi Hall, all established to honor the concept of filial piety. The culture of filial piety in Huishan, initiated by the founder Hua Bao, has been venerated throughout history, consistently cherished by the descendants of the Hua family and the local populace.

The halls of chastity are the most numerous within the hall cluster and are specifically built to commemorate virtuous women. Historically, the local government established five main halls of chastity in Huishan, located in the east, south, west, north, and center, to collectively honor virtuous women from various regions. In addition, there are many halls and memorial arches dedicated to specific virtuous women, who often remained nameless in earlier times, typically referred to by their husbands' surnames. Examples include the Zhang Jiefu Hall, Yang Jiefu Hall, Rong Zhenlie Hall, Ma Zhen Nü Arch, and Qin Xiaozhen Nü Arch. These halls usually feature memorial arches to celebrate the unwavering adherence of these women to their roles and their steadfastness, earning the respect and admiration of the public.

The Halls of the Righteous were primarily established to honor those of noble character who were charitable and benevolent. Examples in Huishan include the Zhang Yishi Hall and Zhu Taishou Hall, with memorial arches inscribed with phrases like "Benevolence" and "Charity" to recognize their good deeds, and the Xue San Yishi Hall is also among them.

4. Ancestral Halls

Ancestral halls are significant sites for commemorating ancestors and promoting family culture in Chinese society. They can be categorized into four types based on scale and scope: ancestral halls, clan halls, branch halls, and family halls. The different levels of ancestral halls reflect the size, status, and influence of the family.

The ancestral hall holds the highest rank, with a scope of worship extending beyond regional limitations. It includes not only those of the same surname and lineage but also families of different branches or surnames who share a blood relationship, symbolizing a collective spiritual bond among extended family members. Examples include the Ziyang Academy, Qian Wusu Hall, and Huabao Hall in Huishan. The clan hall, built collaboratively by families of the same surname within a specific region, serves as a larger symbol of clan culture and spirit. In Huishan, having a clan hall is considered an honor, symbolizing a distinguished lineage. Branch halls are subordinate to clan halls and are established by closer blood relatives for worship, serving as places of ancestor veneration. Family halls are the smallest type, typically located within residential homes for ancestor worship, representing an early form of community and domestic hall.

5. Specialized Halls

Specialized halls are built to honor specific individuals and comprise a significant portion of the Huishan Hall Cluster. The person be hornored here are those who have made significant contributions to the country and the people, establishing a commendable legacy, and are approved by the local government for such honors. Constructing a specialized hall is a mark of distinction, acknowledging ancestors and setting an example for the community, regardless of their era, whether living or deceased. For instance, the Tang Tongqing Hall in Huishan Bank is dedicated to the outstanding relief official Tang Tongqing of the late Qing Dynasty, who aided disaster victims across 51 counties in eight provinces, benefiting countless people. Among Wuxi locals, he holds the record for the most awarded specialized halls.

6. Academy Halls

Academy halls typically honor the head of the academy, where they taught during their lifetime and transformed into a hall after their death. Academy halls are crucial centers for education and scholarly research in ancient times, serving functions such as storing books, reading, teaching, lecturing, and publishing works. Wuxi has a long-standing tradition of valuing teachers and education, and Huishan, as a cultural hub in Wuxi's history, has established five notable academies, including the Shangde Academy, Second Spring Academy (Shaobao Academy), Ziyang Academy, Xishan Academy, and Suichu Academy, as well as the Banshan Yinshi Society, which has a history of over 500 years. These academies not only serve as educational institutions but also as centers for cultural dissemination and academic exchange.

The Shaobao Academy is the most significant in Huishan, founded by the local scholar Shaobao during the Ming Zhengde period. Shaobao was an outstanding writer, philosopher, and upright official in Wuxi's history, known for his integrity, earning him the title of "Master of Thousand Golds." He taught at the Shaobao Academy for eleven years, profoundly impacting the cultural education of Wuxi. After his death, the academy was converted into a hall to honor him but retained its educational functions, becoming a model of academy halls. The Shaobao Academy is also closely associated with the famous couplet by the Donglin scholar Gu Xiancheng: "The sounds of wind, rain, and reading intertwine, caring for family affairs, national issues, and the world at large," which originated within the environment of the Shaobao Academy.

7. Garden Halls

Garden halls refer to halls that feature gardens or were originally gardens that were later converted into halls for various reasons. Upon entering the ancient town of Huishan, visitors are often captivated by the quaint, tranquil, and elegant hall gardens, which leave a lasting impression. These classical gardens, hidden in the bustling city, are also referred to as garden halls. A garden hall serves both the purpose of a hall and as a beautiful garden, providing spaces for residence, appreciation, and recreation. Due to the picturesque scenery of Huishan, many distinguished individuals throughout history, possessing keen insights and refined tastes, flocked to establish gardens, including the Huilu Xiaoyin from the Yuan Dynasty, the Yugong Valley, Jichang Garden, Wang Garden, and Huang Garden from the Ming Dynasty, and the Liugeng Caotang and Siyuan from the Qing Dynasty. Historical research indicates that by 1949, there had been 18 uniquely styled hall gardens in Huishan. However, many of these gardens have vanished, as once the owners encountered misfortunes over the long years, the gardens could no longer be preserved. For instance, Yugong Valley, once one of the four renowned gardens of Jiangnan in the Ming Dynasty, fell into disuse after the owner's death, leaving only a remnant of its former glory today.

What, then, is the secret behind Huishan's most famous garden, Jichang Garden, known for its "unchanging surname for five hundred years"?

Jichang Garden, renowned among classical gardens of

Jiangnan, also functions as a garden-style ancestral hall. It was especially favored by the Qing emperors Kangxi and Qianlong, both of whom visited the site on multiple occasions. Two calligraphic plaques—"Mountain Hues and Stream Light," inscribed by Emperor Kangxi, and "Jade Striking Gold Sprigs," penned by Emperor Qianlong—still hang side by side on the garden's inner wall, testifying to its historical prestige and imperial patronage. It became a must-visit destination for travelers to Jiangnan. Despite undergoing numerous changes throughout history, Jichang Garden has largely been preserved for future generations. The underlying reason for this preservation lies in its status as a family-protected hall. As a hall property, Jichang Garden is a shared asset of the Qin family, which fundamentally safeguards it from being resold or subdivided.

8. Guild Halls

Among the hall cluster in Huishan, there exists a unique category of halls: guild halls and trade halls.

The establishment of guild halls is influenced by historical context as well as geographical factors. During the Ming and Qing Dynasties, Huishan Bang was located not far from the Beitang Rice Market and the Cloth Wharf, where merchants converged along the Grand Canal, prompting various business groups to set up guild halls along the river in the ancient town. Guilds are folk organizations bonded by geographical relationships, often funded by merchants, serving as venues for fellow townspeople to meet and worship, as well as a place for exchanging business information. Among these, the Huizhou Guild Hall, which was notably large, housed the Huizhou Wengong Hall dedicated to Zhu Xi, a prominent Confucian scholar.

Trade halls are dedicated to the ancestors of specific trades, also referred to as trade offices. Examples include the salt trade office and the Wuxi construction trade office, all of which hold regular ritual activities. For instance, the Luban Hall in Huishan serves as the guild hall for the construction industry, dedicated to Lu Ban, an ancient figure renowned for his craftsmanship and revered as the "ancestor of all craftsmen." Across the country, there are various sizes of Lu Ban halls honoring him.

Having discussed this, you may have noticed that the dense cluster of ancestral halls in Huishan, with its diverse categories, is not static. The over one hundred ancestral halls in Huishan have undergone numerous transformations over time, influenced by the rise and fall of dynasties and changing social circumstances, with many different owners and deities being worshipped. The residential houses, villas, temples, Taoist temples, academies, gardens, and guild halls contribute to a myriad of unique hall landscapes. At times splendid, at times dilapidated, the Huishan Ancestral Hall Cluster is in a continuous state of dynamic change, with the unchanging sentiment of "blood ties and ancestral recognition" deeply embedded in the hearts of the people.

家谱里都写了什么

家谱，也被称作族谱、宗谱等。家谱里记载着家的故事、家的文化，一本家谱既可以让你找到自己的根，了解自己的祖先，知道家族的历史渊源，还是了解家族发展过程中的社会、经济、文化的重要典籍。

国有国史，家有家史，重视家谱是中华民族尊重祖先而形成的一种自然美德。梁启超曾指出："我国乡乡家家皆有谱，实可谓史界瑰宝。"中国究竟有多少家谱？有关资料显示，目前存世的中国家谱计有5万多种，其中国内3万多种，海外2万多种。无锡图书馆的家谱收藏相当丰富，已达0.2万余种1.9万余册，所涉姓氏165个，被誉为长三角"查谱中心"。

家谱作为一种特别的书籍，有着自己独特的格式，也称家谱的体例。宋代，欧阳修、苏洵等儒学之士，发"慎终追远"之幽思，起孝敬之心于后人，率先修谱，开创了修家谱的先河，所修家谱体例完备，并成为后世典范。从此确立了以欧阳修、苏洵所修的家谱体例为基本的格式。明清时期的家谱内容更加充实，也有进一步的发展，但基本格式仍以欧、苏二谱式为主，包括：谱序、谱例、谱表、谱系、家训、家诫、家规、祠堂、坟地、义庄、仕谱、人物传记和艺文等内容的比较完善的家谱体制。

欧阳修的家谱体例是先图（家谱称为世系图，属于"世表"的范围），然后列传，是表与传的分别运用。苏洵的家谱体例是谱图下注事实（注人物事迹），五世一揭，是表与传的综合运用。

那么，惠山祠堂保存的家谱里都写了什么呢？

一部完整的家谱，首先记载了本族世系和重要人物事迹。惠山祠堂里的家谱，大都记载着家族先祖到无锡地区世居后的详细情况。重要人物也在家谱中

占据重要篇幅，因为通过对本家族历史人物的记载，可以体现本家族在历史上的地位、作用和影响。

很多家谱，还相当于村史、地方史。几千年来，我国乡村典型的、大量的生活形态是聚族而居，以血缘维系的宗族世世代代在一块土地上生活、繁衍，一村一姓、一村一族的情况比比皆是，要了解村的历史，只需查阅家谱，就几乎可窥全貌。

惠山地区自然风景秀丽，名胜古迹众多，从各家的家谱中，还可以查到不少名胜古迹的典故。

除此之外，家谱里还会记录了本家族的风俗习惯、历史纪事，包括庆典活动的史料。例如，清代乾隆皇帝三次南巡时视察惠山钱王祠的御书诗照片、无锡钱氏湖头支迁锡始祖钱进抵锡1000周年纪念活动就记录在钱氏家谱里，传示后人。

家谱除了记录家史，还规范着子孙的行为。族规、家法、家训多为家谱的组成部分，传统家族的族长，就是根据祖宗制定的家法、家规来行使职权，管理家族，有很大的权威性。在家规、家法中，对成人、嫁娶、丧葬、祭祀等礼仪，乃至日常的衣、食、住、行都有具体的规定。

旧时，汉族人的名字讲究排行字辈，族人入谱，有亲疏长幼之别，为表明代系，方便记忆，同族同辈兄弟取名采用同一个字或同一偏旁，这种做法称排行或排字辈。这些排字的规则也记录在家谱里，常常是一首吉祥庆颂的长诗，也有以五行相生为序的。

在一些比较著名家族的家谱中，还列有仕宦和艺文篇，记载了家族历代官宦名人事迹，包括履历、科第、政绩、功勋、著作、学说、技艺等。许多无名者的好作品在家谱中也得以保存，给研究文学、历史者提供了参考。

What Is Recorded in Genealogies?

Genealogies, also known as clan histories or family trees, document the stories and culture of a family. Holding a genealogy allows individuals to trace their roots, understand their ancestors, and learn about their family's historical origins, as well as significant social, economic, and cultural milestones throughout its development.

Just as nations have national histories, families possess their own histories. The emphasis on genealogies reflects the Chinese culture's respect for ancestors, which is regarded as a natural virtue. Liang Qichao once noted, "Every village and family in our country has its genealogy; it can be considered a treasure in the realm of history." How many genealogies exist in China? Current data indicates that over 50,000 types of genealogies are preserved in China, with more than 30,000 found domestically and over 20,000 abroad. The Wuxi Library boasts an extensive collection of genealogies, numbering over 19,000 volumes encompassing 165 surnames, earning it the title of "Genealogy Center of the Yangtze River Delta."

As a unique type of book, genealogies have their own distinct formats, often referred to as clan records. In the Song Dynasty, scholars such as Ouyang Xiu and Su Xun initiated the recording of genealogies out of a filial piety and a reflective spirit of "revering the past," setting a precedent for future genealogies. Their works established a comprehensive format that served as a model for subsequent genealogies. During the Ming and Qing Dynasties, clan records expanded in content and further developed, yet they remained primarily based on the formats established by Ouyang and Su. These formats typically include elements such as prefaces, examples, tables, lineage charts, family teachings, prohibitions, rules, ancestral halls, burial sites, charitable estates, service records, biographies, and literary contributions, resulting in a fairly complete genealogical system.

Ouyang Xiu's genealogy format begins with a family tree (known as a lineage chart, falling under the category of "genealogical tables"), followed by biographical accounts, distinctly separating charts from narratives. Su Xun's format incorporates annotations under the family tree, detailing significant events, and includes a five-generation overview, blending charts with narratives.

What, then, is written in the genealogies preserved in the Huishan ancestral halls?

A complete genealogy primarily records the lineage of the clan and the significant events of important figures. The genealogies in the Huishan ancestral halls mainly detail the histories of ancestral families after settling in the Wuxi area. Significant individuals occupy notable space within these genealogies, as their accounts reflect the historical status, roles, and influences of the family.

Many genealogies also serve as local histories. For thousands of years, the typical living arrangement in rural China has been clan-based, with families living on the same land for generations, often resulting in villages centered around a single surname or clan. Understanding the history of a village can often be achieved simply by consulting its genealogies.

The Huishan area is renowned for its natural beauty and historical landmarks, and many genealogies reference legends associated with these sites.

Additionally, genealogies often record a family's customs, historical events, and significant celebrations. For instance, the genealogy of the Qian family documents events such as the three southern tours of Emperor Qianlong during the Qing Dynasty, where he inspected the Qian Wang Hall, as well as the commemoration of the 1,000th anniversary of the Qian family's migration to Wuxi, providing valuable historical records for future generations.

Beyond family history, genealogies also regulate the behavior of descendants. Clan rules, family laws, and teachings frequently comprise a genealogy's content. The clan leader traditionally wields authority based on ancestral laws and rules, managing family matters with considerable influence. Specific guidelines regarding ceremonies related to adulthood, marriage, funerals, sacrifices, and even everyday aspects like food, clothing, and living arrangements are typically outlined.

Historically, Han Chinese names often reflect generational order, with distinctions among relatives based on age and closeness. To denote lineage and facilitate memorization, cousins and siblings within the same generation often shared a character or radical in their names, a practice known as generational naming. These naming conventions are recorded in genealogies, often in the form of auspicious poems or sequences based on the Five Elements.

In the genealogies of more prominent families, sections dedicated to official positions and literary achievements detail the accomplishments of historical family members, including their resumes, examination results, political achievements, merits, publications, philosophies, and skills. Many lesser-known but valuable contributions are also preserved within genealogies, providing important references for scholars studying literary history.

祠堂中的涓涓细流是什么水

秦氏双孝祠建于惠山寄畅园旁，祀明成化年间诏旌孝子秦永孚、秦仲孚。乾隆十一年（1746年），裔孙南沙公秦道然等认为："园亭属游观之地，必须建立家祠，始可永垂不朽。"缓步其中，可闻流水潺潺，寻寻觅觅，原是祠园八音涧中有涓涓细水缓缓流出，祠中未有源头，何来活水？

清顺治末，秦德藻将寄畅园合并为一后，请来著名造园专家张涟（南垣）及其侄张鉽来锡将园林改筑。张氏叔侄参照惠山山形地貌，将倾圮假山重新砌垒，模拟惠山连绵逶迤之状，并作为惠山余脉布置，堆成平岗小坡形式，使之与惠山雄浑自然的气势相将。又利用流经墙外的天下第二泉伏流，伴随涧道，引导到假山中来，依据地形倾斜，顺势导流，创造曲涧、澄潭、飞瀑、流泉等水景，使涓涓流水在涧道间产生"金石丝竹匏土革木"八种不同声音，称作"八音涧"，假山也因八音涧的布置增添了生动灵活之趣。

无锡惠山祠堂群密集分布在天下第二泉及其四周泉水群周边，祠堂选址"近泉得水者则为至上"。因此，也可以说天下第二泉的泉水资源、特殊的泉文化和祠堂文化有着千丝万缕的关系，甚至可以说惠山的清泉孕育了古祠堂群落。祠堂，作为中国传统建筑的重要类型，不仅承载着纪念祖先的功能，更是家族文化、宗族观念和社会伦理的重要载体。因泉而聚的祠堂群充分体现了中华民族强大的凝聚力，从个体的事例到群体的协力同心，再到一代一代的接力传承，表现了坚忍不拔、矢志不移的民族精神。这也正是"秦氏双孝祠"这样的祠堂所具有的独特人文价值。

秦氏雙孝祠

What Are the Streams Flowing Through These Ancestral Halls?

The Qin Family Shuangxiao Hall, located adjacent to the Jichang Garden in Huishan, honors the filial piety of Qin Yongfu and Qin Zhongfu, who were recognized during the Ming Chenghua era. In the eleventh year of the Qianlong reign (1746), their descendant, Qindaoran, alongside others, determined that "the garden pavilion belongs to the realm of leisure, and a family hall must be established for it to endure through time." As one strolls through this space, the gentle sound of flowing water can be heard. This is the soft trickle emanating from the Bayin Stream within the hall garden. Yet, without a discernible source within the hall, where does this lively water originate?

At the end of the Shunzhi reign, Qin Dezao merged the Jichang Garden into a unified whole, and invited the renowned landscaping experts Zhang Lian (Nanyuan) and his nephew Zhang Shi to Wuxi to reconstruct the garden. The duo, drawing inspiration from the terrain of Huishan, rebuilt the collapsed artificial hills to mimic the undulating form of Huishan, arranging them as a continuation of its natural contours, thus harmonizing with the majestic essence of Huishan. They also utilized the underground flow of the Second Spring Under Heaven, passing outside the walls, channeling it into the artificial hills. By following the topography, they directed the water flow to create a landscape featuring winding streams, clear pools, cascading waterfalls, and flowing springs. This arrangement produced a variety of sounds that could be categorized into eight distinct types, collectively known as the "Bayin Stream," which added a dynamic charm to the artificial hills.

The Huishan Ancestral Hall Cluster is densely distributed around the Second Spring Under Heaven and its surrounding waters. The selection of sites for the halls is based on the principle that "the closest proximity to water sources is paramount." Thus, it can be asserted that the water resources from the Second Spring Under Heaven are intricately linked to both the unique spring culture and the culture of the halls. The pure waters of Huishan have indeed nurtured this ancient ancestral hall community. As a significant type of traditional Chinese architecture, ancestral halls not only fulfill the function of ancestor worship but also serve as crucial carriers of family culture, clan ideology, and social ethics. The Ancestral Hall Cluster, which has gathered around the spring, embodies the profound cohesion of the Chinese nation, illustrating the resilient and unwavering national spirit through individual stories, collective endeavors, and generations of inherited traditions. This unique cultural value is what defines the Shuangxiao Hall of the Qin family.

祠堂里可不可以有花园

一提到古代的花园，可能很多朋友就会联想到"私定终身后花园"这句话，那么，祠堂这么肃穆的地方，有没有花园呢？

答案是"有的"。根据对无锡惠山祠堂群的考证，很多祠堂都建有花园。小到极简主义的由单座享堂构成的单进、单路祠堂，大到平面布局最为完整的三路四进式祠堂，都可能附有花园，如顾可久祠右部花园、张中丞祠后部花园、王恩绶祠右路花园、杨延俊祠右路花园等。某些祠堂中路还凿有略具园林趣味的泮池水面，如华孝子祠、邵宝祠、唐襄文公祠等，泮池上加条石梁平桥，更能营造出一派幽远宁静的氛围。其中陆宣公祠的享堂与戏台间的院落较小，水池索性溢满整个院落，成为幽深的水院，最为别致。这些大大小小的花园点缀于祠堂群内，形成了极富特色的祠堂园林群。

那么，惠山祠堂群为何会有如此多的花园呢？这就要说到祠堂群的地理位置了。祠堂群位于惠山脚下，惠山有九峰叠翠之胜，地势开阔，山泉成群，古时还能看到芙蓉湖，正所谓"右挹九龙之秀，左望芙蓉如练"。此山、此水自然也是择地造园的好地方，因而逐步形成了"环惠山而园者，若棋布然"的园林群落。到了明代中后期，寄畅园、慧麓小圃、惠岩小筑、黄园、栖隐园、愚公谷、尚德书院、二泉书院等，都发展得颇有规模。

"惠"游祠堂

　　惠山祠堂群,也就"近水楼台先得月",不仅靠山叠石,靠水理池,还得以把周围的美景"借"进祠堂内,使得许多山居园林成为惠山祠堂群中的点缀。早在1989年,著名的园林专家夏泉生和黄茂如两位老先生在编著《无锡寄畅园》时,就注意到惠山祠堂群中出现的这一重要的祠堂园林群现象。群内祠堂除了极为庄严的享堂外,内院、后苑等地方都点缀了山泉水池、曲桥假山、古树名木、奇花异草。经考察统计,到1949年止,惠山古镇历史上先后出现过20多处大小不一、风格各异的祠堂花园。

　　这些花园成为惠山祠堂群的一大特色,给祠堂增加了春夏秋冬四季色彩,也为今天的游客平添了几许闲情与雅趣。

Can Halls Have Gardens?

When ancient gardens are mentioned, many may instinctively recall the phrase "the private garden after the vow of lifelong companionship the secluded gardens often associated with secret vows of Lifelong devotion." But in such a solemn space as a hall, is there a possibility of a garden?

The answer is affirmative. Research on the Huishan Ancestral Hall Cluster in Wuxi indicates that many halls are indeed accompanied by gardens. These range from minimalist single-depth single-route halls consisting of a single main hall to more elaborately designed three-route four-depth, all of which may feature gardens. Examples include the garden to the right of the Gu Kejiu Hall, the garden behind the Zhang Zhongcheng Hall, the garden on the right path of the Wang Enshou Hall, and the garden on the right path of the Yang Yanjun Hall. Some halls also have a central pond that adds a touch of landscape artistry, such as those found in the Hua Xiaozi Hall, Shao Bao Hall, and Tang Xiangwen Hall. Stone bridges across these ponds enhance the serene ambiance. In particular, the courtyard between the main hall and the opera stage of the Lu Xuan Hall is small, with the pond overflowing and creating a deep water courtyard, which is quite distinctive. These various gardens sprinkled throughout the hall cluster form a unique and rich landscape.

So why do so many gardens exist within the Huishan Ancestral Hall Cluster? This can be attributed to the geographic location of the halls. Situated at the foot of Huishan, which features nine emerald peaks and an open terrain abundant with mountain springs, this area once boasted a view of the Furong Lake, aptly described as "with the majestic beauty of the Nine Dragons on the right and the Furong resembling silk on the left." Such mountains and waters naturally provide excellent locations for gardens, leading to the gradual formation of a garden cluster described as "arranged like a chessboard around Huishan." By the mid to late Ming Dynasty, several gardens like Jichang Garden, Huilu Xiaopu, Huiyan Xiaozhu, Huang Garden, Qiyin Garden, Yugong Valley, Shangde Academy, and Second Spring Academy had developed considerable scale.

The Huishan ancestral halls are situated "close to the water's edge," allowing them to draw inspiration from the surrounding scenery. This enables many mountain residences and gardens to serve as embellishments within the hall cluster. As early as 1989, renowned landscape experts Xia Quansheng and Huang Maoru noted the emergence of this significant phenomenon of hall gardens in their monogroph *JiChang Garden in WuXi*. Beyond the solemn halls for ancestor worship, the halls' inner courtyards and rear gardens are adorned with mountain spring pools, winding bridges, artificial hills, ancient trees, and exotic flowers. Statistical surveys indicate that by 1949, there were over 20 hall gardens of varying sizes and styles within the historic Huishan ancient town.

These gardens have become a defining feature of the Huishan ancestral hall conplex, adding vibrant colors throughout the seasons and offering today's visitors a sense of leisure and elegance.

第一篇 邀你进"群"

为什么泥人艺术家出自祠堂

无锡三大特产之一的惠山泥人,常见的圆头圆脑、笑眉笑眼的无锡大阿福,其实是惠山祠堂文化发展中衍生出的一项重要产业。

北有"泥人张",南有惠山泥人,惠山泥人与天津"泥人张"齐名,被誉为彩塑艺术的两颗明珠,但不同于天津泥人的是,惠山泥人不一味追求写实、模仿,而注重造型艺术的夸张和细部的装饰。惠山泥人直接利用惠山古镇宝善桥一带所产的黑泥作原料,依托江南吴文化多彩的民俗风情,因材施技,彩塑结合,抽象与变形相结合,手法简练而生动,是出自惠山古镇的乡土韵味十足的民间艺术瑰宝。

"惠"游祠堂

惠山泥人工艺是依托着古镇祠堂群的发展而衍生出来的。这是为什么呢？原来各地祠堂通常由族内人员负责看管，但惠山祠堂群内有百余家祠堂，所以都是雇用族外的人常年看管，这就促进了就业，有了"祠丁"这种工作。祠堂中为了方便祠丁居住，一般设有简易的生活用房，也算是包住宿了。当然这个差事收入不高，多数祠丁的佣金很低，生活艰难清贫。虽然挣钱不多，但是却不用天天上班，事实上，他们的工作很具季节性特点，也就是在祠丁全年的看管工作中，忙的就是春秋两度的祭扫和祭祀祖宗先人的事宜，其他时候都比较空闲。

钱少，但是可自由支配时间很多，于是，祠丁们开始发挥他们的艺术才能，捏泥人。既有无锡著名的阿福阿喜大胖娃娃，专业说法"粗货"，

又有《珍珠塔》《孟丽君》等手捏戏文，专业说法"细活"。捏出的泥人，就像现在畅销的公仔一样，可以出售，所以祠丁们利用祠堂空间，或祠外公共空间进行设店摆摊，补贴家用。以前调查时，找到了一位年逾九旬的龚炳锡老人，他就是看守倪云林祠堂的老祠丁，是当时为数不多还健在的老祠丁。在他的指导下，对旧惠山祠堂中泥人生产、经营情况进行了一项细致的调查，发现到1949年以前，惠山街上的泥人摊店有48家之多。惠山祠堂文化与惠山泥人艺术之间存在着如此紧密的联系，为惠山祠堂群增添了与众不同的魅力。

  惠山泥人发源于惠山祠堂之中，兴盛于明清至近现代，它不仅是一种独特的艺术形式，更是无锡历史文化的生动体现。对于很多老无锡人来说，惠山泥人承载着他们一代又一代人的情感记忆，连接着过去与现在，如今褪去了历史的尘埃，披上了时代的新装，在新时代能工巧匠的手里，又焕发出新的生命力。

Why do Mud Figurine Artists Emerge From Ancestral Halls?

One of Wuxi's three major specialties is the Huishan mud figurines. The well-known round-headed, round-faced Wuxi Da Afu, characterized by its cheerful demeanor, actually represents an important industry that has emerged from the cultural development of the Huishan ancestral halls.

While "Mud Figurine Zhang" in the north and Huishan Mud Figurines in the south are both recognized as prominent examples of colored sculpture art, the Huishan variety distinguishes itself from its Tianjin counterpart by not merely striving for realism and imitation. Instead, it emphasizes exaggerated artistic forms and intricate embellishments. Made from the locally sourced black clay found around the Baoshan Bridge area of Huishan ancient town, these figurines draw on the rich folk customs of Jiangnan's Wu culture, utilizing various materials and techniques. Their creations combine vibrant colors with abstract and distorted forms, showcasing a lively and straightforward artistic approach, making them a treasure of local folk art that embodies the unique charm of Huishan.

Significantly, the craft of Huishan mud figurines is rooted in the development of the ancestral halls within the ancient town. This connection arises from the fact that these ancestral halls are typically managed by clan members, but with over a hundred halls in the Huishan area, the management often involves hiring outsiders, leading to increased employment opportunities and the emergence of a job known as "ci ding" (hall keeper). To facilitate the living arrangements of these hall keepers, basic accommodations are usually provided within the halls. However, this position tends to offer low income, and many hall keepers struggle financially. Although the income is modest, this role does not adhere to a strict five-day work week. In reality, their work is highly seasonal, centered mainly around the spring and autumn rituals of ancestor worship and tomb sweeping, leaving them with ample free time throughout the year.

With more time at their disposal, these hall keepers began to explore their artistic talents, creating mud figurines that include the famous "Wuxi Da Afu and DaXi"—known in professional terms as "coarse work"—as well as detailed hand-crafted representations from popular local operas such as *The Pearl Tower* and *Meng Lijun*, referred to as "fine work." The figurines they create are marketable, akin to today's popular collectibles, prompting hall keepers to set up stalls either within the halls or in public spaces nearby to supplement their income. During previous research, I encountered a nonagenarian named Gong Bingxi, a former hall keeper of the Ni Yunlin Hall and one of the few remaining elder hall keepers of that era. Under his guidance, a detailed investigation was conducted into the production and sales of mud figurines in the old Huishan ancestral halls, revealing that there were as many as 48 mud figurine stalls on Huishan Street before 1949.

The intricate relationship between Huishan ancestral hall culture and the art of Huishan mud figurines adds a distinctive character to Huishan Ancestral Hall Cluster. Originating within the ancestral halls and flourishing from the Ming and Qing Dynasties to the modern era, Huishan mud figurines represent not just a unique artistic form but also a vivid embodiment of Wuxi's historical culture. For many older residents of Wuxi, these figurines carry the emotional memories of generations, linking the past to the present. Today, having shed the dust of history, they don a new guise, revitalized by the craftsmanship of contemporary artisans, breathing new life into this cherished tradition.

"惠"游祠堂

"马头墙"在无锡叫什么

熟悉古民居的朋友们对"马头墙"一定不陌生,徽州宏村、西递的标志性建筑元素就是错落有致的马头墙。

马头墙在中国传统文化建筑尤其是江南地区的建筑中扮演着非常重要的角色。中国古建筑以木结构为主,这种建筑的好处是防震,有"墙倒屋不倒"的作用,但是也有一个大缺点,就是怕火。除了在庭院中种南天竹,屋顶上雕饰荷花、水草,屋脊接缝处采用龙的儿子鸱吻等象征手段防火外,还采用物理手段防火,马头墙就是其中之一。马头墙实际就是房屋的侧墙,只是这面侧墙在到达屋顶时继续往上升高,将左右两侧相连的房屋有效隔断。如果没有采用马头墙的设计方法,那么一户着火,风助火势,火就极易向两旁蔓延,殃及池鱼。有了马头墙,既隔断了火源,又阻挡了风势,有效防止火势蔓延,所以马头墙又称为封火山墙。

有了这个大体的设计理念和格式后，高出屋顶的部分就可以进行样式的变化。徽州的马头墙就采用了阶梯式层层跌落的样式，既有乐感又省材料，还能象征"昂首奋蹄"的骏马精神。

这种马头墙在无锡惠山祠堂群也能见到，不过更常见的是另一种样式，看着像是两肩耸一帽兜的样子，两肩的样式有一字平肩、美人斜肩、凹陷曲肩。这种山墙形似观音菩萨所戴的兜帽，江南民间流行唤作"观音兜"，王武愍公祠、许文懿公祠、杨藕芳祠都采用了这种样式。

What Is the "Horse-Head Wall" Called in Wuxi?

Those familiar with ancient residences will undoubtedly recognize the term "horse-head wall," a hallmark architectural feature of Huizhou's Hongcun and Xidi, characterized by its staggered formations.

In traditional Chinese architecture, particularly in the Jiangnan region, the horse-head wall plays a crucial role. As most ancient Chinese buildings are primarily wooden structures, this design is advantageous for earthquake resistance, effectively ensuring that "walls may fall, but the house remains standing." However, it has a significant drawback: susceptibility to fire. To mitigate this risk, various symbolic and physical fire prevention methods are employed. For example, planting nandina in courtyards, decorating roofs with lotus and aquatic plant motifs, and incorporating dragon-like ornaments (known as Chiwen) at roof joints serve as symbolic measures. The horse-head wall itself is a practical fire prevention feature; it acts as the side wall of a house that rises above the roof, effectively separating the connected buildings on either side. Without the horse-head wall design, a fire in one household could easily spread to adjacent properties, especially when aided by the wind. The presence of the horse-head wall interrupts the spread of flames and blocks the wind, thus serving as a fire barrier, which is why it is also referred to as a fireproof wall.

Once this fundamental design principle is established, the elevated portions above the roof can be stylistically varied. In Huizhou, the horse-head walls feature a stepped design that cascades downward, providing aesthetic appeal while conserving materials and symbolizing the spirited nature of a galloping horse.

This style of horse-head gable can also be observed among the ancestral halls of Huishan, Wuxi, though a more prevalent variant exists—resembling a hooded cloak with raised shoulders. The shoulder configurations manifest as horizontal straight, elegantly slanted, or concave curved. Resembling the hood adorning Guanyin Bodhisattva, this gable form is colloquially known as the "Guanyin-hood" in Jiangnan folk architecture. Notable examples include the Wang Wumin Hall, Xu Wenyi Hall, and Yang Oufang Hall, all featuring this distinctive design.

第一篇"邀你进'群'"图片来源：惠山古镇、陈鸣谦、金石声、刘楠、上海冷空气、松花江

第二篇 惠风祠话

本篇邀请您深入探索惠山寺祠堂群、横街祠堂群、直街祠堂群、上河塘祠堂群、下河塘祠堂群、惠山浜祠堂群中具有代表性的祠堂，一一揭开这些祠堂背后的故事，让您全面了解惠山祠堂群的丰富内涵，全方位感受惠山祠堂群所蕴含的人文情怀。

AI语音导览

无锡的皇亲国戚

想必大家对驸马已比较熟悉，驸马就是皇帝的女婿，也就是皇帝女儿的丈夫。郡马也是类似的意思，郡马即郡主的丈夫，而郡主就是皇子、皇帝兄弟这些亲王的女儿。因此，过郡马是指当过亲王女婿的过姓人士，这位过姓人士就是过孟玉，他成了徐王棣的郡马。过氏宗族自然也成了无锡的名门望族。

那么过孟玉何德何能，居然能被亲王看上，成为皇族姻亲呢？总结起来，有两大主要原因：一是家庭背景，二是自身条件。

先来说说家庭背景。其实过孟玉的父亲原先不姓"过"，而是姓"任"，叫任象贤，和弟弟任象俊一起被宋高宗赵构录用，做了贴身侍卫。不得不说，赵构选人非常有眼光。南宋建炎元年（1127年），在江苏镇江附近，赵构面临着人生的生死大关，前面有波涛汹涌的大江挡路，后面是杀气腾腾的金兵追击，实在是穷途末路。俗话说，养兵千日，用兵一时，在这生死时速之际，任象贤和任象俊兄弟挺身而出，临危不惧，舍身救主，赵构才得以安全渡江而去。死里逃生，宋高宗非常感念兄弟俩的保驾之功，想要重赏二人。但是两人的回答却是不要重赏，只求复姓，原来他们本姓"过"和"戈"。在遥远的夏代，过国和戈国被一位叫寒浞的人篡灭，两国的人只能改姓"任"，所以兄弟俩恳请宋高宗帮他们复姓，于是高宗就让任象贤恢复过姓，让任象俊恢复戈姓，以褒奖两人的孝心。因为

这件事，这两兄弟复了姓，为子孙后代挣下了一份了不得的家业，也为之后过孟玉被皇家选中奠定了家庭基础。

古人用"孟仲叔季"来表示兄弟姊妹的长幼顺序，"孟"为最长，"季"为最幼。根据孟字推测，过孟玉应该是过象贤的长子。过孟玉的父亲直接救了皇帝的命，但是过孟玉这位"功二代"却并不仰仗父辈救过圣驾的功绩而作威作福，反而是知书达理，尊贤敬老。过孟玉酷爱读书，从小就勤奋苦读，书不离手，更为可贵的是，他读书并不是为了追求功名，而只为家族兴旺。正因为过孟玉德才兼备，拥有美玉般的品质，因

此被皇家相中,做了郡马,还被赐了一大片地,就在无锡锡山的黄藻里,这就解释了为什么原来出生和居住在安徽和州(今安徽和县)的过孟玉会落户到无锡居住。因为身份显赫,他建造的房屋一定会有门楼标志,加上安徽素有"千金门楼四两屋"的说法,这个门楼在当时一定相当轰动,以至于这片地区从此就以"门楼"来命名,并一直沿用到今天。

过孟玉和郡主成家之后,也一直以身作则,虽然贵为郡马,却能勤俭持家,以勤俭教导子孙,而他的子孙们也都以他为榜样,全部诚实勤恳,具备君子风范,并且助人为乐,帮贫济困,兴办义庄,在乡里传为美谈。过孟玉到了老年,也是慈祥平和,情操高尚,这种家风代代相传,也使家族声望日益高涨。过孟玉长子后来去了杭州做官,过孟玉的二儿子则一直生活在无锡,就这样,无锡锡山的过氏子孙绵延不绝,之后逐渐分布无锡各地,再由无锡迁居到北京、上海及世界各地。

祭祀过孟玉的过郡马祠是无锡唯一的皇亲祠堂,和对面的钱武肃王祠,以及惠山寺这座曾经的寺庙祠堂成鼎足之势,成为惠山祠堂群的"门面"和"窗口"。

走进过郡马祠的大门,就是偌大的天井,往前是四开间、古色古香的明清建筑,中间悬挂"南渡褒忠"匾额,点出过氏祖先荣耀之由来,也宣扬了过氏一脉的忠贞气质。中间的木板屏风悬挂都督公和郡马公的彩色画像,两边是一副对联:"胜地有佳山水;善人多贤子孙",正合过孟玉一世为人。两边墙上挂着后代贤人的画像,以及解释过姓由来的书轴,还有锡山过氏家谱总世系图等。

The Imperial Relatives of Wuxi

People are familiar with the title "Princess Consort," which refers to the son-in-law of the emperor, the husband of a princess. Similarly, the Duke Consort is the husband of a "County Princess," who is usually the daughter of a prince, the emperor's son or brother. The phrase "Duke Consort Guo" refers to a person from the Guo family who became a royal son-in-law, specifically Guo Mengyu, who married the daughter of Prince Xu. This marriage elevated the Guo family to the ranks of prominent families in Wuxi.

What qualities did Guo Mengyu possess to become a royal in-law? Two main factors contributed to this: his family background and his personal virtues.

First, let's examine his family background. Guo Mengyu's father was not originally surnamed "Guo" but "Ren," known as Ren Xiangxian. He, along with his brother Ren Xiangjun, served as personal guards to Emperor Gaozong of the Southern Song Dynasty, Zhao Gou. Their loyalty proved crucial during a life-threatening moment for Zhao Gou in the first year of the Jianyan period. When Zhao Gou was pursued by the Jin army near Zhenjiang, facing both a mighty river and fierce enemies that blocked his escape, it was the Ren brothers who risked their lives to save the emperor, ensuring his safe passage. In gratitude for this life-saving act, the emperor wanted to reward them richly, but the brothers only requested the restoration of their ancestral surnames. Originally from the ancient states of Guo and Ge, their ancestors had been forced to change their names to "Ren" during the Xia Dynasty when their states were overthrown. Moved by their filial piety, Emperor Gaozong granted their request, restoring the surname "Guo" to Ren Xiangxian and "Ge" to Ren Xiangjun, thus establishing a prestigious lineage for their descendants and laying the foundation for Guo Mengyu's eventual royal connection.

The ancients used the terms "Meng, Zhong, Shu, and Ji" to indicate the order of seniority among brothers and sisters, with "Meng" being the eldest and "Ji" being the youngest. Based on the character "Meng," Guo Mengyu should be Guo Xiangxian's eldest son, inherited this illustrious legacy. Guo Mengyu was modest and respectful, upholding the values of knowledge and propriety. He was deeply devoted to his studies, not to seek fame or fortune but to bring honor to his family. His virtuous character and intellectual prowess eventually caught the attention of the royal family, and he was chosen as the Duke Consort. The imperial family even granted him a large piece of land in Huangzao, Xishan, Wuxi, which explains why he, originally from Hezhou in Anhui, settled in Wuxi. The grand estate he built, marked by an imposing gate, became so renowned that the area came to be known as "Menlou," a name still used today.

After marrying the County Princess, Guo Mengyu continued to exemplify frugality and diligence, qualities that he instilled in his descendants. Though of noble status, he managed his household with simplicity and taught his children to do the same. His sons followed his example, leading lives of integrity and humility, gaining respect in their community. Guo Mengyu's eldest son later moved to Hangzhou to serve the emperor, while his second son remained in Wuxi, where the Guo family flourished, eventually spreading across the city and beyond to Beijing, Shanghai, and even abroad.

The Guo Duke Consort Ancestral Hall, dedicated to Guo Mengyu, is the only imperial family hall in Wuxi, standing at the forefront of the Huishan Ancestral Hall Cluster. It ranks alongside the Hall of King Qian Wusu and the former Huishan Temple as key cultural landmarks of the region. Entering the hall, one is greeted by a large courtyard and a Ming-Qing style building adorned with a plaque reading "Southward Migration, Loyalty Honored," referencing the Guo family's ancestral glory and highlighting their loyalty and integrity. Inside, portraits of the Guo patriarchs and the Duke Consort are displayed, accompanied by couplets praising the family's virtue and the accomplishments of its descendants. The hall's walls also feature images of notable Guo family figures, explanations of the family's surname origins, and a comprehensive genealogical chart of the Guo lineage.

祠堂群里的"海龙王"

AI语音导览

"海龙王"并非源于无锡本土，乃是源于浙江，这位"海龙王"便是五代十国时期的浙江人钱镠。

那么钱镠为什么会被称为"海龙王"呢？古代多水患，特别是沿海沿江沿河地区。大家都很熟悉作为"浙江文化印记"的钱塘江大潮，它就是钱塘江最终注入东海海口的海潮。钱塘潮虽是千古奇观，却也给周边地区造成了巨大的破坏，很多城镇都曾被海潮整个吞没，湮于大海。因此说当时的百姓生活在水深火热之中，一点也不夸张。不仅潮水袭来之时恐怖，就算平时，也让百姓深受其害，潮患让百姓的饮用水变得越来越

来越咸。因此，想让百姓过上安稳日子，想让地方经济得以发展，必须治理钱塘潮患。传统的方法是用泥土修建堤坝，但是这种做法根本经不住考验，潮水一来，就被那排山倒海之势冲烂，浊浪变得更加泥泞。

因此钱镠摒弃了老旧做法，新创"石屯木桩法"，就是编制很多竹笼，里面装上石头，在海滨整齐码放，堆成防潮大堤，古代称为"海塘"，在海塘前后再打上粗大的木桩进行加固，还在上面压上大石块，这就是钱镠率领工匠建造的"捍海石塘"。这种做法使得海塘十分坚固，直到清雍正时期，依然有一部分屹立在海岸上。钱镠还疏浚钱塘内湖，在太湖地区也设置了专门的治水队——"撩水军"，专门负责浚湖、筑堤，使江浙一带得享灌溉之利。钱镠治水有功，使得原先频受水患之害的地区成为"鱼米之乡"和"丝绸之府"，并为苏州、杭州成为"人间天堂"奠定了坚实的基础。

百姓因钱镠治理水患的功德而感恩于他，称钱镠为"海龙王"，把他建造的"捍海石塘"改称"钱王堤"，并建造祠堂以示纪念。

钱镠在民间被称为"海龙王"，实际上，他的确是"王"，这个"王"就是后梁皇帝朱温封的"吴越王"。过了十几年，又被册封为吴越国王，正式建立吴越国，成为五代十国时期的十国之一。他死后，得到的谥号是"武肃"，因此也被称为钱武肃王。

无锡的钱武肃王祠是宋代迁居到无锡的钱氏后裔所建，如

今已成为全国重点文物保护单位。主殿叫作五王殿，这是因为钱镠过世后传位给了他的儿子钱元瓘，之后又依序传了三位后人，加起来一共是五位国王，也即"五王"。五王殿悬挂"钱武肃王祠"的匾额，两侧悬挂郭沫若书写的对联："功同越水长；德并吴山峙"，堂中还挂着钱氏优秀后代——著名科学家钱伟长题写的"祖德是绳"匾额。步入中堂，有钱武肃王像彩绘屏，这幅画像根据常熟市博物馆的清代画像，用彩绘仿旧白银罩漆真金工艺制成。旁边有钱氏优秀后代——著名书法家、雕塑大师钱绍武所题的长联，左壁有钱镠之外的四位吴越国王以及迁居无锡的钱氏后裔钱进和钱迪的画像和生平简介，右壁是钱氏优秀后代——中国科学院资深院士

钱令希录写的"钱氏家训"。这是一部饱含修身处世智慧的治家宝典，分个人、家庭、社会、国家四个篇章，是钱氏家族的珍贵历史遗产，也是钱氏家族人才辈出的秘诀。

钱武肃王祠的梁上彩绘同样弥足珍贵，这种木构件彩绘在惠山祠堂群极为罕见。彩绘是古建筑装饰的一种手法，按级别可分为和玺、旋子和苏式彩画。前两种常见于宫殿，后者多见于园林。据说钱氏后代在建造祠堂时，考虑到钱镠的身份地位，所以采用了彩绘艺术来提升祠堂的整体格调，虽然年代久远，但仔细辨认，仍能看到寓意"太平有象"的大象图案、寓意"平升三级"的三戟花瓶图案等。除了"画栋"，祠堂还采用了"雕梁"的技艺，通过透雕工艺将戏文展现得淋漓尽致。

"Dragon King of the Sea" of the Ancestral Hall Cluster

In fact, this "Dragon King of the Sea" did not originate in Wuxi but rather in Zhejiang. The title refers to Qian Liu, a prominent figure from Zhejiang during the Five Dynasties and Ten Kingdoms period.

So why was Qian Liu called the "Dragon King of the Sea"? In ancient times, flooding was a common problem, especially in areas near the coast, rivers, and lakes. The Qiantang tidal bore, which is a hallmark of Zhejiang's natural phenomena, is a striking example. This spectacular tidal event, where the Qiantang River flows into the East China Sea, was both awe-inspiring and devastating, often submerging towns and causing immense destruction. The locals suffered greatly, as the tides not only brought flooding but also made their drinking water increasingly saline. Thus, controlling the tides was essential for the well-being of the people and the economic development of the region. The traditional method of constructing mud dikes proved ineffective, as they were easily washed away by the powerful tides, offering little more than a muddy barrier.

Qian Liu abandoned these outdated methods and innovated by introducing the "stone cage and wooden piling method." This technique involved filling bamboo baskets with stones and arranging them along the shore to form a solid sea wall, referred to in ancient times as a "seawall." Large wooden piles were driven into the ground both before and behind the seawall to reinforce it, and heavy stones were placed atop the structure to secure it. This sea defense, known as the "Qian's Seawall," was exceptionally sturdy, and parts of it remained standing even into the Qing Dynasty during the reign of Emperor Yongzheng. Qian Liu also dredged the Qiantang River and established specialized water management teams, known as the "Water Patrol Army," in the Taihu region to manage irrigation and flood control. His efforts transformed the previously flood-prone areas into fertile lands, rich in rice and silk production, laying the foundation for Suzhou and Hangzhou to become the "paradise on earth" they are known as today.

The people, grateful for Qian Liu's contributions to flood control, honored him by calling him the "Dragon King of the Sea" and renamed the seawall he constructed as the "Qian King Dike." They also built halls to commemorate him.

While Qian Liu was revered as the "Dragon King of the Sea" among the populace, he was indeed a king in reality as well, having been granted the title "King of Wuyue" by Zhu Wen, Emperor of the Later Liang Dynasty. Years later, he was officially enfeoffed as the King of Wuyue, establishing the Kingdom of Wuyue as one of the Ten Kingdoms during the Five Dynasties and Ten Kingdoms period. After his death, he was posthumously named "Wusuh," and hence he is also referred to as King Qian Wusuh.

The Qian Wusuh King Ancestral Hall in Wuxi was built by the descendants of the Qian family who had migrated to Wuxi during the Song Dynasty, and it is now a nationally protected cultural heritage site. The main hall is called the "Five Kings Hall," as the throne was passed down from Qian Liu to his son, Qian Yuanguan, and subsequently to three more generations, resulting in a total of five kings. A plaque inscribed "Qian Wusuh King Ancestral Hall" hangs in the hall, with a couplet written by Guo Moruo displayed on both sides: "Merits as long as the waters of Yue, virtues as towering as the mountains of Wu." Additionally, a plaque bearing the words "The Legacy of Our Ancestors" was inscribed by Qian Weichang, a distinguished scientist and descendant of the Qian family. In the central hall, a portrait of King Qian Wusuh is displayed on a painted screen, based on a Qing Dynasty mage from the Changshu Museum, crafted using a traditional technique that involves painting over an antique silver base with lacquer and gold leaf. Adjacent to it is a long couplet written by Qian Shaowu, a renowned calligrapher and sculptor from the Qian family. The left wall features portraits and biographies of the other four Kings of Wuyue, as well as of Qian Jin and Qian Di, two descendants who migrated to Wuxi. The right wall contains the "Qian Family Instructions," inscribed by Qian Lingxi, an esteemed academician of the Chinese Academy of Sciences. This family code, which includes teachings on personal conduct, family management, social responsibility, and national loyalty, remains a cherished part of the Qian family's heritage and has contributed to the family's remarkable legacy.

The beam paintings in the Qian Wusuh King Ancestral Hall are also of great historical value, as painted wood beams are rare in the Huishan Hall Cluster. These paintings, which adorn the wooden components of the structure, follow the traditional styles of the "He Xi," "Xuanzi," and "Su-style" paintings, with the first two styles commonly found in imperial palaces, and the latter typically seen in gardens. It is said that the Qian family adopted these decorative techniques to enhance the hall's grandeur, in accordance with Qian Liu's royal status. Though the artwork has aged, one can still discern the symbolic imagery: elephants representing "peace and prosperity" and vases adorned with three halberds symbolizing the wish for rapid promotion. In addition to the "painted beams," the hall also features intricate "carved beams" with openwork sculptures depicting opera scenes in vivid detail.

祠堂群里的抗金英雄

进入古华山门，往里走，来到香花桥，伫立南望，翠柏掩映下，那座巍然矗立的祠堂——李忠定公祠，纪念的就是抗金英雄李纲。李纲生于北宋元丰六年（1083年），字伯纪。熟悉历史的朋友可能知道这位抗金英雄就是无锡人，所以号梁溪先生。他病逝于绍兴十年（1140年），死后谥号"忠定"。谥号是古代有地位的人死后，朝廷根据其生平表现给予的综合评价。按照宋代对谥号的规定，虑国忘家曰"忠"，安民大虑曰"定"，"忠定"两个字体现了宋代皇室对李纲一生功业的充分肯定。

这座纪念忠定公的祠堂门楼为两层结构，硬山顶，面阔三间。进门后，左侧墙面上刻有李纲后世子孙世系图，右侧刻有李纲生平年表。从这张年表上，可以对李纲有更多的了解。比如，李纲少年时在无锡胶山寺（胶山位于现在的无锡锡山区安镇）读书，19岁时母亲去世，他在惠山上为母亲筑庐守墓三年，空余时间，他在山上种植松树十余万棵，留下惠山大松坡这一名胜。39岁时其父亲去世，李

AI语音导览

纲将其父母合葬在惠山上，丁忧三年期间，又在原万松林中继续植树万棵。1993年，惠山森林公园获评国家森林公园，这份荣耀的背后，也有李纲一份功劳。

当然，李纲最受世人推崇的还是他的爱国情怀。在祠堂东墙的漏窗下，有一块大名鼎鼎的"揩泪碑"，便是最好的见证。揩泪的是李纲，揩的不是儿女情长之泪，而是忧国忧民之泪。绍兴二年（1132年），李纲因主张抗金被贬，路经福建宁化县城，当时天色已晚，他便在当地的草苍庙过夜。恍惚间，他想起靖康年间东京汴梁被金人攻破，徽宗、钦宗两位皇帝被掳至北国至今未还，大好国土仍在敌人的铁蹄之下，而自己请求恢复中原的建议又未被朝廷采纳，眼看着复兴无望，不禁慨然长叹，泪湿衣襟。片刻之后，李纲揩去泪水，要来纸笔，挥毫写下："不愁芒屦长南谪，满愿灵旗助北征。酹彻一杯揩泪眼，烟云何处是三京？"后人把李纲这首诗和诗后的自序刻碑留存，这就有了大名鼎鼎的"揩泪碑"。不过，现在大家见到的这块碑是后人仿建的。

进入享堂，可以看到很多历史人物对李纲的评价。门前擎檐柱上刻有一副对联："至策大猷，垂法戒于万世；孤忠伟节，奠宗社于三朝。"这副对联原本是宋代著名的理学大师朱熹题写的。门匾上刻着"一世伟人"，也出自朱熹对李纲的评价："孤忠伟节，一世之伟人。"门柱上还有一副对联："进退一身关社稷；英灵千古镇湖山"，则出自林则徐之手。享堂神龛内画着李纲官服坐像，上悬"千古流芳"匾额，两侧对联"望重三朝持亮节；书成十事秉丹心"，则由乾隆年间兵部、工部尚

书费淳题写。对联中频繁提到的三朝，说的是李纲一生历经徽宗、钦宗、高宗三朝，可谓名副其实的"三朝元老"。墙上"其道则隆，其运则剥"出自文天祥《忠定公赞》，意思是用李纲的治国之道，则国运昌盛，否则就国运颓废。

其实，李忠定公祠原先并不是建造在这里，而是建于李纲少年读书的胶山北麓，废弃后进行了重建。明正德年间，南京礼部尚书无锡人邵宝，在惠山开办尚德书院和二泉书院，刻了"五贤遗像"以纪念这位先哲。邵宝去世后，他的家人又将李纲祠建于纪念邵宝的邵文庄公祠内，以示崇敬。清代，李纲后人在惠山上河塘择地建祠，康熙五年（1666年），才从上河塘移建到此处，乾隆二年（1737年），皇帝又下令修缮。现在的李忠定公祠则是2006年以后在原址重建的。祠堂修建重建的历史就刻在庭院东面的几方古碑上，只是字迹已经模糊，不太好辨认。

名人评价也好，几修祠堂也好，都说明李纲作为抗金英雄的代表，受到世人褒扬，后人景仰。现在庭院中间还放置着一尊青铜方鼎，仿的是后母戊大方鼎式样，这是现代无锡李氏宗亲联谊会捐建的，底座和鼎身分别刻着篆书铭文"万古长青"和"千秋万代"。李纲，如今依然活在人们心中。

The Anti-Jin Hero of the Ancestral Hall Cluster

Entering the ancient Huashan gate, proceeding inward, reaching the Xianghua Bridge, looking south, you will find the imposing Li Zhongding Hall, which commemorates the anti-Jin hero Li Gang. Born in the sixth year of the Yuanfeng era of the Northern Song Dynasty (1083), Li Gang was also known as Boji. Those familiar with history may know that this anti-Jin hero hailed from Wuxi, earning him the name Mr. Liangxi. He passed away in the tenth year of Shaoxing (1140) and was posthumously honored with the title "Zhongding." This title, granted to individuals of status after death, reflects a comprehensive evaluation based on their life achievements. According to the Song Dynasty's rules for posthumous titles, "loyalty" is expressed as loyalty to the state over family, and "stability" refers to significant concern for the people. Thus, "Zhongding" embodies the Song royal family's high regard for Li Gang's life and accomplishments.

The entrance to the hall dedicated to Li Gang features a two-story structure with a gable roof and three bays. Inside, the left wall displays a family tree of Li Gang's descendants, while the right features a timeline of his life. From this timeline, we gain deeper insights into Li Gang. For instance, he studied at the Jiaoshan Hall in Wuxi during his youth (Jiaoshan is located in the present-day Anzhen of Wuxi's Xishan District). After his mother passed away when he was 19, he built a hut on Huishan to guard her grave for three years, during which he planted over 100,000 pine trees, creating the scenic site known as Dongsongpo. At the age of 39, after the death of his father, Li Gang had his parents interred together on Huishan and continued to plant another 10,000 trees during the three years of mourning. In 1993, Huishan Forest Park was designated a national forest park, a recognition to which Li Gang undoubtedly contributed significantly.

Li Gang is most revered for his patriotic spirit. A well-known stone called the "Tear Wiping Tablet" is found under a window on the east wall of the hall, serving as poignant evidence of this sentiment. The tears he wiped were not those of familial sorrow, but rather of patriotism and concern for the people. The story behind this is as follows: In the second year of Shaoxing of the song Dynasty(1132), after being demoted for advocating resistance against the Jin, Li Gang passed through Ninghua County, Fujian. As night fell, he stayed overnight at the local Caocang Hall. In a moment of reverie, he recalled how the Jin had breached the city of Bianliang during the Jingkang era, capturing the Huizong and Qinzong emperors, who had yet to return, while the homeland continued to suffer under enemy occupation. Despite his proposals to restore the Central Plains being ignored by the court, he felt a sense of hopelessness about the possibility of revival and could not help but sigh deeply, wetting his clothes with tears. After a moment, Li Gang wiped away his tears, took up paper and brush, and wrote: "Not worried about my shoes being long for exile; I only wish my divine banner would aid the northern campaign. Pour a cup for my tearful eyes; where is the three capitals amidst the smoke and clouds?" Later generations engraved this poem and its preface on a tablet, which became the famous "Tear Wiping Tablet." The current tablet is a replica built by later generations.

Upon entering the main hall, one can see numerous historical evaluations of Li Gang. The pillars supporting the eaves at the entrance are engraved with a couplet: "Through great strategies and guidelines, he sets a precedent for future generations; with solitary loyalty and noble character, he establishes the foundation of the state across three dynasties." This couplet was originally penned by Zhu Xi, a renowned Neo-Confucian master of the Song Dynasty. The plaque above the door reads "Great Person of a Generation," also derived from Zhu Xi's assessment of Li Gang as "a solitary loyal and noble figure, a great person of his time." Another couplet inscribed on the door pillars, "Advancing and retreating, my life concerns the state; heroic spirits endure through the ages," was written by Lin Zexu. Within the hall, a painted statue of Li Gang in official attire can be found, suspended with a plaque that reads "Eternal Fame," flanked by couplets "Respected across three dynasties for his upright character; recounting ten virtues, holding a loyal heart," inscribed by Fei Chun, a minister of war and works during the Qianlong period. The "three dynasties" mentioned in the couplets refers to the three reigns—Huizong, Qinzong, and Gaozong—through which Li Gang lived, earning him the title of "veteran of three dynasties." The inscription on the wall, "If the method is honorable, the fate will prosper; if the method is flawed, the fate will decline," comes from Wen Tianxiang's *Praise for Zhongding*, suggesting that under Li Gang's governance, the nation would thrive; otherwise, it would face decline.

In fact, the Li Zhongding Hall was not originally built at its current location but was situated at the northern foot of Jiaoshan, where Li Gang studied in his youth. After falling into disrepair, it was rebuilt during the Ming Dynasty. During the Zhengde era, Shao Bao, a native of Wuxi and Minister of Rites in Nanjing, established the Shangde Academy and Second Spring Academy in Huishan and carved "Portraits of the Five Worthies" to honor this philosopher. After Shao Bao's death, his family built the Li Gang Hall within the Shao Wenzhuang Hall, dedicated to Shao Bao, as a mark of respect. During the Qing Dynasty, descendants of Li Gang chose a site on Huishan, constructing the hall. In the fifth year of Kangxi (1666), it was relocated from Shanghetang to its current site, and in the second year of Qianlong, the emperor ordered repairs. The present Li Zhongding Hall was reconstructed after 2006 at its original location. The history of the hall's construction and renovations is inscribed on several ancient tablets in the eastern courtyard, although the inscriptions have become somewhat illegible.

The acclaim of notable figures and the repeated renovations of the hall both illustrate Li Gang's enduring legacy as a national hero, respected and admired by later generations. In the courtyard, there now stands a bronze square ding, modeled after the famous Simuwu Ding, which was donated by the modern Wuxi Li Clan Association. The base and body of the ding are inscribed with the seal script phrases "Evergreen through the Ages" and "Eternity Across Millennia." Thus, Li Gang continues to live on in the hearts of the people.

三让天下的圣人

惠山祠堂群有一座圣人祠堂，祠堂中为一位被圣人誉为圣人的人物，他就是开创了吴地历史的泰伯。司马迁在《史记》中记载，孔圣人曾赞誉泰伯："太伯，其可谓至德也已矣"，这里的"太伯"就是泰伯。泰伯是陕西人，在交通极不发达的上古时代，从陕西千里迢迢来到江南一带，成就了一段流芳千年的佳话，这就是"泰伯奔吴"的故事。

商朝末年，陕西岐山有个姬姓周部落，看过《封神演义》的朋友可能立马联想到了姜子牙辅佐的周文王姬昌，没错，周部落的首领周太王古公亶父就是姬昌的爷爷。古公亶父颇具慧眼，当时就相中了之后灭掉无道商纣王的姬昌，为了传位给姬昌，自然要先传位给姬昌的父亲，也就是他的三儿子季历。在古代，通常都是顺位继承，大儿子泰伯才是法定继承人，泰伯之后，也应该轮到二儿子仲雍，最后才轮到小儿子季历。为了这事，周太王左右为难，经常念叨一句话："我世当有兴者，其在昌乎？"这意思再明显不过。泰伯知道后，不但没有心生嫉妒，反而成全了他父亲的心意，放弃唾手可得的王位，带着二弟仲雍，

找了个为父亲治病采药的借口，奔江南来了。一路上，他们风餐露宿、忍饥挨饿，历尽艰险、长途跋涉，最后在离家乡岐山1500千米之遥的梅里（今无锡梅村）落了户。当时的梅里与中原相比，还处于蛮荒阶段，泰伯不畏艰辛、勇于开拓，将中原先进的农业技术传到江南，并兴修水利，开凿了中国历史上第一条人工河"伯渎河"，数年之间，人民殷富，附近几千户居民听到泰伯如此贤能，纷纷投奔而来，奉立泰伯为君主，建立了"句吴"国，后来成为吴国，并在春秋时期称霸。从泰伯开始，到最后一位吴王夫差结束，吴国共传了二十五世。

其实，泰伯定居梅里后，不是没有回过故乡，在他父亲周太王去世的时候，泰伯就为料理父亲后事回去过，这时候，家族中就有人提出让他继承大统，但他拒绝了。后来，他的三弟季历又找到泰伯，劝说他接受这个王位，但泰伯推说自己已经

成了江南人，不再像个周王了，坚决不肯回去。这样算起来，连同他父亲健在时的"预先让位"，泰伯一共"让"了三次，这就是"三让天下"的故事。后世孔圣人听说这个故事后十分感慨："太伯，其可谓至德也已矣，三以天下让，民无得而称焉。"就是说，泰伯的道德高到了极处，他曾经三次将天下让给弟弟，百姓不知道要如何称颂他的至高德行啊！

正因为泰伯的"至德"，纪念泰伯的祠堂并没有用姓氏命名，而以"至德"命名。至德祠位于著名景点"天下第二泉"的东边，兴建于清代乾隆三十年（1765年），最初并不在此处，泰伯墓在今鸿声鸿山（古谓皇山），泰伯庙在今梅村，因城乡间交通不便，明洪武年间（1368—1398年）在无锡城中大娄巷另建泰伯祠。乾隆三十年（1765年），大娄巷泰伯祠年久失修而倾圮，无锡知县吴钺、浙江遂安知县吴培源等捐资，于惠山东麓二泉亭外东向购得邹园炼石阁、绳河馆旧址，移建至德祠。门额"至德祠"为吴钺所书。此后，此处至德祠几经损毁、复建，现仅存泰伯殿。

至德祠是惠山祠堂群中十个核心祠堂之一，2006年被国

家文物局列为全国重点文物保护单位，2012年又被公布为世界文化遗产预备名录。作为纪念先哲的专祠，至德祠并不属于某个家族所有，而是吴地百姓怀念先祖泰伯，传承至德文化之所。

今天，我们依然感激泰伯，因为他"三让天下"的至德，成就了吴文化三千多年的历史，也成就了无锡作为吴文化发源地的美名。今天的梅村，每逢农历正月初九泰伯的生日，还会举办泰伯庙会，2014年，泰伯庙会被列入国家级非物质文化遗产名录，2024年，作为春节文化组成部分入选联合国教科文组织人类非物质文化遗产代表作名录。

The Sage Who Thrice Yielded the Throne

The Huishan Ancestral Hall Cluster has a hall for a saint who was praised by Confucius as a saint himself. He is Taibo, the founder of the history of Wu region. In the *Records of the Grand Historian* by Sima Qian, Confucius praised Taibo as "Taibo, he can be called a person of supreme virtue." Taibo. He was a native of Shaanxi, and in the ancient times when transportation was not very developed, he traveled thousands of miles from Shaanxi to the southern part of the Jiangnan region. This journey became a legendary story that has been passed down through the ages, known as "Taibo's Journey to Wu."

During the late Shang Dynasty, there was a Zhou tribe with the surname Ji in Qishan, Shaanxi. Those who have read *Fengshen Yanyi* might immediately think of Jiang Ziya assisting King Wen of Zhou, Ji Chang. Indeed, the leader of the Zhou tribe, King Tai of Zhou, Gu Gong Danfu, was Ji Chang's grandfather. This wise grandfather foresaw the potential of Ji Chang, who would later overthrow the tyrannical Shang. To pass the throne to Ji Chang, he first needed to pass it to Ji Chang's father, his third son, Ji Li. Everyone knows that in ancient times, succession typically followed the order of birth, meaning the eldest son, Taibo, was the rightful heir. After Taibo, it would be the turn of the second son, Zhongyong. There was no way it would fall to the youngest son, Ji Li. Because of this, King Tai of Zhou was torn, often murmuring the phrase, "The one who will bring prosperity to our dynasty, is it Chang?" The meaning was crystal clear. When Taibo learned of this, not only did he not become jealous, but he also actually fulfilled his father's wish by relinquishing the throne that was his for the taking. He took his younger brother Zhongyong with him and, using the excuse of gathering medicinal herbs for their father's illness, ventured to Jiangnan region. Along the way, they braved harsh conditions, endured hunger and hardship, faced numerous dangers, and traveled long distances, ultimately settling in Meili (today's Meicun, Wuxi),

1,500 km away from their hometown in Qishan. Compared to the Central Plains, Meili was still in a wild, undeveloped state. He brought advanced agricultural techniques from the Central Plains to Jiangnan, improved water management, and dug China's first artificial river, the Bodu River showing his tenacity and pioneering spirit. Within a few years, the people became prosperous. Hearing of Taibo's wisdom and virtue, thousands of families from nearby areas flocked to join him, and they established the state of Gou Wu, which later became the state of Wu, dominating the region during the Spring and Autumn period. From Taibo to the last King of Wu, Fuchai, the state of Wu was ruled by twenty-five generations.

After settling in Meili, Taibo did return to his hometown when his father, King Tai of Zhou, passed away. During this time, some family members suggested that he should inherit the throne, but he refused. Later, his younger brother Ji Li found Taibo and urged him to accept the kingship. However, Taibo argued that he had become a person of the Jiangnan and no longer resembled a Zhou king. He steadfastly refused to return. Counting the times he had renounced the throne while his father was still alive, Taibo had relinquished the throne three times in total. This is the story of "Thrice Yielding the Throne." Confucius, upon hearing this story, was deeply moved and remarked, " Taibo can be said to have reached the utmost virtue. He thrice yielded the throne, and the people do not know how to extol his supreme moral conduct."

Due to Taibo's "supreme virtue," the hall dedicated to him was not named after his surname but rather called the "Shrine of Supreme Virtue" (Zhide Hall). It is located to the east of the famous scenic spot "Second Spring Under Heaven." The shrine was built in the 30th year of the Qianlong era of the Qing Dynasty (1765), but it was not originally located here. Taibo's tomb is in present-day Hongsheng, Hongshan (formerly known as Huangshan), and the Taibo Temple is in today's Meicun (also called Meili). Due to inconvenient transportation between the rural and urban areas, a new Taibo Hall was built in Dalou Alley in Wuxi city during the Hongwu era of the Ming Dynasty (1368–1398) . By the 30th year of the Qianlong era (1765), the Taibo Hall in Dalou Alley had fallen into disrepair. Wuxi County Magistrate Wu Yue, along with Wu family members Zou Qi and others, the ninth main editor of the family genealogy, Qianlong Ding Si Imperial Scholar, and Zhejiang Sui'an County Magistrate Wu Peiyuan, funded the relocation of the hall. They purchased the former sites of Lian Shi Pavilion and Sheng He Pavilion in the Zou Garden, east of the Second Spring Pavilion, at the eastern foot of Huishan, and moved the Hall of Supreme Virtue there. The plaque reading "Hall of Supreme Virtue" was written by Wu Yue. Since then, the hall has been destroyed and rebuilt several times, and only the Taibo Hall remaine now.

The Hall of Supreme Virtue (Zhide Hall) is one of the ten core halls in the Huishan Ancestral Hall Cluster . In 2006, it was designated as a National Key Cultural Relics Protection Unit by the State Administration of Cultural Heritage, and in 2012, it was listed on the Tentative List of World Cultural Heritage Sites. As a hall dedicated to commemorating the sage Taibo, the Zhide Hall does not belong to any specific family but serves as a place for people in the Wu region to honor their ancestor Taibo and to carry on the culture of supreme virtue.

Today, we still hold deep gratitude towards Taibo, for his supreme virtue in "Thrice Yielding the Throne," which has contributed to over three thousand years of Wu culture and established Wuxi's reputation as the birthplace of Wu culture. Every year on the ninth day of the first lunar month, Taibo's birthday, a temple fair is held in Meili to honor him. In 2014, the Taibo Temple Fair was listed as a national intangible cultural heritage by the State Council. In 2024, it was selected as part of the Spring Festival culture and included in the UNESCO Representative List of the Intangible Cultural Heritage of Humanity.

古人有多孝

百善孝为先，孝道是中国传统文化中极具生命力和影响力的核心价值观。

据考证，商代就有了"孝"字，金文的"孝"字，字形是一个孩子托着老人，作服侍状。西周以后，孝文化日臻成熟。历朝历代都有大量关于孝的文献记载和民间口头文学。其中，以《孝经》和《二十四孝》为重要代表。孝道文化也成为儒家的伦理基石。孔子特别重视孝道，他认为孝是仁之本、德之始。在儒家经典《论语》中，"孝"出现了19次。《论语》共有二十章，涉及"孝"的内容就占了一半。

"孝心一开，百善皆来。"把孝作为仁之本，爱人首先从爱父母做起，然后爱族人、爱长上、爱民族、爱国家。这种推己及人的自然亲情，符合人的认识与情感发展规律。在古代中国，孝是治国安民的主要精神基础。

首推的是有孝祖祠之称的华孝子祠。在无锡惠山祠堂群里，"华孝子祠"是最古老，占地面积最大，也是21世纪第一个有后裔出资修缮的祠堂。

华孝子祠始建于唐代，祀东晋无锡孝子华宝。华宝生于东晋，成长于宋，逝世于齐。据载，华宝幼年丧母，父亲华豪于东晋义熙末年随刘裕防守长安，临行前告诉年仅八岁的儿子华宝，待自己卫戍期满回乡便为儿子行成人礼、娶亲。然而长安陷落，华豪死于战争。华宝恪守与父亲的约定，直至70多

岁仍未戴冠成亲,此事在民间传为佳话。时人把故事的着眼点放在"孝义"上,成就了华宝的孝义之名,华宝也成为无锡第一位被写入国史的平民百姓,华氏后人也秉承忠孝节义的祖训,成为造福地方的大族。

华孝子祠位于天下第二泉景点东侧。门前立四面牌坊,有一座木石结构、藻饰精美的亭子,四根直径大约40厘米的花岗岩石柱支撑着木质亭顶,俗称无顶亭。无顶亭和一般的亭子不一样,上面中空,抬头可望天,雨水也会从中空处落入亭内井中,这在无锡是独一无二的,恐怕在全国也鲜少有这样的亭子。"无顶"意为"无冠",亭子没有"帽子",以纪念终生"未冠"未娶同样没有"帽子"的孝子华宝。无顶亭系华氏宗族表忠孝节义及科第的纪念建筑物,建于清乾隆十三年(1748年)。祠内有始建于明代

的石桥、楠木享堂，有珍贵的《真赏斋法帖》及文徵明所绘《纺绩督课图》、所书《春草轩辞》以及元以来历代祠堂修复碑记。

另一处值得一书的祠堂是位于无锡惠山古镇南朝古刹惠山寺香花桥南侧、邹忠公祠旁、寄畅园对面的李忠定公祠，它纪念的是前文所述宋代抗金名臣李纲。

首先，李纲对母亲可谓至孝。李纲19岁时，母亲去世。李纲在母亲下葬时，手书"释氏妙法《莲华经》"七卷置于棺椁中。他在家乡惠山上为母亲筑庐守墓三年，亲情感动乡里。空余时间，他在山上种植松树十余万棵，留下惠山大松坡这一

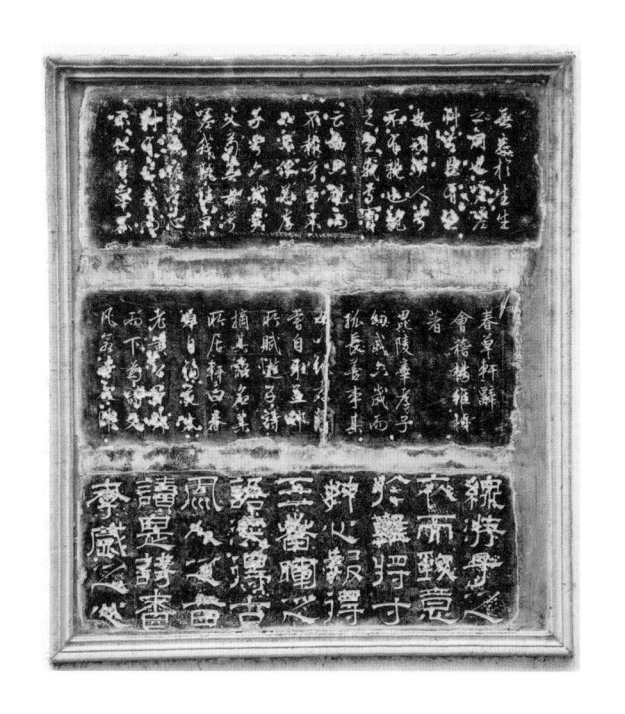

名胜。宣和三年（1121年）李纲之父李夔病故，李纲于当年八月将父亲的灵柩运至无锡，在母亲的坟墓中同穴下葬。并上书敕封母亲为"韩国夫人"。其次，李纲对吴家也深怀至亲之情，他每年都会带着兄弟四人给姨母扫墓，亲写祭文，他在《祭姨母吴宜人文》写"每见夫人，如我母存"，今人看了，都无不为之动容。相关文献记载，在李纲去世时，其小舅父吴彦举也在受荫补之列，这是他能为吴家做的最后一件事，可见他至死都想念着外婆家。

《孝经》开宗明义第一章就说："孝始于事亲，终于事君。"如果没有对亲人长辈的孝，就没有对国家的忠，可见，李纲忠君爱国、刚正不阿的品格，是有其家族渊源的，是在忠孝文化熏陶下形成的。

How Filial Were the Ancients?

The concept of filial piety has deep roots in Chinese culture, often considered the important virtue. The character for "filial piety" (孝) can be traced back to the Shang Dynasty, depicted in bronze inscriptions as a child supporting an elder, symbolizing care and service. By the Western Zhou period, filial culture had reached maturity, with extensive documentation in literature and oral traditions across various dynasties. Key texts such as *The Classic of Filial Piety* and *The Twenty-four Filial Exemplars* stand out as significant representations of this virtue. Confucius emphasized filial piety, regarding it as the foundation of benevolence and morality. In *the Analects*, the term "filial piety" appears 19 times, underscoring its importance, as nearly half of the text's twenty chapters address this theme.

The saying "When filial piety flourishes, all virtues follow" encapsulates the idea that love for others begins with love for one's parents and extends to family, elders, the nation, and the country. This natural progression of affection aligns with human cognitive and emotional development. In ancient China, filial piety served as a crucial spiritual foundation for governance and social stability.

The first is the Hua Xiaozi Hall, considered the oldest and largest among the Huishan Ancestral Halls, and the first to be restored in the current century with funds from its descendants.

Founded in the Tang Dynasty, the hall honors Hua Bao, a paragon of filial piety from the Eastern Jin Dynasty, who lived through the

Song Dynasty and died in the Qi Dynasty. Hua Bao, born in Wuxi, lost his mother at an early age. His father, Hua Hao, was called to defend Chang'an during the Later Jin, promising his son that he would return to conduct his coming-of-age ceremony. However, after Chang'an fell, Hua Hao perished in battle, and Hua Bao honored his father's promise, remaining unmarried and unadorned until the age of seventy, earning widespread acclaim for his steadfastness. This story, emphasizing filial devotion and righteousness, cemented Hua Bao's legacy, making him the first commoner from Wuxi to be documented in national history. His descendants upheld the values of loyalty, filial piety, and integrity, becoming prominent benefactors of the local community and founding the Huashi clan of Dangkou, Wuxi.

The Hua Xiaozi Hall is located to the east of the Second Spring Under Heaven, featuring four archways at its entrance. A beautifully decorated pavilion, supported by four granite columns, each approximately 40 cm in diameter stands in front of the hall, distinctive for its open roof—commonly referred to as the "roofless pavilion." This unique structure allows rainwater to fall into an interior well, a rarity not only in Wuxi but across the nation. The pavilion's name symbolizes Hua Bao's lifelong status of being "unadorned"—a fitting tribute to his filial piety. The hall, constructed in the thirteenth year of the Qianlong reign (1748), serves as a monument to the Hua clan's commitment to loyalty, filial piety, integrity, and scholarly achievement. Inside the hall, one can find a stone bridge and a hall made of camphor wood from the Ming Dynasty, alongside treasured artifacts such as the *Zhenshangzhai Calligraphy* and works by the Ming artist Wen Zhengming.

Another significant ancestral hall is the Li Zhongding Hall, located to the south of Huishan Hall, near the fragrant flower bridge and adjacent to the Zou Zhonggong Hall. It commemorates Li Gang, a renowned statesman of the Song Dynasty who resisted the Jin invasion.

Li Gang's filial devotion was profound; he mourned his mother deeply, and at the age of 19, he placed copies of *the Lotus Sutra* in her coffin upon her death. He dedicated three years to guarding her grave, earning the affection of his community. After his father's passing, he ensured that both parents were buried together, posthumously honoring his mother with the title of "Lady of Han." He also maintained close ties with his maternal relatives, honoring his aunt with annual visits to her grave, which he personally marked with heartfelt memorials.

The *Classic of Filial Piety* articulates the principle that filial duty to parents is foundational to loyalty to one's sovereign. Thus, Li Gang's loyalty to the state and his unwavering integrity were deeply rooted in his family's values and shaped by a culture steeped in compassion and filial piety.

与陆游齐名的无锡诗人

从小学到高中,我们学了不少陆游的诗作,与陆游同时代,还有一位与陆游齐名的诗人,他就是尤袤。尤袤和陆游以及另外两位大家也非常熟悉的诗人——杨万里、范成大并称为"南宋四大家"。

尤袤是南宋的著名诗人,他的诗作秀丽婉约、淡泊优雅,著有《遂初小稿》《内外制》《老子音训》《乐溪集》《全唐诗话》等,只可惜保留下来的不多。尤袤出生于无锡,从小聪明过人,5岁就能咏诗作对,被四方乡邻称为"神童",长大后自是满腹经纶、才华横溢,更关键的是还极富创造力。这样一位人才参加科举考试,中个状元好比囊中取物。只因他得罪了当时大权在握的奸臣秦桧,结果被降为三甲37名,实在可惜!之后他一路做官,因为抗金有功,还做到了礼部尚书。由于功勋卓著,皇帝让他延迟退休,直到70岁才终于放他告老还乡。他就在惠山造了几间房屋,用作读书之处,取名为"锡麓书堂",又在他祖父建造的"依山亭"旧址,建造了"遂初书院"。书院建立后,立刻吸引了许多慕名前来拜师的学子,其中一位学生还中了状元,这就是无锡历史上第一个状元——蒋重珍。学生得中状元,对尤袤来说,也算是一种补偿、一种证明。

"遂初书院"的匾额是宋光宗亲题赐给他的,足见皇帝对他的厚爱。"遂初"是尤袤的号,可以理解为"不忘初心"的意思,尤袤的初心一定与书有关,因为尤袤是位极爱看书之人,他曾经把书籍比作"代肌之肉,寒之裘,寂处之朋友,幽忧之金石琴瑟",足见他嗜书如命。晚年的尤袤,一心向书,就闭门谢客,宅在家里以抄书为乐,不仅自己抄得不亦乐乎,还让弟子、婢仆和他一起抄,这么抄啊抄,居然抄出了三万多卷,真是"抄书破万卷"了。为了把这些书收藏起来,他还在城中的房子里专门建造了"万卷楼",因为藏书丰富,且其中不少善本、珍本和孤本,所以他的万卷楼也成了南宋著名的藏书楼,他也被人戏称为"尤书橱"。更为别出心裁的是,他还

按照经史子集4部44小类的顺序，为体量庞大的藏书编撰了书目，首开中国书目著录版本之先河，这就是著名的《遂初堂书目》。在"子"部下面，他又开创性地增加了"谱录"这一类别，用来收藏文房、印玺等图谱之书。清代纪晓岚在编纂《四库全书总目》时还学习了他这一创举。

这样一位爱书的功臣自然受到后人敬重。朱元璋当上皇帝没多久，尤袤的后人就在惠山建祠堂来纪念文简公尤袤，就叫"锡麓书院"，旁边重新建造了"锡麓书堂"，之后在清代、民国时期数次重建。

现在的尤文简公祠已被评为全国重点文物保护单位。祠堂位于天下第二泉庭院的南侧山坡上，东接"垂虹廊"，北接天下第二泉，南接碧山吟社。整个建筑飞檐翘角，雕花门窗，古色古香。现存的万卷楼、遂初堂均用了尤袤所起的旧名，以志纪念。

现在这里不仅是中华尤氏宗亲祭祀、寻根之地，更成了人们品茗赏泉的绝佳去处。

A Poet From Wuxi Renowned Alongside Lu You

We studied extensively from elementary to high school, however, contemporaneous with Lu You was another eminent poet, You Mao, who, along with Lu You and two other well-known figures, Yang Wanli and Fan Chengda, are collectively referred to as the "Four Great Poets of the Southern Song Dynasty."

You Mao, a prominent poet of the Southern Song era, is celebrated for his elegant and refined poetry, which includes works such as *Sui Chu Xiao Gao*, *Nei Wai Zhi*, *Laozi Yin Xun*, *Le Xi Ji*, and *Quan Tang Shi Hua*, although only a limited number of his writings have survived. Born in Wuxi, You Mao displayed exceptional intelligence from a young age, composing poetry and couplets by the age of five, earning the title of "child prodigy" among his peers. As he matured, he became a well-rounded scholar, rich in knowledge and creativity. Given his talents, passing the imperial examination and becoming a top scholar seemed almost assured. Unfortunately, due to a falling out with the powerful corrupt official Qin Hui, he was demoted to the 37th position in the third rank, a tragic turn of fate. He later served in various government positions, ultimately attaining the role of Minister of Rites due to his contributions to the anti-Jin resistance. His exemplary service led the emperor to grant him an extended retirement, allowing him to return home only at the age of 70.

In his later years, he constructed several buildings at the foot of Huishan Mountain for scholarly pursuits, naming one "Xilu Shutang." He also established the "Sui Chu Academy" on the site of an old pavilion built by his grandfather. The academy quickly attracted students from near and far, one of whom eventually became the first top scholar in Wuxi's history—Jiang Zhongzhen. The success of his students served as a form of compensation and validation for You Mao.

The plaque of "Sui Chu Academy" was personally inscribed by Emperor Song Guangzong, underscoring the emperor's deep appreciation for You Mao. The name "Sui Chu" can be interpreted as "staying true to one's original aspirations," which aligns with You Mao's love for books. He was known for his profound admiration of literature, famously comparing books to "flesh for the body, warmth for the cold, companions in solitude, and treasures of silence," reflecting his lifelong passion for reading. In his later years, You Mao devoted himself entirely to literature, isolating himself from guests to find joy in transcribing texts. Remarkably, he completed over thirty thousand scrolls, a testament to his dedication. To house his extensive collection, he built the "Wan Juan Lou" (Ten Thousand Scrolls Pavilion) in the city. His library became renowned not only for its volume but also for its many rare and unique editions, leading him to be playfully referred to as "You Shuchu" (You the Bookcase). Additionally, he organized his vast collection according to the four categories of classical literature, creating a bibliographic catalog known as *the Sui Chu Tang Shu Mu*, which set a precedent for bibliographic practices in China. Notably, he introduced the category of "Pu Lu" (Genealogies) to catalog texts related to literary implements and seals. This innovation was later adopted by the Qing Dynasty scholar Ji Xiaolan when compiling *the Complete Catalogue of the Four Treasuries*.

A figure revered for his love of books, You Mao was honored by his descendants shortly after the rise of Zhu Yuanzhang, who built a hall in Huishan dedicated to the venerated scholar, named "Xilu Academy." Adjacent to it, the "Xilu Shutang" was reconstructed multiple times during the Qing Dynasty and the Republic of China era.

Today, the You Wenjian Hall has been designated as a national key cultural relic protection unit. The hall is situated on the southern slope of the garden surrounding the "Second Spring Under Heaven," with the "Chuihong Corridor" to the east, the Second Spring Under Heaven to the north, and Bishan Yinshe to the south. The architecture features elegant eaves, intricate wooden carvings, and an antique ambiance. The existing Wan Juan Lou and Sui Chu Tang retain the names originally bestowed by You Mao, commemorating his legacy.

Currently, this site serves not only as a place for the descendants of the You family to pay their respects and trace their roots but also as a popular destination for tea tasting and enjoying the spring.

祠堂群里的茶圣是谁

大家都知道，无锡有个著名的"天下第二泉"，是全国只此一家的"第二泉"。那么这个"天下第二"是谁评定的呢？

他就是唐代的陆羽。陆羽是湖北人，从小被寺庙的禅师收养，但陆羽并没有皈依佛门，他是在给师傅打杂煮茶的过程中，爱上了茶文化，所以长大后选择游历天下，遍访名茶。现代人喝茶大多不太讲究，自来水烧开泡泡即可，但是古人喝茶讲究"名泉配名茶"，喝好茶，水一定要好，否则就有焚琴煮鹤之嫌。因此，陆羽也同时考察名泉。在这一过程中，他写了一本著作《茶经》，十分轰动，他也就成了"茶圣"。后来证明，这本《茶经》也是世界上第一部茶叶专著。

无锡惠山就是他考察过的地方之一。当时正值安史之乱，陆羽一为考察，二为避乱，就躲进了江南一带的山林中。他每天穿着纱巾短褐，脚上踏着草履，独自在山野间游走，深入农家茶园，探寻茶叶与泉水的奥秘。他时而挥杖击打林木，时而伸手探弄流水，直到夜幕降临，才心满意足地回家。回的这个"家"，其实就是惠山寺，为此，他还写下了著名的《惠山寺记》，并对惠山泉水进行了品评，将其列为"天下第二"。"天下第二泉"最早就是因为陆羽而成名，因此也称为"陆羽泉""陆子泉"。此后，二泉日益名盛，不断得到专家、茶客的赞誉，例如著名词人苏东坡就一定要来到二泉才肯泡他珍贵的"小团月"茶饼。

纪念陆羽的祠堂就叫陆子祠，最早是北宋时建造的，就建在二泉亭的上坡，之后曾经加入了悯农诗人李绅、爱情诗人秦观、著名画家倪云林等另外九位著名人物，成了"十贤祠"。1996年，才又恢复为"陆子祠"。里面有《陆羽品茶图》的漆画，画上陆羽悠然自得地横靠在山石间，煮茶品茶，上面还写着《茶经》中的名句："其水，用山水上、江水中、井水下……"两边挂着大型屏书《惠山寺记》。檐廊前有一副对联，"试第二泉，且对明亭暗窦；携小团月，分尝山茗溪茶"，这是由苏东坡诗句"独携天上小团月，来试人间第二泉"改写而来的。

这副对联也成了天下第二泉的新广告，您不妨也带上中意的名茶，在这山野美景中，试试茶圣评定的"天下第二泉"。

视频 陆子祠

Who Is the Tea God of the Ancestral Hall Cluster?

As we all know, Wuxi has a famous "Second Spring Under Heaven," which is the only "second spring" in our country. So who determined this "second under heaven"?

It was Lu Yu, a Tang Dynasty person. Lu Yu was from Hubei and was adopted by a monk at a hall when he was young. However, Lu Yu did not become a Buddhist monk. Instead, he fell in love with tea culture while serving tea to his master and decided to travel around the country to visit famous teas after he grew up. Modern people don't pay much attention to drinking tea, they just boil tap water and drink it, but ancient people drank tea by matching famous springs with famous teas. Good tea needs good water, otherwise it would be like cooking a zither and boiling a crane. Therefore, Lu Yu also examined famous springs at the same time. In this process, he wrote a book called *The Classic of Tea*, which caused a great sensation. He also became known as the "Sage of Tea." Later it was proved that this book *The Classic of Tea* was also the world's first book on tea.

Wuxi Huishan is one of the places he visited. At that time, the Anshi Rebellion was happening, so Lu Yu went there either to investigate or to escape from the chaos. He hid himself in the mountain forests of the southern part of Jiangsu. Every day, he wore a gauze headscarf and a short jacket, and wore straw sandals on his feet. He traveled alone in the mountains and fields, visiting tea gardens in rural areas and exploring the secrets of tea and springs. Sometimes he would beat the trees with his stick, and sometimes he would touch the water with his hand, until he was satisfied and went home at night. The "home" he returned to was actually the Huishan Temple, so he wrote the famous article *Record of Huishan Temple*, in which he evaluated the Huishan spring water and ranked it as the second best in the world. Thus, the Second Spring Under Heaven first became famous because of Lu Yu and is also known as

"Lu Yu Spring" or "Lu Zi Spring." Since then, the spring has gained increasing fame, continuously receiving praise from experts and tea enthusiasts. For example, the renowned poet Su Dongpo insisted on coming to the spring to brew his precious "Xiao Tuan Yue" tea cakes.

The Hall dedicated to Lu Yu is called the Lu Zi Hall, originally built in the Northern Song Dynasty, situated uphill from the Second Spring Pavilion. Later, nine other famous figures, including Li Shen, the poet of compassion for farmers, Qin Guan, the poet of love, and the famous painter Ni Yunlin, were included, making it the "Hall of Ten Worthies." In 1996, it was restored to the Lu Zi Hall. Inside, there is a lacquer painting titled "Lu Yu Tasting Tea," depicting Lu Yu leisurely reclining among the rocks, brewing and tasting tea. The painting also features a famous quote from *The Classic of Tea*: "For water, use mountain water as the best, river water as the second, and well water as the least."

On both sides hang large inscriptions of "Huishan Temple Record." In front of the veranda is a pair of couplets: "Try the Second Spring Water, and face the bright pavilion and dark holes; carry a small moon, and share the mountain tea and creek tea." This couplet is derived from Su Dongpo's poem "Carrying a small moon from heaven, I came to try the second best spring water on earth."

This couplet has also become a new advertisement for the Second Spring. You might as well bring your favorite fine tea and try the "Second Spring Under Heaven" in this beautiful mountain scenery, as judged by the Sage of Tea.

"惠"游祠堂

无锡最大的清代祠堂建筑

昭忠祠也称淮湘昭忠祠，是淮军修建的首座昭忠祠，也是无锡现存最完整的清代祠堂建筑。根据《无锡地方资料汇编》记载："清朝咸丰至同治年间，李鸿章的淮湘军曾与太平军在江南一带激战，惠山的寺院毁于战火，仅存寺门匾额。"同治三年（1864年），太平天国战事基本结束不久，李鸿章即奏请清廷为阵亡将士在无锡县城外惠泉山麓天下第二泉之侧修建淮军昭忠祠，同治四年（1865年）五月，昭忠祠在被毁的惠山寺基址上建成。2002年，无锡在原址重修惠山寺，淮湘昭忠祠就位于惠山寺的后部，也就形成了一种独特的祠中有寺、寺中有祠的布局。

昭忠祠坐西朝东，依山而筑，布局对称，层次丰富，雕镂精美。祠前有一口梁代大同井，见证了"南朝四百八十寺，多少楼台烟雨中"的历史。大门建在两重崇台上，歇山顶，面阔三间，门前有双狮戏珠图案的抱鼓石一

AI语音导览

对，门上悬挂李鸿章亲题的"昭忠祠"匾额，原匾在1949年后被毁，现在的匾额是近年集字而成的。

进入二门即仪门之后，是一座碑亭，木石结构，歇山顶，碑亭中矗立着《敕建惠山昭忠祠碑》，碑高2.2米。正面刻着同治三年清政府同意李鸿章建昭忠祠这一请求的碑文，背面刻的是五龙戏珠图案。

大殿面阔三间，进深七架，硬山顶。南北两侧的墙上，有李鸿章、李鹤章撰写的修建该祠的碑文。碑文既写出了淮军将士与太平军激战的场景，也写出了他们战死后故乡眷属的悲戚境遇。昭忠祠后部还有起居殿，西殿院中还有戏台一座。

昭忠祠，并不是一般的家族祠堂，这里纪念的是一群阵亡之士，按照清代礼制，昭忠祠祭祀属于"群祀"，一共祭祀多少人呢？根据牌位推算，大概超过了1600人。这些被祭祀的人员又分为正祀和袱祀两种。正祀也叫列祀，祭祀的是那些军衔较高的军官。袱祀也称附祀，无疑就是祭祀军衔不高的小军官或者普通战士，还有一般殉难民众。因为祭祀的对象有高低之分，所以祭祀的级别就有显著差异。您看，被安放在昭忠祠显著位置的、牌位尺寸比较大的，就是正祀，像程学启、张遇春、陈忠德、韩正国、张行科等人，都供在前正殿和后正室。而安放在不太显著的位置或两边走廊、左右屋子的就是袱祀，牌位尺寸也比较小，有的甚至几十人合用一个牌位。当然袱祀还有另一种特殊情况，就是原来属于淮军系统的将领或文员，病故后经李鸿章上奏，清廷允准，也可以放在这里

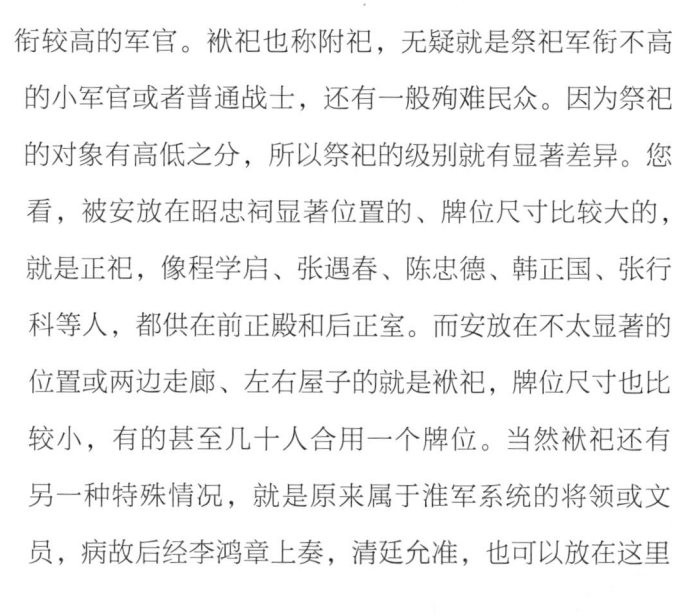

祭祀。

惠山的昭忠祠是淮军修建的首座昭忠祠，从建筑形制到祭祀规制等方面，都起到了引领示范作用，也对淮军历史及晚清抚恤制度产生了重要影响。日后淮军虽然不断在各地修建昭忠祠，但再无李鸿章撰文的碑刻，可见无锡惠山昭忠祠的重要地位。

根据顾文璧、钱宗奎《无锡最大的清代祠堂建筑——淮湘昭忠祠》一文记载，该祠是无锡地区现存最完整、规模最大、规格最高的清代祠堂建筑。主要建筑都有雕刻装饰，集中反映了晚清无锡地区砖、石、木雕工艺水平。你要是感兴趣，不妨去昭忠祠走一走，看一看。如果你看到昭忠祠后的一面墙头上装饰有西游记中的沙和尚和猪八戒，千万不要觉得奇怪，这是无锡市非物质文化遗产灰塑，是能工巧匠数百年来精湛技艺的延续。据记载，灰塑在唐代就已经出现，明清时期，祠堂、寺观和豪门大宅建筑盛行用灰塑做装饰，灰塑除了最基本的装饰作用外，还是趋吉避凶、消灾祈福的一种象征，表达了人们对美好生活的追求与向往。

The Largest Ancestral Hall of the Qing Dynasty in Wuxi

The Zhaozhong Ancestral Hall, also known as the Huai-Xiang Zhaozhong Hall, is the first of its kind built by the Huai Army and stands today as the most complete surviving ancestral hall structure from the Qing dynasty in Wuxi. According to the Compilation of Local Materials of Wuxi, "During the reigns of Xianfeng and Tongzhi in the Qing Dynasty, Li Hongzhang's Huai-Xiang Army engaged in fierce battles with the Taiping forces across Jiangnan. Most of the temples on Mount Hui were destroyed by war, leaving only the temple gate and its inscribed plaque." In 1864, just after the conclusion of the Taiping Rebellion, Li Hongzhang petitioned the imperial court to construct a Zhaozhong Hall at the foot of Huishan Mountain, beside the "Second Spring under Heaven," to commemorate fallen soldiers. Completed in 1865, the hall was built on the ruins of the old Huishan Temple. In 2002, Huishan Temple was reconstructed on its original site, with the Zhaozhong Hall located to its rear, forming a distinctive architectural layout in which the temple and ancestral hall are interwoven.

Facing east and backed by the mountain, the Zhaozhong Hall features a symmetrical layout with a rich spatial hierarchy and intricate carvings. In front of the hall lies the Datong Well, dating back to the Liang Dynasty, a silent witness to the "Three Hundred and Eighty Temples of the Southern Dynasties, cloaked in rain and mist." The main gate, perched atop two tiers of raised platforms, has a xieshan-style roof and three bays. In front of the gate stands a pair of stone drum piers adorned with motifs of lions playing with a ball. Above the gate hangs a plaque bearing the inscription "Zhaozhong Hall," personally written by Li Hongzhang. Although the original was destroyed after 1949, the current version was recreated based on historic calligraphy.

Beyond the second gate, the Yimen, lies a stele pavilion constructed of wood and stone with a xieshan roof. Inside stands the "Stele for the Imperial Edict to Construct the Huishan Zhaozhong Hall," which is 2.2 meters tall. The front records the Qing government's approval in 1864 of Li Hongzhang's proposal, while the reverse features an intricate design of five dragons playing with a pearl.

The main hall, comprising three bays in width and seven purlins in depth, has a gabled roof. On the interior side walls, one finds inscriptions authored by Li Hongzhang and his brother Li Hezhang detailing the fierce battles between the Huai Army and the Taiping forces, as well as the grief endured by the families of the fallen. Behind the main hall are residential quarters, and within the western courtyard stands a traditional performance stage.

Unlike typical ancestral halls that honor a single lineage, the Zhaozhong Hall is a memorial dedicated to a collective—those who died in service. According to Qing ceremonial norms, this constitutes a qunsi, or collective sacrifice. Based on the number of spirit tablets, the hall is estimated to commemorate more than 1,600 individuals. These are divided into zhengsi (principal commemorations) and fusi (subsidiary commemorations). The former includes high-ranking officers and is marked by larger, more prominently placed tablets—such as those honoring Cheng Xueqi, Zhang Yuchun, Chen Zhongde, Han Zhenguo, and Zhang Xingke. The latter honors lower-ranking officers, ordinary soldiers, and civilians who perished, often sharing a tablet or being enshrined in more peripheral locations. In some cases, former Huai Army officers who died of illness were also commemorated through imperial approval granted upon Li Hongzhang's recommendation.

As the earliest Zhaozhong Hall established by the Huai Army, the Huishan structure set a precedent in both architectural form and ritual practice, exerting significant influence on the Huai Army's commemorative culture and the broader Qing system of posthumous recognition. Although more such halls were built later across China, none bore inscriptions personally authored by Li Hongzhang, underscoring the exceptional historical status of the Wuxi Huishan Zhaozhong Hall.

According to the research of Gu Wenbi and Qian Zongkui in The Largest Qing Dynasty Ancestral Hall in Wuxi: Huai-Xiang Zhaozhong Hall, this hall remains the largest, most complete, and most refined example of Qing ancestral architecture in the region. Its intricate decorative carvings in brick, stone, and wood collectively reflect the superb craftsmanship of late Qing artisans in Wuxi. A visit to the Zhaozhong Hall offers more than architectural appreciation—on the rear wall, one may spot figures like Sha Wujing and Zhu Bajie from Journey to the West. These are not anomalies, but rather part of Wuxi's intangible cultural heritage: huīsù (lime plaster sculpture). With roots tracing back to the Tang dynasty and flourishing during the Ming and Qing periods, this art form not only served decorative purposes but was also imbued with auspicious symbolism, embodying the people's hopes for peace, protection, and a prosperous life.

"惠"游祠堂

"事事关心"的人

盘点中国古代著名的书院，必定少不了无锡东林书院。跟东林书院一起闻名天下的还有那副对联，"风声雨声读书声，声声入耳；家事国事天下事，事事关心"。有意思的是，这副"三声三事"联也已传扬了"三生三世"，最早是顾宪成祠的镇祠之宝，1946年才从祠中移至东林书院。

顾宪成是无锡人，26岁那年参加乡试，也就是省级考试，夺得了第一名，人称解元。会试考中了进士，开始了从政之路。以顾宪成的个性，注定不会在官场有多大起色。翻翻他的从政履历，最高也就是郎中，正五品官职，其他大多数时间都在六品级别徘徊。因为经常担任类似副职的推官，还赢得了

AI语音导览

"天下推官第一"的名声。当然这个"天下第一"前面还有一个"公廉寡欲"的定语,基本就是顾宪成个性的写照。正应了中国那句古话"无欲则刚",他太过"寡欲",自然就成了无比刚直的人。他明知万历皇帝和前大学士王家屏不对付,却偏要推举王家屏入阁,触怒龙颜。也是因为这件事,顾宪成被罢官回家,从此成了一介平民。

明代很多被革职的文官,回乡后,基本就开始了不问世事、提前养老的另一种生活,例如无锡望族秦家的秦燿回来后就掇山理水,重修寄畅园,过起了比老庄还老庄的生活,苏州拙政园主人也是如此,所以明代园林十分兴盛。但是,顾宪成与众不同。他非但没有"不问世事",反而"事事关心",他和弟弟顾允成、同乡高攀龙先是讲学,讲了三年之后,人气大增,四年后又拉到了政府资助,便修复了大名鼎鼎的东林书院,顾宪成也被称为"东林先生"。他们在书院不仅讲解儒经,切磋义理,而且讽议朝政,指斥时弊,其影响力可以用震动朝野来形容。固定讲课的八位先生以顾宪成为负责人,组成了一支在朝在野、结构合理的师资队伍,时称"东林八君子",还制定了"东林会约",形成了固定的会议制度。东林书院以其"宁折不弯、务实爱国"的精神感染了大批志同道合之士,产生了一般书院难以产生的巨大的政治影响力。

顾宪成逝世后第二年,也就是明万历四十一年(1613年),他的后人就建造了纪念他的"顾端文公祠",地点就在惠山寺旁边的听松坊。顾端文公祠原有墙门、照壁、正殿、庑房、享堂、芙蓉亭等多处建筑,清代又增加了"积书岩"这处

建筑，这是顾宪成一位非常有出息的后代建造的，这位后代就是纳兰性德的挚友、明末清初的"词家三绝"之一顾贞观，他退休回乡后就来到老祖宗祠堂藏书读书。1949年后，顾端文公祠被民居所占，多有损毁。2001年，政府将祠堂主体部分进行了修复，现在已基本恢复原貌。

祠堂里悬挂多副对联，最著名的当然还是：

"风声雨声读书声，声声入耳；家事国事天下事，事事关心。"

A Person Who Cares About Everything

When discussing the renowned academies of ancient China, Wuxi's Donglin Academy undoubtedly ranks among the most significant. Alongside the academy, a famous couplet often cited is "The sounds of wind, rain, and reading are all in the ear; matters of family, state, and the world are all of concern." Interestingly, this couplet, known as the "Three Sounds and Three Matters," has transcended its original context, becoming popularly associated with the phrase "Three Lifetimes." Initially, it was a treasured artifact of the Gu Xiancheng Hall and was not relocated to Donglin Academy until 1946.

Gu Xiancheng, a native of Wuxi, achieved first place in the provincial examination at the age of 26, earning the title of "Jieyuan." After successfully passing the imperial examination and becoming a Jinshi, he embarked on a political career. However, given Gu Xiancheng's character, it was clear he would not achieve significant advancement in the bureaucracy. A review of his official career reveals that he reached only the position of Langzhong, a fifth-grade official, while spending most of his time at the sixth-grade level. His frequent role as an assistant judge garnered him the reputation of being "the foremost judge in the world." This title, however, came with the qualifying phrase "public, honest, and selfless," which aptly reflects Gu Xiancheng's nature. In line with the Chinese proverb "Without desire, one remains steadfast," his excessive selflessness rendered him remarkably upright. Despite knowing of the tensions between Emperor Wanli and the former Grand Secretary Wang Jiaping, he insisted on recommending Wang Jiaping for a position in the cabinet, thereby incurring the emperor's wrath. Consequently, Gu Xiancheng was dismissed from his official post and returned home, living as an ordinary citizen thereafter.

Typically, many scholars dismissed during the Ming Dynasty would retreat into a life of leisure upon returning home, disengaging

顧端文公祠

from worldly affairs. For instance, Qin Yao of the prominent Wuxi family returned to cultivate gardens and restore the Jichang Garden, leading a life akin to that of Laozi and Zhuangzi. The same can be said for the owner of the Suzhou's Zhuozheng Garden, contributing to the flourishing of gardens during the Ming era. However, Gu Xiancheng diverged from this norm. Instead of becoming detached from worldly matters, he took an active interest in them. Together with his brother Gu Yunchen and fellow townsman Gao Panlong, he engaged in teaching. After three years, their popularity soared, and four years later, they secured government funding to restore the renowned Donglin Academy, where Gu Xiancheng became known as "Master Donglin." Within the academy, they not only taught Confucian classics and debated moral principles but also critiqued political affairs and condemned social injustices, wielding an influence that could be described as shaking both the court and the common people. The eight instructors who held regular lectures, led by Gu Xiancheng, formed a well-structured teaching team known as the "Eight Worthies of Donglin," and they established the "Donglin Association," creating a formal meeting system. The academy's spirit of "bending without breaking, pragmatism, and patriotism" resonated with many like-minded individuals, generating a significant political impact seldom seen in other academies.

The year following Gu Xiancheng's death, in the 41st year

of the Wanli reign (1613), his descendants constructed the "Gu Duanwen Hall" to honor him, located beside Huishan Temple in Tingsongfang. Originally, the Hall comprised walls, a screen wall, a main hall, a corridor, a worship hall, and a Hibiscus Pavilion. During the Qing Dynasty, an additional structure known as "Jishu Rock" was built by one of Gu Xiancheng's illustrious descendants, Gu Zhengguan, a close friend of Nalan Xingde and one of the "Three Absolute Poets" of the late Ming and early Qing periods. After retiring, Gu Zhengguan came to the ancestral hall to read and collect books. After 1949, the hall was encroached upon by residential buildings, resulting in considerable damage. In 2001, the government restored the main structure of the hall, and it has since largely regained its original appearance.

The hall houses numerous couplets, with the most famous being:

"The sounds of wind, rain, and reading are all in the ear;
matters of family, state, and the world are all of concern."

明代的"千金不受先生"

顾端文公祠隔壁，就是邵文庄公祠。邵文庄公祠纪念的是无锡人邵宝，别看这个名字颇有些乡土气息，但邵宝却一路做到浙江右布政使、右副都御史总督漕运，就算开罪小人被弹劾回乡，再度起用也被任命为南京礼部尚书，正二品官衔，去世后还被封了"太子太保"，又升一级。

在无锡，邵宝绝对是个具有传奇色彩的人物。民间很多传说都与邵宝有关，令人印象最深刻的就是关于惠山石门的传说。据说石门可以打开，里面堆积着很多金银财宝。善良的人因为不贪心，所以进去拿了就能在规定时间内出来。现在的石门当然是打不开了，因为有个极为贪心的人进去后横竖拿不完，最后被惩罚永远关在石门里头了，而要想这道石门再度打开，就非要等邵宝来了不可，"若要石门开，要等邵宝来"的民谣在无锡可谓家喻户晓。这个传说说明，邵宝是

AI语音导览

一个嫉恶如仇、公允正直的人。

邵宝为人刚正不阿,为官清正廉洁。他有句传世箴言,"何以守官,曰敬与廉。敬则不忽,廉乃有严"。就是说为官要做到敬业和廉洁,敬业则不马虎,廉洁才有威严。邵宝不仅这样说,而且不折不扣地这样做。正德四年(1509年),邵宝受朝廷委派总督漕运。当时有个粮长凭借手中的权力,贪赃枉法,被揭发后请人送了一千两黄金给邵宝,要邵宝为他开脱。结果,邵宝严词拒绝,并告诫说,他这样做,要罪上加罪。这件事情也为邵宝赢得了一个"千金不受先生"的荣誉称号。

邵宝一生酷爱看书,根据民间说法,他的同学读书都读得"头昏眼花",只有邵宝越读越嫌少,所以他一生的学术成就也十分了得,写了《定性书说》《学史》《简端录》等上百卷

书。邵宝还热衷于修建讲学之所，他任职期间，在江西修白鹿洞书院，建一峰书院。退休回家后，又在家乡建尚德书院、二泉书院等，附带创建了惠山二泉风景名胜。乡亲们都称他为"笃行君子""二泉先生"。

再来看看纪念这位"千金不受先生"的祠堂。邵文庄公祠始建于明正德十一年（1516年），现在也在听松坊内，这里松涛如鼓，泉飞成云，池山古木，翠竹如屏，环境十分清幽。最为可贵的是，祠堂还保留着几处邵宝遗迹。

一处就是邵宝所建的"二泉书院"，清代几经重修。匾额是由邵氏家族后代、做过清政府知县的邵涵初题写的。因为邵宝曾经修建过白鹿洞书院，所以后廊两侧门楣上的砖刻"洗砚""藏书"就用了白鹿洞书院的典故。

另一处是邵宝所建"点易台"，是用石头叠成的形如八卦的石台，一块圆石，象征太极，两块狭长的隳石象征着两仪，还有四块隳石象征四象。邵宝喜欢坐在这里读书，边读边用朱笔点批，而石台上的一方天然砚台正好供邵宝蘸朱砂使用，这块砚台也就有了个名字"研朱石"。点易台的下面还有一眼"滴露泉"，旁边有石头茶几、石头茶座。看书累了，正好到这里喝茶休息。滴露泉旁边是"海天亭"，从亭子往上走几百步，有块平石，叫作"望阙岩"，阙就是京城。晚年的邵宝，经常让人扶着登上去，朝着京城拜祝。点易台山坡上还保存了"青

壁丹崖""人间天上"的题刻。

再一处是两株高大的明代古银杏，现在邵文庄公祠第二进院落的天井里。

还有一处就是香积池，池水来自惠山寺前的金莲池，源头当然也是二泉水，池边有个古老的石龙头，也叫螭吻。以池命名，但实际还是泉，属于惠山九龙十三泉之一。香积池现在第三进院落中，这里还立着两米多高的邵宝塑像。往后走有长长的碑廊，里面有邵宝的《题十贤祠诗》《海天亭记》等珍贵碑刻。

视频　二泉书院

The "Master Who Would Not Accept a Thousand Gold Pieces" in the Ming Dynasty

Adjacent to the Gu Duanwen Hall is the Shao Wenzhuang Hall, dedicated to Shao Bao, a notable figure from Wuxi. Although his name may seem somewhat rustic, Shao Bao achieved significant heights in his career, serving as the Right Governor of Zhejiang and later as the Right Vice Minister of War, overseeing grain transportation. Even after falling into disfavor and being impeached back to his hometown, he was subsequently reinstated and appointed as the Minister of Rites in Nanjing, holding the second-ranking official title. After his death, he was posthumously awarded the title "Grand Tutor to the Crown Prince," elevating his rank further.

In Wuxi, Shao Bao is certainly regarded as a legendary figure, with many local tales associated with him. One of the most memorable stories involves the Shimen (Stone Gate) at Huishan, which was said to be capable of opening to reveal a treasure trove of gold and silver. Those of good character, who were not greedy, could enter and exit within the stipulated time, whereas a particularly greedy individual who entered could not leave and was punished by being trapped inside forever. According to local folklore, the gate would only open again when Shao Bao returned, leading to the saying, "To open the Stone Gate, one must wait for Shao Bao." This legend illustrates Shao Bao's esteemed status among the people Furthermore, it highlights his reputation as someone who despised evil and was fair-minded.

Shao Bao was known for his integrity and uprightness, maintaining a clean and honest governance. He famously stated, "How to uphold one's official duties? Through respect and integrity. With respect, one is not negligent; with integrity, one commands authority." This means that a public servant must be diligent and incorruptible, as diligence prevents carelessness, while integrity ensures respect. Shao Bao not only espoused these principles but also lived by them rigorously. For instance, in the fourth year of the Zhengde era (1509), he was appointed by the court to oversee grain transport. At that time, a grain inspector abused his power and, upon being exposed, attempted to bribe Shao Bao with a thousand taels of gold to secure his exoneration. Shao Bao firmly refused, warning that such an act would only compound his crimes. This incident earned him the honorific title of "the master who would not accept a thousand gold pieces."

Throughout his life, Shao Bao had a profound love for reading. According to folklore, while his classmates would read until their eyes grew weary, he felt that he could never read enough. Consequently, his academic achievements were remarkable, resulting in numerous works, including *Dingxing Shushuo, Xueshi, Jiandan Lu*, and *Huangchao Juyanhang Lu*, among others, totaling over a hundred volumes. He also took a keen interest in building educational institutions. During his tenure, he renovated the Bailudong Academy in Jiangxi and established the Yifeng Academy. After retiring to his hometown, he founded the Shangde Academy and Second Spring Academy, along with the scenic area of Huishan Spring. His fellow villagers affectionately referred to him as "a gentleman of integrity" and "Mr. Second Spring."

Now, let us examine the hall that commemorates this "master who would not accept a thousand gold pieces." The Shao Wenzhuang Hall was first established in the eleventh year of the Zhengde era (1516) and is now located in Tingsongfang, a serene place filled with the sounds of rustling pines, flowing springs, ancient trees, and green bamboo. Notably, the hall preserves several relics associated with Shao Bao.

One significant site is the Second Spring Academy, originally built by Shao Bao and later renovated multiple times during the Qing Dynasty. The plaque was inscribed by Shao Bao's descendants, including Shao Hanchu, who served as a magistrate under the Qing government. Because Shao Bao had previously restored the Bailudong Academy, the brick carvings on the door frames of the rear corridor, reading "Wash Inkstone" and "Store Books," reference the traditions of Bailudong Academy.

Another noteworthy feature is the "Dianyi Platform," constructed of stone in the shape of the Bagua (eight trigrams). This platform includes a circular stone symbolizing the Taiji, flanked by two long stones representing the two principles, and four additional stones symbolizing the four phenomena. Shao Bao enjoyed sitting here to read books, annotating the text with a vermilion brush, while a natural inkstone on the platform conveniently served for dipping his brush. This inkstone was aptly named "Yanzhu Stone." Below the Dianyi Platform lies the "Dilu Spring," accompanied by stone tea tables and chairs. It provides a perfect resting spot for enjoying tea after reading. Adjacent to the spring is the "Haitian Pavilion," and a few hundred steps up leads to a flat stone called "Wangque Rock," which refers to the capital city. In his later years, Shao Bao often needed assistance to climb up, where he would bow towards the capital. The hillside of the Dianyi Platform also features inscriptions reading "Green Walls and Red Cliffs" and "Heaven on Earth."

Another notable feature is the pair of tall ancient ginkgo trees from the Ming Dynasty, located in the courtyard of the second entrance of the Shao Wenzhuang Hall.

Additionally, there is the Xiangji Pond, with water sourced from the Golden Lotus Pond in front of the Huishan Temple, which in turn derives from the second Spring. The pond is adorned with an ancient stone dragon head, also known as a chiwen. Although named a pond, it is fundamentally a spring and is one of the thirteen springs of Huishan. Xiangji Pond is currently located in the third courtyard, where a statue of Shao Bao stands over two meters high. Continuing further leads to a long corridor of steles, featuring precious inscriptions such as Shao Bao's *Poem on the Ten Worthies' Temple* and Record of Haitian Pavilion.

邵宝最珍贵的墨宝

邵宝手书的点易台四面碑,是现存邵宝最大的亲笔书法刻石,珍贵至极。邵宝是高官没错,学问好也没错,而且书法也很厉害,那么,邵宝的老师是谁呢？他就是明代书法家李东阳,当然李先生还有"茶陵诗派"核心人物、明代文学家、内阁首辅、礼部尚书、户部尚书、太子少保、太子太保、大学士等众多头衔。

李东阳先生擅长篆书、隶书、楷书、行书、草书,可以说中国书法的各种书体,李东阳先生均游刃有余。而且他还对明代中期书法风格的形成起到了承上启下的作用。明代初期,出于公文写作的需要,书法风格务求方方正正、大小一致、乌黑光洁,也就是说,书法要写得跟印刷体一般,这就是台阁体;而明代中期盛行吴门书法,就是以祝枝山、文徵明等为代表的抒发个人色彩、彰显鲜明个性的书法。李东阳先生生活在明代初期和中期的过渡时期,他的书法已经摆脱了台阁体这种规正字体的束缚,加之李先生书法的巨大影响力,自然对后来的书风产生了重要影响。

李东阳的书法被赞誉为"长沙公大草,中古绝技也！玲珑飞动,不可按抑,而纯雅之色,如精金美玉,毫无怒张蹈厉之癖,盖天资清澈,全不带渣滓以出"。跟着这样的书法大家学习,邵宝的书法理所当然不会差,确切地说,邵宝的书法也是闻名遐迩。他的老师是书体全才,邵宝则是更加擅长行书和草书。据说他的行草以篆书和隶书为底蕴，用笔方中见圆，一点一画饱满深厚；精力内含，字体伟岸雄强；遒劲舒和，气息古朴苍劲；一提一按一顿一挫中，更觉骨力峻爽。可以说邵宝的书法拙中见巧，飘逸脱俗。不仅深得他老师李东阳书法精髓，甚至被明代书法家朱谋垔称赞为"深得颜鲁公笔意"。所以，邵宝虽然并没有被正式冠以书法家名衔，但其书法造诣之高是有目共睹的。

这块邵宝手书的点易台四面碑也因此闻名。

Shao Bao's Most Precious Calligraphic Work

The four-sided stele of the "Dianyi Platform," hand-inscribed by Shao Bao, stands as the largest extant stone engraving of his calligraphy and is of immense value. As we know, Shao Bao held a high official position and possessed considerable scholarly knowledge, he also was proficient in calligraphy.

So, who was Shao Bao's teacher? He was Li Dongyang, a renowned calligrapher of the Ming Dynasty, whose distinguished credentials also include being a core figure in the "Chaling Poetry School," a prominent literary figure of the Ming era, as well as holding numerous high-ranking positions such as Prime Minister, Minister of Rites, Minister of Revenue, and various honorary titles including Grand Guardian of the Heir Apparent.

Li Dongyang excelled in various scripts including seal script, clerical script, regular script, running script, and cursive script. In essence, he mastered the full spectrum of Chinese calligraphy. Furthermore, he played a crucial role in bridging the early and mid-Ming calligraphic styles. This is significant because, in the early Ming period, the style was dictated by the need for formal document writing, which demanded a square, consistent, and glossy appearance akin to printed text—this style is known as "Taige Ti." By contrast, the mid-Ming period saw the rise of the Wumen calligraphic style, represented by figures such as Zhu Zhishan and Wen Zhengming, who emphasized personal expression and distinct individuality in their work. Living during this transitional period, Li Dongyang's calligraphy transcended the rigid constraints of Taige Ti, and his profound influence naturally impacted later calligraphic trends.

Li Dongyang's calligraphy has been praised as "the epitome of the Changsha style, a unique skill of ancient times! Its elegance is lively and dynamic, impossible to suppress, with a pure and refined quality akin to exquisite gold and jade, entirely free from any coarseness, stemming from a clear and untainted talent." Learning from such a master, it is no surprise that Shao Bao's calligraphy is also highly regarded. To be precise, Shao Bao's work is well-known in its own right. While his teacher was a versatile calligrapher, Shao Bao particularly excelled in running and cursive scripts. It is said that his running script draws upon the foundations of seal and clerical scripts, characterized by a roundness that emerges from a square structure, with each stroke being full and profound. His energy imbues the characters with a robust and majestic quality; they exhibit a vigorous yet gentle grace, echoing an ancient and powerful breath. The interplay of pressure and release in his strokes further enhances the strength and elegance of his writing. One could argue that Shao Bao's calligraphy embodies a blend of clumsiness and sophistication, exuding an ethereal and transcendent quality. He not only grasped the essence of his teacher Li Dongyang's style but was also praised by the Ming calligrapher Zhu Moudan for being "deeply attuned to the brush strokes of Yan Lugong." Thus, although Shao Bao has not been formally titled as a calligrapher, his high level of expertise is evident to all.

The stone stele of the "Dianyi Platform," inscribed by Shao Bao, is famous for it and you certainly should not miss.

祠堂群里的驱虫专家

"虫神祠"是惠山最有趣的祠堂之一,位于五中丞祠旁。刘猛将祠主刘锜原是南宋抗金名将,曾大破金兀术的"拐子马",后来遭秦桧构陷,被贬到地方当官。在任期间治理水患,尤其驱蝗有功,被后世尊为"虫神"。

据说,但凡无锡某方出现虫灾,老百姓就会到虫神祠祭祀。其实,不只是无锡,旧时江南一带农村很多地方都有刘猛将祠,每年正月过了十五,当地百姓就开始筹办刘猛将庙会来田间驱蝗,吴地方言"轧闹猛"也由此衍生而来。有趣的是,惠山祠堂群中,这间祠堂最小,祠门狭窄,连清道光年间所赐"福佑康年"匾额都容不下。

将刘猛将升级为虫神,并为他设立专门的祠堂,寄托着无锡百姓对防治虫害最为质朴的愿望,更反映了民间对农业丰收的期盼,也体现了人们对英勇善战、为民除害的英雄人物的崇敬。

AI语音导览

The Expert in Pest Control of the Ancestral Hall Cluster

The "Insect God Hall," dedicated to the Valiant General Liu, is one of the most intriguing halls in Huishan, located beside the Wuzhong Cheng Hall. Liu Meng is revered as the spirit of pest control and is based on the historical figure Liu Qi, a renowned general of the Southern Song Dynasty known for his victories against the Jin dynasty's general, Wanyan Aguda. Liu Qi later fell victim to political intrigue by Qin Hui and was demoted to a local official. During his tenure, he successfully managed water disasters and was particularly noted for his effective measures against locusts, leading later generations to honor him as the "Insect God."

According to tradition, whenever a locust plague arises in any part of Wuxi, the residents flock to the Insect God Hall to offer prayers. This practice was not limited to Wuxi; many rural areas in Jiangnan once featured Liu Meng Halls. After the fifteenth day of the first lunar month each year, local people would organize hall fairs at the Liu Meng Hall to perform pest control rituals. The Wu dialect term "ga nao meng," which means to create a lively atmosphere, also derives from these activities. Interestingly, among the Huishan Ancestral Hall Cluster, this hall is the smallest, with a narrow entrance that even the plaque bestowed during the Daoguang era, reading "Blessings for a Healthy Year," cannot fit.

Upgrading the Valiant General Liu to the status of an Insect God and establishing a dedicated hall for him embodies the simple hopes of the people of Wuxi for pest control. This also reflects the community's expectations for agricultural abundance and signifies their reverence for heroic figures who valiantly protect the populace from harm.

被"送来送去"的惠山寺

惠山寺是惠山古迹区的重要组成部分，也是通往天下第二泉的必经之路。本来，惠山寺和祠堂没什么关系，因为出家人没有子孙后代，也就不会有孝子贤孙为祭祀先祖而建立祠堂的说法。但是惠山寺很特别，因为被"送来送去"就不再单纯是寺庙了，也成了祠堂，当然是特殊的祠堂类型，夏泉生先生称为"寺院祠"。

在北宋靖康元年（1126年），宋钦宗曾经将惠山寺赐给了前篇说到的抗金英雄李纲作为"功德院"，算是对他多次击退金兵、保卫都城开封战功的奖赏。惠山寺不仅被宋钦宗送给过李纲，5年之后，也就是宋高宗赵构在位时期，又被送了一次。那一年，有一位特殊人物去世了，她就是指定赵构坐上皇帝宝座的孟皇后，当然，她去世时已经是太后了。为了纪念这位昭慈圣献孟太后，宋高宗把惠山寺赐给了据说是孟太后侄子的信安郡王孟忠厚。

AI语音导览

既然北宋时期，就被拿来"送人"了，说明，惠山寺起码在"送人"之前就已经存在了，那么，它最早是什么时候建立的呢？

这就要说到中国历史上一个特殊的时期，南朝。南朝，实际上是刘宋、南齐、南梁、南陈四个朝代的总称，这个时期，时局动荡不安，政局更迭频繁，人们生活困难，为佛教的广泛传播奠定了坚实的社会基础，再加上帝王推崇，就有了"南朝四百八十寺"的说法。而惠山寺，正是南朝刘宋景平元年（423年）建立的。当时惠山有一处名胜叫作"历山草堂"，那一年被改成了僧舍，称为"华山精舍"，后来，高僧僧显法师来到无锡，就住在华山精舍，还带来了一种奇特的花卉——千叶金莲，并将它种在寺庙的方池之中。这方池塘如今也成了惠山寺的一处名胜，就是金莲桥下的金莲池。每逢盛夏，池中满目苍绿，绿色中星星点点缀满了金色小花，景象奇绝。

到了梁朝大同三年（537年），华山精舍正式改名"惠山寺"，其实原本用的是智慧的"慧"字，但是因为"慧"和"惠"相通，加上这里在晋代的时候已经被称为惠山，所以之

"惠"游祠堂

后就一直叫作"惠山寺"了。

惠山寺接待过很多名人，像唐代的茶神陆羽，写下"谁知盘中餐，粒粒皆辛苦"的唐代悯农诗人李绅，北宋大词人苏东坡等。

今天重修过的惠山寺，分为中路、北路两路建筑。中路包括唐宋石经幢、金刚殿、香花桥和日月池、天王殿、金莲桥和金莲池、乾隆题诗的御碑亭、听松石床、古银杏、钟楼、大雄宝殿。面对大雄宝殿右转，进入不二法门后，就是北路建筑，包括罗汉堂、大悲阁、藏经楼、地藏殿、五观堂、惠山寺图书馆等。

如今的惠山寺虽然不大，却承载着千年的历史沧桑，蕴藏着深厚的文化底蕴，古老的石阶上留下了无数名人的足迹，一砖一瓦都似乎在低语着过去的事情。

The Transience of Huishan Temple

Huishan Temple is an integral part of the Huishan historical site and serves as a crucial passage to the Second Spring Under Heaven. Ordinarily, Huishan temple and ancestral halls do not have much in common, as monks do not have descendants who would build ancestral halls to worship their ancestors. However, Huishan Temple is unique. After being "passed around," it evolved from merely being a temple to also functioning as an ancestral hall, albeit a special type termed "Temple Ancestral Hall" by scholar Xia Quan Sheng.

In the first year of the Jingkang era (1126) of the Northern Song Dynasty, Emperor Qinzong conferred Huishan Temple to the aforementioned anti-Jin hero, Li Gang, as a "Meritorious Institute," honoring his repeated victories against the Jin forces and his efforts in defending the capital, Kaifeng. In fact, the Huishan Temple was not only given to Li Gang by Emperor Qinzong; five years later (1131), during the reign of Emperor Gaozong Zhao Gou, it was conferred again. That year, a notable figure passed away: Empress Meng, who had designated Zhao Gou as emperor. At the time of her death, she held the title of empress dowager. To honor the late Empress Meng, Emperor Gaozong granted Huishan Temple to her purported nephew, Prince Meng Zhonghou of Xin'an.

Given that Huishan Temple was being "passed around" as early as the Northern Song period, it indicates that it must have existed prior to this practice. So, when was it originally established?

This brings us to a significant period in Chinese history known as the Southern Dynasties. The term "Southern Dynasties" refers to the collective name of the four dynasties: Song, Qi, Liang, and Chen. During this tumultuous time, marked by political instability and frequent changes in government, the people faced hardships, which laid a solid social foundation for the widespread dissemination of Buddhism, further supported by the emperors' patronage. This era is often referred to as the period of "Four Hundred and Eighty

Temples in the Southern Dynasties." Huishan Temple was founded in the first year of the Jingping era (423) during the Liu Song period of the Southern Dynasties. At that time, there was a scenic spot on Huishan called "Lishan Caotang," which was converted into a monk's residence named "Huashan Jing She." Later, the eminent monk Sengxian arrived in Wuxi and took residence at "Huashan Jing She," bringing with him a rare flower known as the Thousand-Leaved Golden Lotus, which he planted in the temple's square pond. This pond has since become a renowned attraction of the Huishan Temple, known as the Golden Lotus Pond beneath the Jinlian Bridge. In the height of summer, the pond is lush green, dotted with golden flowers, creating a breathtaking scene.

In the third year of the Datong era (537) of the Liang Dynasty, Huashan Jing She was officially renamed "Huishan Temple." Originally, the temple was referred to using the character for "wisdom" (慧), but due to the phonetic similarity between "Hui"(慧) and "Hui" (惠), combined with the fact that it had already been called Huishan (惠山) during the Jin Dynasty, it has since retained the name Huishan Temple (惠山寺).

Over the years, Huishan Temple has hosted many notable figures, including Lu Yu, the Tea Sage, the Tang Dynasty poet Li Shen, who wrote the poignant poem "Who knows the meal in the plate, every grain comes with hard work," and the prominent Northern Song lyricist Su Dongpo.

Today, the restored Huishan Temple comprises two main sections: the central and northern routes. The central route features the Tang-Song Stone Sutra Pillar, the Vajra Hall, Xianghua Bridge, Sun-Moon Pool, Hall of Heavenly Kings, Jinlian Bridge and Golden Lotus Pond, the royal monument inscribed with Qianlong's poetry, the Listening to Pine Stone Bed, the ancient ginkgo, the Bell Tower, and the Mahavira Hall. Turning right from the Mahavira Hall and entering the Gate of Non-Duality leads to the northern route, which includes the Arhat Hall, Great Compassion Pavilion, Sutra Collection Building, Ksitigarbha Hall, Five Contemplations Hall, and Huishan Temple Library.

Although modern Huishan Temple may not be large, it bears the weight of a millennia of history and embodies rich cultural connotations. The ancient stone steps are imprinted with the footprints of countless notable individuals, and every brick and tile seems to whisper stories of the past.

祠堂群里最美的祠堂

AI语音导览

寄畅园，是始建于明代时期的古园。这座园林做到了"五百年来不移姓"！可千万别小看这一"不移姓"，这可是园林保存完整且保留固有风貌的关键。同样建于明代的苏州园林——拙政园，就曾数易其主，有时是因为子孙不争气一夜豪赌把园林输给了他人，有时是因为后代衰落把园林卖给了他人，不管哪种原因，频繁更换园主让拙政园几度荒废，改换门庭后，也因为新主人的文化修养和习惯爱好不同，几经重修，导致园林局部风格不统一。在《长洲县志》中就有记载，说拙政园"廿年来数易主，虽增葺壮丽，无复昔时山林雅致矣"。原来浑然一体、统一规划的拙政园，因为频繁更换园主，最终演变为东、中、西部三个相互分离、自成格局的园林。更有甚者，换了主人后，园林直接湮没。

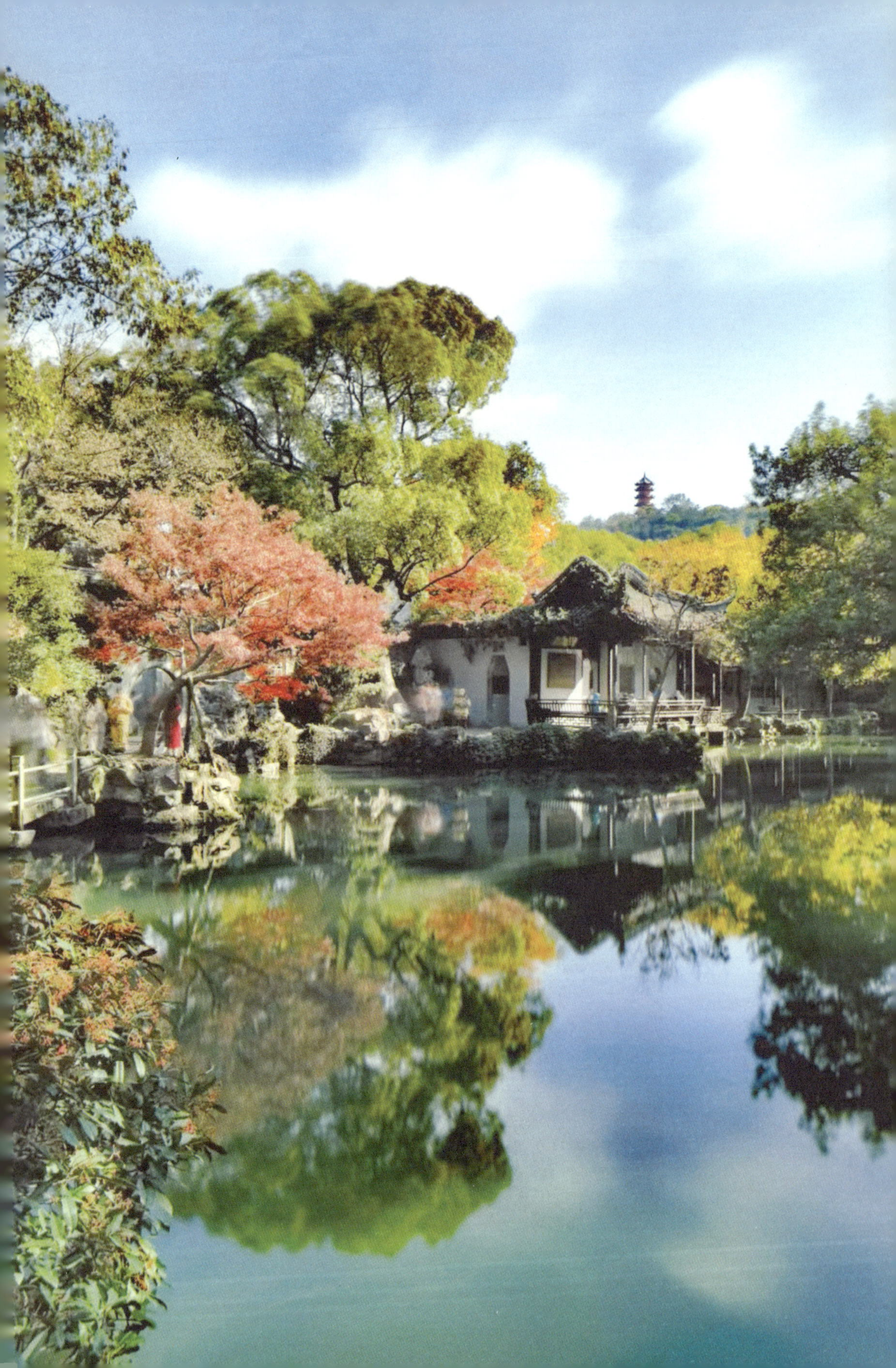

这样看来，寄畅园能做到"五百年来不移姓"实在太不容易！那么，是不是拥有寄畅园的秦家比较幸运，子孙后代都很有出息呢？其实，寄畅园在历史上也曾几度濒危。例如万历三十二年（1604年），也就是寄畅园历史上说得着的第四代园主秦燿逝世那年，寄畅园就面临过一次"分关"危机，当时寄畅园这份祖产被作为遗产进行分割，园林被一切四，一代名园差点被毁。还有一次是政治危机，当时第五代园主秦德藻，也是寄畅园史上数得着的人物，他的大孙子曾被康熙选入宫中当第九子胤禟的老师，后来继位的是第四子，也就是雍正皇帝，秦家遭到牵连，寄畅园也被充公了。

所以，寄畅园也面临过危机，那么，寄畅园传承五百年且不移姓的秘诀又是什么呢？这就与寄畅园除园林之外的另一个身份——祠堂直接相关了。用《寄畅园祖祠改建公议》来解释，"惟是园亭究属游观之地，必须建立家祠，始可永垂不朽"。说白了，园林毕竟是供人娱乐消遣的地方，地位不会特别高，就像历史上真实发生的那样，能被当作豪赌的赌注或者变卖的家产，难以代代相传，唯有改作地位极高的祠堂，才能在精神上约束子孙后代，得以长久保存。事实上，寄畅园正是靠了这一妙招才得以"永垂不朽"，这在国内外也算得上是个孤例。

《寄畅园祖祠改建公议》明确将寄畅园改为祖祠，家族共同管理，确立了寄畅园稳固的宗族所有地位，避免再次被族人据为私产导致被破坏或断送的命运。寄畅园充公被皇帝发还之后，秦家立刻付诸行动，将寄畅园的嘉树堂改建为双孝祠，纪念颇有

孝心的两位秦氏先人，以继承双孝遗风，并约定各房捐祭田，其中一房世代掌管园产，寄畅园自此成为秦氏共有的祠园。

正因如此，本是园林的寄畅园理所当然成了惠山祠堂群里最美丽的祠堂。

从第一代园主五部尚书秦金开辟这里建造"凤谷行窝"开始，就奠定了寄畅园山林野趣的基本格调。第四代园主秦燿罢官回乡后，寄情山水，根据王羲之"寄畅山水阴"的诗句，将"凤谷行窝"改名为"寄畅园"，并修建了"知鱼槛""锦汇漪""嘉树堂""卧云堂""邻梵阁""鹤步滩""先月榭""含贞斋""凌虚阁"等二十个园景，成就了寄畅园今天的主要风貌。第五代园主秦德藻又增添了"八音涧""七星桥""美人石"等景观，为寄畅园锦上添花。

游览寄畅园，有几处地方一定能引发您诗意的联想。一处是凤谷行窝南门厅，在这一角宁静的院落中，时间仿佛停止了，周围杂树垂荫，云淡烟轻，两棵高大的金桂遮天蔽日，不禁让人联想到"人闲桂花落，夜静春山空"的诗意。另一处是八音涧，走在涧道中，抬头古树苍苍，低头清泉潺潺，颇有"明月松间照，清泉石上流"的诗意。快到八音涧的尽头，石壁挡路，一转身，眼前豁然开朗，锦汇漪明媚动人，真有"山重水复疑无路，柳暗花明又一村"的诗意。站在知鱼槛，观望锦汇漪、远处假山和借入的连绵惠山，又不禁让人联想到"青山隐隐水迢迢"的诗意。

寄畅园，就是一首诗！难怪，康熙、乾隆两位皇帝次次下江南，必游寄畅园，并御赐"山色溪光""玉戛金摐"两块匾

额，一静一动、一观一听，道出了寄畅园无尽的诗意。乾隆皇帝甚至还画了图纸带回去，在皇家园林颐和园中建造了园中园"惠山园"，也就是今天的"谐趣园"。

寄畅园，这座享誉中外的名园，祠堂群里最美的祠堂，一草一木都透露着岁月的痕迹，一砖一瓦都见证了家族的兴衰，在这里，自然与人文交织，历史与现实相融，构成了一幅幅诗意盎然的画卷。

视频 寄畅园

"惠"游祠堂

The Most Beautiful Hall of the Ancestral Hall Cluster

  The Jichang Garden is a historic site in Wuxi dating back to the Ming Dynasty. It is precisely due to this transformation that it has been preserved, managing to achieve the remarkable feat of remaining within the same family lineage for over five hundred years! This unchanging lineage is not a trivial matter; it is the key to the garden's preservation in its original form. For comparison, the Suzhou garden, Zhuozheng Garden, which was also established in the Ming Dynasty, has changed ownership multiple times. This was sometimes due to descendants squandering their fortunes through gambling, while at other times, it was because of family decline leading to its sale. Regardless of the reasons, the frequent changes in ownership led to Zhuozheng Garden falling into neglect, and renovations by new owners often resulted in a lack of stylistic unity.

Historical records, such as *the Chronicle of Changzhou County*, note that despite renovations that made it more splendid, the garden had lost its original charm and elegance. Originally a harmonious and unified landscape, the garden eventually evolved into three distinct sections due to ownership changes. In some cases, gardens have even disappeared entirely after changing hands.

Given this context, the ability of Jichang Garden to remain "unchanged in lineage for five hundred years" is indeed remarkable! You might think that the Qin family, as the current owners of Jichang Garden, were particularly fortunate, with descendants who thrived. In reality, Jichang Garden has faced several near-catastrophes throughout its history. For instance, in 1604, the year of the fourth generation's owner, Qin Yao's death, the garden was threatened by a "division crisis." At that time, the ancestral property was at risk of being divided among heirs, putting the garden's integrity in jeopardy. Additionally, during a political crisis involving the fifth-generation owner, Qin Dezhao—an important figure in the garden's history—his grandson was selected as a tutor for the ninth son of Emperor Kangxi. However, following the ascension of the fourth son, Emperor Yongzheng, this grandson was implicated, resulting in the confiscation of Jichang Garden.

So, what is the secret behind Jichang Garden's ability to pass down through generations without changing ownership? This is closely related to its dual identity as a garden and an ancestral hall. *The Proposal for the Reconstruction of the Ancestral Hall at Jichang Garden* states, "The garden is ultimately a place for leisure; it is imperative to establish an ancestral hall for it to be eternally honored." In essence, a garden, being primarily a recreational space, does not hold a particularly elevated status; it can easily become a gambling stake or be sold off, jeopardizing its generational legacy. Only by transforming it into an esteemed ancestral hall can the spiritual bonds be established to guide descendants, ensuring its longevity. In fact, it is this clever strategy that has allowed Jichang Garden to achieve its "eternal glory," making it a unique case both domestically and internationally.

The Proposal for the Reconstruction of the Ancestral Hall explicitly designated Jichang Garden as an ancestral hall, to be managed collectively by the family. This solidified its status as a family-owned property, preventing it from being claimed as private property by any individual, which could lead to its destruction or loss. Following the garden's restoration to the Qin family after imperial confiscation, they swiftly took action to convert Jichang Garden's Jia Shu Hall into a Double Filial Piety Hall, commemorating two of their ancestors known for their filial piety, thus inheriting the tradition of double filial piety. They agreed that each branch of the family would contribute to its maintenance, with one branch tasked with the management of the garden, establishing Jichang Garden as a shared ancestral estate of the Qin family.

For this reason, Jichang Garden, with its origins as a garden, naturally emerged as the most beautiful ancestral hall within the Huishan Ancestral Hall Cluster. Beginning with the first-generation owner, the Minister of War, Qin Jinkai, who established "Fenggu Xingwo," the basic aesthetic of Jichang Garden was set. After the fourth-generation owner, Qin Yao, returned to his hometown from official duties, he infused his passion for nature into the garden, renaming "Fenggu Xingwo" to "Jichang Garden," inspired by Wang Xizhi's poem "Jichang Mountain and Water Shadow." He also constructed 20 various scenic spots, including Zhiyu Pavilion, Jinhui Yi, Jia Shu Hall, Woyun Hall, Lin Fan Pavilion, Hebu Beach, Xianyue Pavilion, Hanzhen Hall, and Lin Xu Pavilion, shaping the garden's primary landscape as we see it today. The fifth-generation owner, Qin Dezhao, further enhanced the garden by adding features like Bayin Stream, Seven Stars Bridge, and Beauty Stone.

If you visit Jichang Garden, certain locations are bound to evoke poetic imagery. One such spot is the southern entrance hall of Fenggu Xingwo. In this tranquil courtyard, time seems to stand still; the surrounding trees provide ample shade, and the sky is serene and misty, with two towering osmanthus trees casting their shade. This atmosphere evokes the poetic sentiment of "In the tranquility of the night, the osmanthus flowers fall, the mountains are quiet, and the spring is empty." Another location is Bayin Stream. Walking along the path, you see ancient trees towering overhead and hear the gentle flow of clear springs beneath. This evokes the imagery of "The bright moon shines through the pines, and the clear spring flows over the stones." Near the end of Bayin Stream, a stone wall blocks the path. However, turning around, you are greeted with an expansive view of Jinhui Yi, which is captivating and reminiscent of "In the face of mountains and rivers, the path seems lost; in the shadowy willows and blooming flowers, there lies another village." Standing at Zhiyu Pavilion, overlooking Jinhui Yi, the distant rockery, and the cascading Huishan, one cannot help but recall the poetic imagery of "The green mountains hide the waters that stretch endlessly."

Jichang Garden is a poem unto itself! It is no wonder that both Emperor Kangxi and Emperor Qianlong visited it every time they traveled south. They even bestowed the garden with the plaques "Mountain Color and Stream Light" and "Jade Tinkling and Gold Clanking," encapsulating the endless poetic essence of Jichang Garden through a harmonious blend of stillness and movement, observation and listening. Emperor Qianlong even sketched plans to construct an inner garden, Huishan Garden, at the Summer Palace, known today as "Xiequ Garden."

Jichang Garden, a renowned garden recognized both domestically and internationally, stands as the most beautiful ancestral hall among the hall cluster. Every tree and every stone bears witness to the passage of time, and each brick and tile recounts the rise and fall of the family. Here, nature and culture intertwine, and history and reality merge, creating vivid.

冒死反对"花石纲"的斗士

许显谟祠位于惠山古镇横街37号,与寄畅园隔街相望,祀主为北宋时期的著名学者和官员许德之。许德之,原名焕,字振叔,号文懿,生于1076年,卒于1142年,无锡许舍人,原籍河南,由祖父许旦从徙地高邮再迁无锡,成为锡山许氏二世祖。许舍位于无锡雪浪山麓,原名"鹤溪",正是因为宣和五年(1123年)许德之写了一篇《许舍记》而改名"许舍",无锡人称为许舍里,这个地名一直流传到今天。

许德之出身名门,是唐代睢阳太守许远的第十一世孙,自幼聪慧过人,北宋绍圣元年(1094年)高中进士,从此步入仕途,曾任扬州法曹,后迁任太常寺少卿,以显谟阁学士衔出任婺州(今浙江金华)知府,与晁咏之、韩韶、苏象先一起,号称"维扬四俊"。

许显谟祠原本在南泉方湖寺旁边,而我们现在所见的这座祠堂,则是在清乾隆三十七年(1772年),由许德之的后裔许岱崧奉旨在此建造,主祀许德之,配祀其后人——朝廷旌表的孝子许培元。祠堂门楼为观音兜山墙式,原为一路两进,面阔均为四间,为硬山顶有封火山墙的平房建筑,内有孝德堂、塔院和两庑,现仅存一进,2009年9月对其进行了修复。

许德之才学出众,为官清廉,心系百姓,更以耿直敢言著称。宋徽宗曾在便殿召见他,询问治国之策。他毫不犹豫地答道:"治道无多术,唯进贤退不肖。有贤不能用,与非贤而遽信,虽勤不治。"这段话的意思是说,治国之道没有太多复杂的方法,关键在于提拔贤能人才,罢免不称职者。如果放着贤才不任用,反而轻率信任无能之辈,即便君主勤于政务,国家也无法得到有效治理。这番话深得徽宗赞许,也展现了他卓越的政治见解和勇气。

在许德之的一生中,最为人津津乐道的是他反对"花石纲"的事迹。当时,宋徽宗为了满足自己的奢靡生活,下令在全国范围内搜罗奇花异石,运往汴京修建园林。这一举措给百姓带来了沉重的负担,民不聊生。许德之毅然冒死上书徽宗,痛陈"花石纲"之弊,请求停止这一劳民伤财的举动。虽然他

的奏章没有得到立即回应，但他并没有放弃，而是继续通过各种方式向朝廷进谏。最终，他的勇气和担当赢得了百姓的广泛赞誉。

许德之曾公开反对权臣秦桧的卖国行径而屡遭排挤，后为避报复，辞官回乡。高宗赵构即位后，他又被重新启用，继续为官。他去世后，被追赠为户部尚书，谥号"文懿"，以表彰他一生的功绩和品德。

许氏一门四进士，许德之为北宋绍圣初年（1094年）进士，其弟许衍之为南宋绍兴二年（1132年）进士，特奏名第一。其子许伸，南宋绍兴十二年（1142年）进士，其孙许寿，南宋绍兴十八年（1148年）进士，彰显了无锡许氏"诗书传家"的门风，让人不禁对许氏一门的学识和才华肃然起敬。

许显谟祠不仅是一座祭祀先贤的祠堂，更是一座承载着深厚文化底蕴的历史遗迹。它见证了许德之一生的辉煌与坎坷，也见证了无锡这片土地上的文化繁荣与发展。修复后的祠堂内，辟有非物质文化遗产泥人展，让大家在感受历史文化的同时，也能领略到国家级非遗惠山泥人的独特魅力。

The Courageous Opponent of the "Huashi Tribute": A Tribute to Xu Dezhi

The Xu Xianmo Ancestral Hall, located at No. 37 Hengjie Street in the historic Huishan Ancient Town, sits directly opposite the celebrated Jichang Garden. It is dedicated to Xu Dezhi, a renowned scholar and official of the Northern Song dynasty. Born Xu Huan in 1076 and later known by his courtesy name Zhenshu and literary name Wenyi, Xu Dezhi hailed from the prestigious Xu family of Wuxi. Although his ancestral home was in Henan, his grandfather Xu Dan migrated first to Gaoyou and then resettled in Wuxi, establishing Xu Dezhi as the second-generation ancestor of the Xu lineage in Xishan. The family estate, originally named "Hexi" and situated at the foot of Xuelang Mountain in Wuxi, was renamed "Xushe" following Xu Dezhi's composition of A Record of the Xu Estate in 1123 (5th year of the Xuanhe reign). Locally, the area became known as Xusheli—a name that has endured to this day.

A descendant of the Tang dynasty's famed Governor of Suiyang, Xu Yuan, Xu Dezhi was the eleventh-generation heir of this illustrious lineage. Exceptionally gifted from a young age, he ranked among the top in the imperial civil service examination in 1094, the first year of the Shaosheng reign, thereby commencing a distinguished official career. He served as legal officer in Yangzhou and later as Vice Minister of Rites at the Imperial Ancestral Temple. Appointed Prefect of Wuzhou (modern-day Jinhua, Zhejiang), he was granted the honorary title of Scholar of the Xianmo Pavilion. Alongside noted contemporaries such as Chao Yongzhi, Han Shao, and Su Xiangxian, he earned recognition as one of the "Four Talents of Weiyang."

The original ancestral hall of Xu Xianmo stood beside Fanghu Temple in Nanquan. The current structure was commissioned in 1772 (37th year of the Qianlong reign in the Qing dynasty) by imperial edict and built by Xu Dezhi's descendant Xu Daisong. The hall venerates Xu Dezhi as the principal deity and includes a secondary shrine to his filial descendant Xu Peiyuan, who was formally recognized by the imperial court. The gate tower features a Guanyin-doushan-style gable wall. Originally a two-section hall, each section spanned four bays and featured single-story structures with gabled roofs and firewalls. The layout included the Hall of Filial Virtue, a pagoda courtyard, and flanking side halls. Today, only one section survives, which was restored in September 2009.

Xu Dezhi was widely admired for his literary brilliance, incorruptible character, and concern for the welfare of the people. He was also celebrated for his moral rectitude and fearless candor. On one occasion, Emperor Huizong of Song summoned him to the inner palace for counsel on statecraft. Xu offered his advice without hesitation: "Good governance requires no intricate methods, only the promotion of the virtuous and the dismissal of the unworthy. To possess talent but not employ it, or to hastily trust the unfit, renders even the most diligent rule ineffective." This concise yet profound statement won the emperor's favor and reflected Xu's political insight and boldness.

Among his many achievements, Xu Dezhi is perhaps best remembered for his courageous opposition to the Huashi Gang—the imperial initiative that forced the nationwide collection and transportation of rare stones and exotic flora to embellish imperial gardens in Bianjing (present-day Kaifeng). This extravagant scheme imposed unbearable burdens on the populace, driving many to destitution. Risking his life, Xu submitted multiple memorials to Emperor Huizong, criticizing the policy's extravagance and urging its termination. Though initially ignored, he remained steadfast, continuing to voice dissent through various channels. His moral fortitude and unwavering advocacy ultimately earned him widespread admiration among the people.

Xu also openly denounced the traitorous conduct of the powerful court official Qin Hui, which led to repeated marginalization. To escape political retribution, he eventually resigned and returned to his hometown. After Emperor Gaozong (Zhao Gou) ascended the throne, Xu was recalled to official service. Upon his death, he was posthumously awarded the title of Minister of Revenue and given the honorific name "Wenyi" in recognition of his lifetime of service and integrity.

The Xu family produced four generations of jinshi (successful candidates in the highest imperial examination). Xu Dezhi achieved this distinction in 1094; his younger brother Xu Yanzhi obtained the same honor in 1132 as the top candidate of a special imperial decree. Xu's son, Xu Shen, became a jinshi in 1142, followed by his grandson Xu Shou in 1148. The family's sustained scholarly excellence epitomizes the Xu lineage's commitment to the Confucian ideals of transmitting knowledge and moral cultivation—a tradition that continues to inspire profound respect.

More than a site of ancestral veneration, the Xu Xianmo Ancestral Hall stands as a vital historical monument enriched with cultural depth. It bears witness to Xu Dezhi's extraordinary life of virtue and valor, and to the enduring cultural flourishing of Wuxi. The recently restored hall now houses an exhibition of Huishan clay figurines—a form of national-level intangible cultural heritage—allowing visitors to experience both the grandeur of history and the charm of traditional folk artistry.

哪个家族是无锡民族工商业的先行者

悠久而厚重的工商文化是无锡的精神根脉,百年工商精神传承至今,无锡第一个创办企业的工商业家族不是大家熟悉的荣氏家族,而是杨氏家族。

光绪二十一年(1895年),杨宗濂(字艺芳)、杨宗瀚(字藕芳)兄弟在运河畔羊腰湾创办了无锡第一家工厂,兄弟俩取古训"业精于勤荒于嬉"之意,为工厂取名"业勤",业勤纱厂于次年开工生产。这是近代无锡第一家机器工厂,也是全国第一家商办纱厂,标志着近代工商业从此在无锡兴起,之后荣家、周家、薛家的面粉、棉纺、机器、缫丝业相继出现,无锡工商业蓬勃发展。

杨宗濂、杨宗瀚当年商议创办业勤纱厂的地方就是这座杨四褒祠。杨四褒祠,始建于清光绪八年(1882年),原是一座典雅的杨氏别墅花园,是清末无锡优秀别墅园林之一。光绪二十年(1894年),杨宗濂将其改建为祠堂,以纪念其父母、叔婶,因此得名"杨四褒祠"。原祠楼底层纪念杨延俊(号菊仙)、杨延鹭(号菊人)兄弟,楼上配祀侯氏(杨延俊妻)、杜氏(杨延鹭妻)。

杨宗濂的父亲杨延俊,清道光二十七年(1847年)与李鸿章为同榜进士,历任山东汜城等地知县。杨延俊当年的考卷现在就收藏在无锡市图书馆。据说当年会试时,杨延俊与李鸿章住在同号宿舍,李鸿章大病,杨延俊悉心照料,李、杨两家

因此结下深厚情谊，杨延俊去世后，李鸿章先后任用了他的儿子杨宗濂、杨宗瀚。

杨宗濂是杨延俊的长子，随李鸿章征战太平军、捻军，筹建北洋武备学堂，开办天津自来火公司，会办上海机器织布局。光绪十八年（1892年），其母去世，杨宗濂丁忧回家，在此期间在潜庐（又名留耕草堂）与三弟杨宗瀚商议创办业勤纱厂。

"潜庐"源于《易经》"潜龙勿用"之典，主厅留耕草堂，坐北朝南，为歇山顶建筑，面阔三间，中有屏门，东西开有花窗，堂外回廊蜿蜒曲折，回环往复，纳锡、惠两山秀色于园内，另有望山楼、丛桂轩、门厅及戏台等建筑，花园结构紧

凑，布局精巧，清幽雅致，极尽江南园林之妙。留耕草堂门厅在上河塘临龙头下，上悬"潜庐"匾额，由民国十七年（1928年）7月许国凤题并隶书。2006年5月25日，留耕草堂被作为惠山镇核心祠堂园林列入全国重点文物保护单位。

可惜的是杨氏兄弟创办的业勤纱厂在1937年被日军焚毁，抗日战争胜利后，杨氏后人杨世骏奉命回无锡谋求战争赔偿，准备重建业勤纱厂，最终却未能如愿。杨氏家族作为近代民族工商业先驱，以民族工商业而兴，然而子孙后辈却以研究学问而著称，最为大家熟知的大概是中国历史上第一位女性大学校长杨荫榆、音乐史家杨荫浏以及中国现代作家、文学翻译家杨绛。

作为杨氏兄弟商议创办无锡第一家工厂的地方，杨四褒祠不仅是一座祠堂，还是一段家族荣耀与历史传承的见证，与惠山祠堂群内另外三座杨氏祠堂——杨忠襄公祠、杨宗濂祠和杨宗瀚祠，共同传递着无锡民族工商业家族务实创新、经世致用的精神，成为惠山祠堂群的一道独特风景。

Which Family Pioneered Ethnic Industry and Commerce in Wuxi?

The rich and profound industrial culture is the spiritual backbone of the city. The century-long spirit of Wuxi's industry and commerce has been passed down through generations. The family that the first to establish a business in Wuxi is not the well-known Rong family, but rather the Yang family.

In the 21st year of the Guangxu era (1895), brothers Yang Zonglian (styled Yifang) and Yang Zonghan (styled Oufang) founded Wuxi's first factory in Yangyaowan along the Grand Canal. The brothers named the factory "Yeqin" to embody the ancient saying "Diligence in work brings success; idleness leads to failure." The Yeqin Cotton Mill began production the following year. This marked the establishment of the first machine factory in modern Wuxi and the first commercially operated cotton mill in the country, signifying the rise of modern industry and commerce in Wuxi. Subsequently, the Rong, Zhou, and Xue families entered the flour, cotton spinning, machinery, and silk reeling industries, contributing to the flourishing of Wuxi's industrial sector.

The place where Yang Zonglian and Yang Zonghan discussed the establishment of the Yeqin Cotton Mill is the Yang Sibao Ancestral Hall. Constructed in the eighth year of Guangxu (1882), this elegant hall was originally a Yang family villa garden and is considered one of Wuxi's finest gardens from the late Qing Dynasty. In the 20th year of Guangxu (1894), Yang Zonglian converted it into an ancestral hall to commemorate his parents and uncles, hence the name "Yang Sibao Ancestral Hall." The main hall honors brothers Yang Yanjun (styled Juxian) and Yang Yanzhi (styled Juren), with their wives, from the Hou and Du families, worshipped on the upper level.

Yang Zonglian's father, Yang Yanjun, passed the imperial examination in the 27th year of Daoguang (1847) alongside Li

Hongzhang and held the position of county magistrate in various places, including Feicheng, Shandong. Yang Yanjun's examination papers are now preserved in the Wuxi City Library. It is said that during the examination, Yang Yanjun and Li Hongzhang shared a dormitory. When Li fell seriously ill, Yang cared for him, forging a deep friendship between the two families. After Yang Yanjun's death, Li Hongzhang appointed his sons, Yang Zonglian and Yang Zonghan, to significant positions.

As the eldest son of Yang Yanjun, Yang Zonglian fought alongside Li Hongzhang against the Taiping Army and the Nian Army, participated in establishing the Beiyang Military Academy, and managed the Tianjin Gas Company and Shanghai Machine Weaving Bureau. After his mother passed away in 1892, Yang Zonglian returned home in mourning. During this time, he and his brother Yang Zonghan discussed the establishment of the Yeqin Cotton Mill at their residence, known as Qianlu (also called Liugeng Caotang).

The name "Qianlu" originates from the *I Ching*, specifically the phrase "the hidden dragon does not act." The main hall of Liugeng Caotang, oriented south with a hip roof design, consists of three bays, featuring a screen door and flower windows to the east and west. The exterior is adorned with a winding corridor that encircles the garden, integrating the beautiful scenery of Xishan and Huishan mountains. Additionally, structures such as the Wangshan Pavilion, Conggui Pavilion, entrance hall, and stage enhance the garden's compact structure and exquisite layout, embodying the elegance of Jiangnan gardens. The entrance hall of Liugeng Caotang is situated near the Longtoudi on Shanghe Pond and features the inscription "Qianlu," written in seal script by Xu Guofeng in July 1928. On May 25, 2006, Liugeng Caotang was designated a key national cultural relic protection unit.

Unfortunately, the Yeqin Cotton Mill established by the Yang brothers was destroyed by the Japanese army in 1937. After the victory in the War of Resistance, Yang Shijun, a descendant of the Yang family, was tasked with returning to Wuxi to seek war reparations and prepare for the reconstruction of the mill, but ultimately, this did not come to fruition. The Yang family, as pioneers of modern ethnic industry and commerce, rose to prominence through their contributions to industry; however, their descendants became renowned for their scholarly pursuits. The most notable figures include Yang Yinyu, China's first female university president; Yang Yinliu, a music historian; and Yang Jiang, a modern Chinese writer and translator.

As the site where the Yang brothers deliberated on establishing Wuxi's first factory, Yang Sibao Ancestral Hall stands not only as a place of worship but also as a testament to family honor and historical heritage. Together with three other Yang ancestral halls in the Huishan Cluster—the Yang Zhongxiang Hall, the Yang Zonglian Hall, and the Yang Zonghan Hall—they collectively convey the spirit of practical innovation and application that characterizes Wuxi's ethnic industrial and commercial families, becoming a unique feature of the Huishan Ancestral Hall Cluster.

把日子过成"朝如青丝暮成雪"的地方

在中国古代，坚贞守节、忠贞不渝、从一而终、为夫守节可谓是封建社会的女性本色。惠山祠堂群中数量很多的一类祠堂，就是为了纪念这些贞节的妇女，这就是节妇祠，又叫贞节祠。这些祠堂都是由礼部或者祠堂授权的机构批准设立，不是家族随便可以建造的，显示出这一"褒奖"的官方权威性。

在惠山二泉里中部、听松坊南端、观墩之后、惠山浜东端和烧香浜顶等，遍及惠山古镇东南西北中就有五所贞节总祠，另外还有不少节妇祠、贞节祠、节烈祠、节孝祠等贞节专祠，如唐素女祠、华节妇祠、荣孝贞节女祠、单姬祠等，每个不同的女性背后都是相同的命运，在封建礼教中消耗自我，在寂静岁月中慢慢枯萎，何时镜中一瞥，只能感慨"朝如青丝暮成雪"。

位于惠山古镇横街上的贞义单姬祠堂，就是这样一座具有广泛代表意义的女性贞义祠堂。这里原先是一处贞节祠，而单姬原本在惠山古镇寄畅园后面的听松坊内，有独立的祠堂，但年久失修，难以恢复旧貌，因此，无锡单氏便将单姬并入了现在的祠堂。

单姬是无锡历史上一位传奇女性，她8岁被许配给沈家，12岁还没出嫁，丈夫便亡故了。于是单姬剪了头发，发誓终身不嫁，守贞到85岁去世。明清历代名贤先后为单姬题匾、写碑、作赞，褒扬其贞义。现在的祠堂共三进，主要陈列着单氏

家谱、单氏名人事迹、单氏后人捐赠的家族珍贵文物等,当然最重要的是传承古代节义的内容。在几千年的封建宗法社会里,在"三从四德"制度下,在"贞烈两全"的礼教中,多少女性传承着这样的"美德"殉节而亡,由青丝变成白发,由青年转成暮年。

　　幸好那一年代已随风逝去,如今的中国,"妇女能顶半边天",女性在社会和家庭中的地位达到了历史新高度。

The Place Where Days Pass Like "Black Hair in the Morning and Snow in the Evening"

In ancient China, fidelity and loyalty of women reflected the expectations of a feudal society. In the Huishan Hall Cluster, there exists a significant category of halls dedicated to the commemoration of these virtuous women, known as "Jiefu Hall" or "Chastity Hall." These halls established under the approval of the Ministry of Rites or authorized organizations, signifying the official recognition of this honor.

Throughout the ancient town of Huishan, there are five main chastity halls located in the southeastern, southwestern, northeastern, and northwestern areas, as well as numerous specialized halls dedicated to chastity, including the Tang Sunu Hall, Hua Jiefu Hall, Rongxiao Zhenjienu Hall, and Shan Ji Hall. Each of these women embodies a similar fate—consumed by the rigid confines of feudal moral teachings, they gradually withered away in silence. Upon catching a glimpse of themselves in the mirror, they could only sigh, "Black hair in the morning, snow in the evening."

The Shan Ji Hall, located on Heng Street in the ancient town of Huishan, serves as a representative hall dedicated to female chastity and loyalty. Originally established as a chastity hall, Shan Ji's hall was situated in the Tingsongfang area behind the Jichang Garden in Huishan. However, it fell into disrepair over time and could not be restored to its former glory. Thus, the Shan family of Wuxi integrated Shan Ji into the current hall for veneration.

Shan Ji is a legendary figure in Wuxi's history; she was betrothed at the age of eight and lost her husband at twelve before marriage. Consequently, she cut her hair and vowed never to remarry, maintaining her chastity until her death at the age of eighty-five. Renowned scholars from the Ming and Qing dynasties honored Shan Ji with plaques, inscriptions, and eulogies, extolling her virtue. The current hall features three main halls displaying the genealogy of the Shan family, notable achievements of its members, and precious family artifacts donated by descendants, with the primary aim of perpetuating the virtues of chastity in ancient time. In the thousands of years of feudal patriarchal society, under the constraints of the "Three Obediences and Four Virtues" system, and within the oppressive moral codes that demanded both chastity and loyalty, countless women upheld such "virtues" to their detriment. Their lives transitioned from youthful vigor to old age.

Fortunately, that era has long passed. In contemporary China, where "women hold up half the sky," the status of women in society and family has reached unprecedented heights.

"晚到"的祠堂

这座"晚到"的祠堂纪念的是浦长源。浦长源是元末明初的无锡人，但是纪念他的祠堂却是清康熙年间修建的，整整晚了327年。那么，为什么隔了300多年才建呢？这是因为康熙四十二年（1703年），康熙宣布了一件事情，要对天下所有"忠孝节义之人，有功名教之士"进行表彰，过去称作"旌表"，所有申请通过的人，都可以奉旨建造祠堂，将这一项目提升到远高于私人家族建造的国家级水平。浦长源的祠堂就是这么来的。

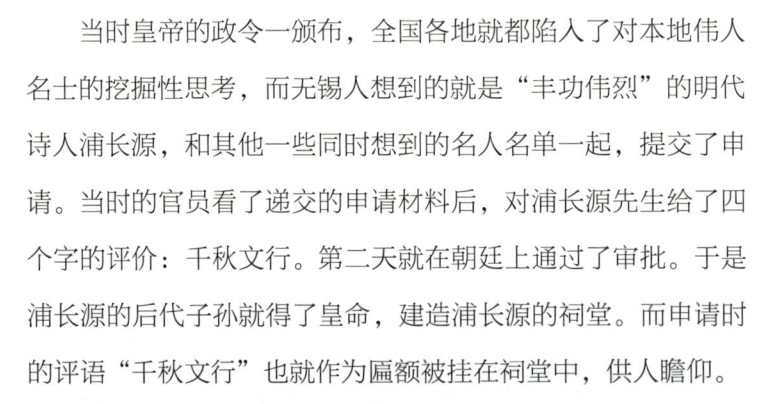

当时皇帝的政令一颁布，全国各地就都陷入了对本地伟人名士的挖掘性思考，而无锡人想到的就是"丰功伟烈"的明代诗人浦长源，和其他一些同时想到的名人名单一起，提交了申请。当时的官员看了递交的申请材料后，对浦长源先生给了四个字的评价：千秋文行。第二天就在朝廷上通过了审批。于是浦长源的后代子孙就得了皇命，建造浦长源的祠堂。而申请时的评语"千秋文行"也就作为匾额被挂在祠堂中，供人瞻仰。

那么，无锡人为什么会想到浦长源呢？其实他是无锡本土一位出色的诗人，本名是浦源，长源是他的字，号东海生。据说他少年时就崭露头角，表现出非凡的才华，所谓"少负奇才"，同时还博览群书。天赋加上努力，使得他诗书画俱佳。诗有唐诗的韵味，书法有王羲之、王献之的笔意，小楷和草书写得特别好。因此他得了"吴下十才子之一"的名声，还作为

人才被引进了朱㭎的晋王府,当了引礼舍人。

之后,他因为仰慕福建才子林鸿的才华,翻山越岭前去拜访。当时,林鸿的学生为了考考来访者,就让他献诗,于是浦长源即兴发挥,连着写了好几首诗,其中有两句"云边路绕巴山色,树里河流汉水声"简直是神来之笔,两位学生看到这两句,拍案叫绝,赞叹不已,立时进去禀报了师傅林鸿,林鸿一听也是十分满意,认为和自己的诗风十分接近,立刻请进来上座,并且邀请浦长源加入他办的诗社,因此,浦长源还是"闽中十才子"之一("闽中十才子"也有其他版本)。

可惜的是,天妒英才,浦长源在36岁时英年早逝。他在去陕西办差时,遇到大风浪,轮船失事,因公殉职了。临死之际,还想到自己完不成工作,浦长源先生的人品可见一斑。

The "Belated" Ancestral Hall

This "belated" ancestral hall is dedicated to Pu Changyuan. Pu was a native of Wuxi during the late Yuan and early Ming dynasties, but his ancestral hall was built during the reign of Emperor Kangxi in the Qing Dynasty, a full 327 years later. Why the delay of over three centuries? The reason lies in a decree issued by Emperor Kangxi in 1703 (the 42nd year of his reign), in which he called for the recognition of "loyal, filial, virtuous, and righteous individuals, as well as those who contributed to the cultivation of moral values and education." Historically referred to as "Jingbiao," this formal recognition allowed individuals who met the criteria to apply for and receive imperial approval to build ancestral halls in their honor. It was through this process that Pu Changyuan's hall came to be built.

When the emperor's edict was announced, local officials across the empire engaged in a reflective evaluation of their region's notable historical figures. Wuxi citizens immediately thought of Pu Changyuan, a revered Ming Dynasty poet known for his significant contributions. Together with other names, Pu's candidacy was submitted for review. After examining the application, the government official responsible for cultural affairs praised Pu with four characters: "A model of literary conduct for eternity." The final review was swiftly approved by the court, and Pu's descendants were granted the imperial order to construct his ancestral hall. While they were responsible for funding the project, the hall's national significance was clear. The phrase "A model of literary conduct for eternity," used in the initial review, was inscribed on a plaque inside the hall for all to see.

So why did Wuxi residents think of Pu Changyuan? He was an accomplished poet from Wuxi, originally named Pu Yuan, with the courtesy name Changyuan and the sobriquet Donghaisheng. It is said that from a young age, he displayed exceptional talent, earning the reputation of being a "prodigy." He was widely read and skilled in various artistic disciplines, excelling in poetry, calligraphy, and painting. His poetry evoked the charm of Tang dynasty verse, and his calligraphy reflected the influence of masters Wang Xizhi and Wang Xianzhi, with particular mastery in small regular script and cursive script. His reputation as one of the "Ten Talents of Wuxi" grew, and he was recruited by Zhu Gang, the Prince of Jin, to serve in his court as a ceremonial official.

Later, Pu embarked on a journey to visit Lin Hong, a renowned scholar from Fujian, whose literary talents he deeply admired. To test the young poet's abilities, Lin Hong's disciples asked Pu to recite some of his own poetry. Pu responded on the spot, composing several poems in quick succession. Among them, two lines stood out: "The mountain path winds through misty peaks, the river murmurs beneath the trees," which were met with astonishment by the students. Impressed, they immediately reported Pu's talent to Lin Hong, who, upon hearing the verses, recognized Pu's poetic style as closely aligned with his own. Lin warmly welcomed Pu, inviting him to join his poetry society. Thus, Pu also became known as one of the "Ten Talents of Minzhong," though various versions of this group exist.

Tragically, Pu Changyuan's life was cut short at the age of thirty-six. While traveling on official business to Shaanxi, Pu's boat encountered a violent storm and capsized, leading to his untimely death. Even in his final moments, he was also remembered his responsibilities. His character is thus forever etched in history as one marked by loyalty and integrity.

著名画家是位美食博主

　　从古华山门出发,沿惠山直街向东而行,不出50米,便来到高士里1号楼,这里就是著名的倪云林先生祠,又名倪高士祠。这是一座建于清康熙三十年(1691年)的祠堂,纪念的是元代画家、诗人倪云林(1301—1374),由云林先生的裔孙倪凤来等奉檄在明王大益园废址上建造。后经乾隆十一年(1746年)、道光二十六年(1846年)、民国四年(1915年)三次修葺,祠堂内有思敬堂、雪渚斋、鹤情楼,后园有池沼、假山、琴舫等建筑。

　　云林先生是无锡梅里祇陀村人(今无锡市锡山区云林街道

云林社区），名瓒，字元镇，号云林，是世界文化名人、元四家之一、中国古代十大画家之一、无锡倪氏七世祖。倪云林诗书画三绝，尤以画为三绝之冠，他对中国画理论和技法发展做出了开创性贡献，画作多取景太湖山水，意境高雅，被后世推崇为中国文人山水画的最高境界。

如果说，太湖美景成就了倪云林的画，那么，太湖风物更孕育了一位初代"美食博主"。云林先生日常喜好精研美食，还把制作心得记录下来，集结成册。《云林堂饮食制度集》中记载了多则元代末期苏南无锡一带食物的制作之法，是目前可追溯的最早记载无锡饮食文化的古籍，也是唯一一本系统反映元末明初江南饮食生活场景和烹饪制作技艺的文献。从这一则则食物记录中可以感受到云林先生身为美食家的高雅品位，同时，书中记录的食材和制作技法还折射出他的饮食文化思想，对研究当代江南饮食有重要价值。

云林先生留下的"美食博客",流传至今,对无锡菜的影响十分深远。在总结无锡菜以及讲到传承江南美食文化时,都要提到几个重要的问题,比如无锡菜"咸出头,甜收口"。云林先生所写的40%左右的菜肴,都要先用酒和盐将食料腌制一下再烹饪,咸出头,甜收口。云林先生还多次使用"渨"字,表示浸泡的含义,沿用至今,意思也一点没变。

同时,在云林先生的"煮鲤鱼"和"鲻鱼"等菜中可以看到无锡菜浓油赤酱的影子,无锡菜除了老烧鱼、鳝糊等经典水鲜菜,豆制品、面筋、生麸类的菜式也多是浓油赤酱。比如说烤麸,云林先生所录"煮麸干"的烧法就类似于现在烤麸与"着酱面筋"的烧法,也是用十几种调料,这些调料只是跟现在的稍微有点区别,但都丰富且入味。

云林先生的食谱取料,丰富而全面,还有很大的包容性,充

分体现了江南吴文化地区饮食文化兼收并蓄的特点，如梭子蟹，用海鲜的原料。其风味特点还说明了无锡菜渊源的问题。无锡菜是什么时候变甜的，元代就甜，云林先生记录的菜有四分之一都是甜的，由此可见无锡饮食文化的传承。

  漫步在今天的惠山古镇，抬眼是青砖黛瓦错落有致，鼻端是各色美食满街飘香，卤汁鲜甜的小笼馒头、香美甘甜的桂花酒、酥软绵甜的糖芋头、软韧香甜的梅花糕、皮薄汤鲜的小馄饨、爽滑劲道的银丝面、酥松脆软的油酥饼、软润嫩滑的豆腐花、外脆里糯的玉兰饼，还有各色享有盛名的正宗无锡味道，诱人垂涎。

A Renowned Painter as a Culinary Blogger

Starting from the ancient Huashan Gate and heading east along Huishan Zhijie for less than 50 meters, one arrives at Building No. 1, Gaoshi Li, which houses the renowned memorial hall of Mr. Ni Yunlin, also known as the Ni Gaoshi Hall. This ancestral hall, established in the 30th year of the Kangxi Emperor's reign (1691), honors the Yuan Dynasty painter and poet Ni Yunlin (1301–1374). It was constructed at the site of the abandoned Deyi Garden under the auspices of Ni Fenglai, a descendant of Ni Yunlin. The hall underwent three renovations during the 11th year of the Qianlong Emperor's reign (1746), the 26th year of the Daoguang Emperor's reign (1846), and the 4th year of the Republic of China. Inside the hall, there are areas named Jingsi Hall, Xuezhu Studio, and Heqing

Tower, while the back garden features a pond, rockery, and a qin boat.

Ni Yunlin hailed from Qituo Village in Meili, Wuxi (now part of the Yunlin Community in Wuxi's Xishan District). His personal name was Zan, courtesy name Yuanzhen, and he was known as Yunlin. He is celebrated as a world cultural figure, one of the Four Masters of the Yuan Dynasty, one of the top ten ancient Chinese painters, and the seventh ancestor of the Ni family in Wuxi. Ni Yunlin excelled in poetry, calligraphy, and painting, with his paintings considered the pinnacle of his talents. He made pioneering contributions to the development of Chinese painting theory and techniques, often depicting the landscapes of Taihu Lake with elegant artistic conceptions, earning him admiration as an exemplar of literati landscape painting in China.

While the beautiful scenery of Taihu Lake shaped Ni Yunlin's art, the region's culinary culture also nurtured a pioneer of early "food blogging." Ni Yunlin had a profound interest in gastronomy, documenting his culinary experiences and compiling them into a volume. *The Yunlin Hall Dietary Regulations* records various methods of preparing dishes from the late Yuan Dynasty in the Suzhou and Wuxi areas, representing the earliest traceable documentation of Wuxi's culinary culture. It is also the only systematic literature reflecting the dining customs and culinary techniques of Jiangnan during the late Yuan and early Ming Dynasties. Through these food records, one can appreciate YunLin refined tastes as a gourmet. Moreover, the ingredients and cooking techniques recorded in the book reflect his culinary philosophy, holding significant value for contemporary research on Jiangnan's cuisine.

The "culinary blog" left behind by Ni Yunlin continues to influence Wuxi cuisine profoundly. When summarizing Wuxi dishes and discussing the inheritance of Jiangnan's culinary culture, several key issues arise. For instance, Wuxi cuisine is characterized by a "salty start and sweet finish." Approximately 40% of the dishes described by Ni Yunlin involve marinating ingredients with wine and salt before cooking, Ni Yunlin frequently used the term "yin" (浥), meaning to soak, a practice that endures to this day without any change in meaning.

Furthermore, in Ni Yunlin's recipes for "boiled carp" and "brine fish," we see the influence of rich and robust flavors typical of Wuxi cuisine. In addition to classic aquatic dishes like braised fish and eel, Wuxi cuisine features various preparations involving bean products, gluten, and raw dough. For instance, Ni Yunlin's method of preparing "boiled gluten" is reminiscent of today's practices for making baked gluten and "sauce-coated gluten," utilizing over a dozen seasonings. Although some of these seasonings differ slightly from modern ones, they are still rich and flavorful.

Ni Yunlin's recipes are diverse, comprehensive, and highly inclusive, showcasing the eclectic nature of the culinary culture in the Wu cultural region of Jiangnan. The use of river crab as a seafood ingredient highlights the origins of Wuxi cuisine. Historically, Wuxi cuisine has been sweet, with one-quarter of the dishes recorded by Ni Yunlin classified as sweet. This underscores the transmission of Wuxi's culinary culture through the ages.

内相经纶，清风传家

绣嶂街15号是惠山祠堂群一张响亮的名片，论年头，这是古镇里可以进前五的宋代古建筑遗址；论人物，这里纪念的是唐代宰相，他的才华学问、气节品德无不令人折服，《资治通鉴》中连篇收录其政论达39篇，震古烁今；论影响，这位贤相死后800多年，乾隆还为褒奖他亲笔题写匾额，这就是历经近900年风霜的古镇核心保护祠堂——陆宣公祠。

作为无锡陆氏传承家风的总祠堂，陆宣公祠里除了唐代名相陆贽，更荟聚了历代陆氏名贤，且个个都称得上彪炳千古、清风照人。

陆宣公祠一如老谱所记，坐北朝南，四开三进，砖木结构，花鸟脊饰。祠门前的砖雕祠额"陆宣公祠"四个大字为当代书法名家陆修伯手迹，彰显着祠堂的古朴庄严。走进祠堂内，可以看到右手墙嵌石碑上一句陆贽的格言——"吾上不负天子，下不负吾所学，不恤其他"，是南宋爱国诗人陆游为叔父陆贽所书，在白墙映衬下格外醒目。

二进享堂，木窗上方是乾隆御赐的"世代忠良"和"内相经纶"两块匾额，这不仅是对陆贽的赞誉，也是对陆氏家族历代忠良的肯定。在外厅东眺，只见传说中无锡文风文脉的象征——锡山上龙光宝塔如点睛之笔；看厅内，两侧墙上的16位陆氏历代名贤祖像，果真是满门忠良。这里有汉代首位力倡儒学的思想家陆贾；有清廉为民的吴县县令陆烈；有三国时期

"惠"游祠堂

的东吴"社稷之臣"陆逊；有隋炀帝也敬重三分的隋代名臣陆知命；有父子宰相，父亲是深受武则天信任，两度为相的陆元方，儿子是度量恢宏、推行仁政的陆象先；有撰写中国第一部农具专著《耒耜经》的唐代文学家陆龟蒙；有南宋理学家、心学奠基人、陆王学派的开创者陆九渊；有无锡陆氏始祖、南宋抗金英雄廉吏陆寘；有著名的南宋文学家、爱国诗人陆游；有南宋左丞相、抗元名臣陆秀夫；有山水画名家、元四家之冠、《富春山居图》的作者黄公望；有明末清初江南大儒陆世仪；有被誉为"天下第一清廉"的清代理学家陆陇其；有民国江西吏治研究所所长陆士奎；还有以笔为武器传播马克思主义的新中国第一位宣传部部长陆定一。这些陆氏先贤，每一位都是中华民族的骄傲、江山社稷的脊梁，这一脉相承、代代相传的浩

AI语音导览

然正气和廉洁清风,令人缅怀先德之余,敬意油然升腾。

　　陆氏人才济济,尤其是清官代出,光耀千秋,翻开文史典籍,陆氏著名文学家、医学家更是人才辈出,群星璀璨。打开世代相传的陆氏家训,我们似乎看到了奥秘,陆氏家训中说:"教子有方,朝夕苦读,必成其才,为国献力。宁静致远,洁身自好,穷不失志。"字字珠玑,以这样的家规家风,弘扬祖德,教育后人,怪不得代代陆氏有英才,朗朗清风满乾坤。

　　陆宣公祠不仅是陆氏家族的宗祠,也是学习优秀传统文化,传承良好家规家风的所在。这里没有商业化的喧嚣,只有宁静与祥和,在此漫步盘桓,瞻仰贤堂先祖伟业,观四水归堂精巧天井,赏石梁飞架幽深水院,听玲珑戏台风雅曲音,感受那份来自历史深处的清风。

Internal Harmony Governs the State, Integrity Passes Through Generations

No. 15 Xiuzhang Street serves as a striking emblem of the Huishan Ancestral Hall Cluster, being one of the top five remaining Song Dynasty architectural sites in the ancient town. It honors the memory of a Tang Dynasty chancellor whose scholarly talents and moral integrity command deep respect. His political essays, numbering thirty-nine in the *Comprehensive Mirror in Aid of Governance*, have resonated throughout history. Over 800 years after his death, Emperor Qianlong personally inscribed a plaque in his honor. This is the Lu Xuan Gong Hall, which has weathered 890 years, standing at the core of the town's cultural heritage.

As the primary ancestral hall for the Wuxi Lu family, the Lu Xuan Gong Hall is dedicated not only to the renowned Tang statesman Lu Zhi but also houses the legacies of various eminent figures from the Lu lineage, each deserving of eternal remembrance and integrity.

The Lu Xuan Gong Hall, as recorded in the old family scriptures, faces south with a layout of four openings and three courtyards, constructed of brick and wood, adorned with floral and avian motifs on its ridge. The brick carving above the entrance, inscribed with "Lu Xuan Gong Ci," is penned by the contemporary calligrapher Lu Xiubo, showcasing the hall's ancient and solemn character. Upon entering, one can find a stone tablet on the right wall bearing a famous saying by Lu Zhi: "I am neither ungrateful to the emperor above nor neglectful of my studies below, caring not for others." This inscription, written by the patriotic Southern Song poet Lu You for his uncle, stands out prominently against the white wall.

In the second courtyard's hall, above the wooden windows, are two plaques granted by Emperor Qianlong: "Generations of Loyalty" and "Internal Affairs Management," which not only honor Lu Zhi but also affirm the loyalty of the Lu family across generations. From the eastern part of the hall, one can gaze at the Longguang Pagoda on Xishan Mountain, symbolizing Wuxi's cultural heritage. Observing the portraits of sixteen distinguished ancestors of the Lu family on the walls, one can truly appreciate the legacy of loyalty. Among them are the Han Dynasty scholar Lu Jia, the incorruptible county magistrate Lu Lie, the Eastern Wu minister Lu Xun from the Three Kingdoms period, the esteemed official Lu Zhiming from the Sui Dynasty, who was respected by Emperor Yang, and the father-son duo of Lu Yuanfang, trusted twice by Empress Wu Zetian, and his son Lu Xiangxian, who advocated benevolent governance. There is also Lu Guimeng, the Tang literary figure who authored China's first treatise on agricultural tools, *the Classic of the Pow and Rake*; the Neo-Confucian scholar Lu Jiuyuan, a founder of the Lu-Wang school of thought; Lu Shao, the ancestor of the Wuxi Lu clan and a hero against the Jurchen invaders during the Southern Song; the famous Southern Song poet and patriot Lu You; the Southern Song Left Chancellor and anti-Yuan minister Lu Xiufu; the renowned landscape painter Huang Gongwang, the leader of the Four Masters of Yuan and the author of *Develling in the Fachun Mountains*; the late Ming and early Qing Confucian Lu Shiyi; the Qing Neo-Confucian scholar Lu Longqi, revered as "the most incorruptible official in the world"; Lu Shikui, the head of the Jiangxi Institute of Civil Service during the Republic; and Lu Dingyi, the first propaganda minister of the People's Republic of China, who spread Marxism with his pen. Each of these Lu ancestors is a source of pride for the Chinese nation, serving as the backbone of the country, especially the moral integrity and noble spirit passed down through generations, evoking deep respect for their virtues.

  The Lu family has produced a wealth of talent, particularly in the realm of virtuous officials who have left an indelible mark on history. The illustrious contributions of Lu scholars, writers, and physicians shine brightly in literary and historical texts. The ancestral teachings of the Lu family reveal the secret: "Educating children properly requires diligent study day and night to nurture their talents for the service of the nation. Tranquility leads to vastness; maintaining personal integrity and ambition, even in poverty." Each phrase carries profound wisdom, and with such family rules and virtues, they promote ancestral virtues and educate future generations, making it no surprise that the Lu family continues to produce exceptional talents and maintains a noble atmosphere across generations.

  The Lu Xuan Gong Hall is not only the ancestral hall of the Lu family but also an ideal venue for learning excellent traditional culture and inheriting fine family values. Here, commercial hustle and bustle is absent, replaced by tranquility and harmony. As we stroll through, paying homage to our esteemed ancestors, we marvel at the intricately designed courtyard where waters converge, admire the stone beams spanning the serene waters, listen to the elegant music emanating from the exquisite opera stage, and feel the refreshing breeze that comes from deep within history.

祠堂群里最迷你的戏台

祠堂中的戏台是宗族祭祀的演出场所,主要满足敬祖的需要。张中丞祠、陆宣公祠、昭忠祠、范文正公祠内均有戏台,春申君祠、王恩绶祠、杨延俊祠内戏台则仅存基址。春申君祠及张、陆两祠戏台位居中轴,利于酬敬祠主。王、杨两祠戏台位居边路,临池挑筑,面向花厅,可供评弹清唱曲艺之用。以前惠山茶会、祠祭期间好戏连台,热闹非凡。最为珍奇的是范文正公祠内的迷你戏台,以其精巧的设计和独特的文化内涵,成为不可错过的一道风景。

范文正公祠位于惠山古镇绣嶂街17号，纪念北宋名相、文学家范仲淹，配祀元迁锡始祖范睎文。清乾隆五十年（1785年），裔孙范章辂等请建于明谈恺慧麓小圃故址，原祠面阔五间五进，咸丰年间毁于兵灾，清末、民国初年先后修葺。

范仲淹（989—1052），苏州吴县（江苏苏州）人。父墉，仲淹两岁而孤，母贫无依，改嫁朱氏，因取朱姓，名说。大中祥符八年（1015年）中进士。母逝，复本姓，更名仲淹，字希文。官至陕西四路安抚使，参知政事。为政敢言直谏。仁宗时，与韩琦率兵同拒西夏，威镇边地。庆历三年（1043年）议行"新政"：考官吏，减冗员，轻薄赋，整军修武。结果为言者所攻，"新政"未得施行，归于失败。此后，范仲淹又因得罪了宰相吕夷简，被贬放河南邓州，庆历六年（1046年），范仲淹受好友滕子京委托，为重修的岳阳楼题写了一篇《岳阳楼记》，留下千古名句"先天下之忧而忧，后天下之乐而乐"。范仲淹工诗、词、散文，有《范文正公集》传世，死谥文正。

范睎文，字景文，号药庄，钱塘人，南宋太学生。咸淳年间（1265—1274年）曾上书弹劾贾似道。元时求贤，睎文与赵俯同荐于朝，任提举杭州学路，转长兴丞，著有《对床夜话》。其子范拱为无锡教授，移居无锡而终。

来到祠前，首先映入眼帘的是门前的抱鼓石，它们古朴庄重，仿佛在诉说着历史的沧桑。进入范文正公祠，仿佛穿越了时空的隧道，回到了那个古老的时代。整个祠堂由三进院落构成，每一进院落都充满了历史的痕迹。

进入门厅，左右两边树立着"范文正公祠堂记""无锡堰

桥祠堂碑记"等石碑，记录着范文正公祠的建祠经过和历史沿革，墙上刻有范仲淹生平以及范氏世系大宗图。

穿过门厅，首先映入眼帘的是"敦叙堂"，两侧木柱之上题写一副对联："源从尧舜祖德流芳传世泽；望出高平宗功浩瀚振家声"。这里是范仲淹的后人聚集议事的地方。堂内太师壁上绘有巨幅范仲淹半身持笏像，面容庄重，眼神深邃。画像之上悬有"德行家传"匾额，画像两侧一副对联："文章传赤县；忠爱数名流"。站在这里，不禁让人想起他那句"先天下之忧而忧，后天下之乐而乐"，感受到范文正公以天下为己任的胸怀和担当。

走过石板桥，来到"后乐堂"，堂内梁枋上悬"济时良相"匾额，堂中太师壁正面是明代大书画家文徵明书写的《岳阳楼记》，背面是岳阳楼全景图。《岳阳楼记》也被后人视为范氏家训。这里不仅是范仲淹后人读书的地方，也是他们修身养性之地。在这里，人们可以感受到那种静谧与宁和，也可以体会到书香门第的文化气息。

来到后花园，一池碧水荡漾其中，沿池曲廊蜿蜒曲折，宛如一条时光隧道，带领人们穿越时空，感受历史的厚重。曲廊转折处有一半亭，名曰"先忧亭"，寓意深远，提醒着人们要时刻关注国家和民族的命运。站在亭中，俯瞰着后花园美景，不禁让人再次感念范公那忧国忧民的情怀。

"报本堂"内有范氏祖先的牌位，展现了范氏家族的世代传承。而堂东甬道沿东墙的"先天下之忧而忧，后天下之乐而乐"行书砖雕，更是点睛之笔，彰显了范公胸怀天下的高尚情操。

"报本堂"东侧有一口井泉，井泉边有一座浚泉亭，左右亭柱刻着一副对联："求木之长者必固其根本；欲流之远者必浚其泉源"。亭对面一汪清澈池水，水草丛生，生机勃勃。

眼前这座浚泉亭就是惠山祠堂群现存戏台中最小的戏台，和其他三座一样，也是单檐歇山顶，但只可供一人在其中弹拉清唱，戏台虽小，功能却不减，同样能起到敬祖的作用。

范文正公祠不仅是范仲淹这位伟大历史人物的纪念场所，更是传承和弘扬中华优秀传统文化的重要载体。在这里，人们可以领略到范公的高尚品质和崇高精神，更可以深刻感受到中华民族悠久的历史和文化底蕴。

The Miniature Stage in the Ancestral Hall Cluster

The opera stage within the ancestral halls serves as a performance venue for clan rituals, primarily aimed at honoring ancestors and entertaining deities. Stages can be found in the Zhang Zhongcheng Hall, Lu Xuan Hall, Zhao Zhong Hall, and Fan Wenzheng Hall, while the stages remain only as foundations at the Chunshen Jun Hall, Wang En Shou Hall and Yang Yan Jun Hall. The stages in Chunshen Jun and the Zhang and Lu halls are centrally located, facilitating respect for the hall masters, whereas the Wang and Yang halls feature stages positioned along the sides, adjacent to ponds, facing the flower halls, suitable for performances of narrative ballads and other traditional arts. Historically, during the Huishan incense fairs, tea gatherings, and ancestral rituals, lively performances filled the air. Of particular note is the miniature stage located in the Fan Wenzheng Hall, which, due to its exquisite design and unique cultural significance, has become a must-see attraction.

Situated at 17 Xiuzhang Street in the ancient town of Huishan, the Fan Wenzheng Ancestral Hall venerates the renowned Northern Song statesman and literary figure Fan Zhongyan, along with the ancestral founder Fan Xiwen. Constructed at the site of the Ming Dynasty's Tan Kai Hui Lu Garden in the fifth year of the Qianlong era (1785) by descendants such as Fan Zhanglu, the original hall featured five bays and five main sections. It was destroyed during military conflicts in the Xianfeng period but underwent restoration at the end of the Qing Dynasty and the beginning of the Republic of China.

Fan Zhongyan (989-1052), hailing from Wu County, Suzhou (Jiangsu), lost his father at the age of two and was raised by his impoverished mother, who remarried, thus adopting her new husband's surname, Zhu. In the eighth year of the Dazhong Xiangfu era (1015), he became a jinshi (the highest degree in the imperial examination). After his mother's death, he reverted to his original surname and changed his name to Zhongyan, with the courtesy name Xiwen. He rose to the position of pacification commissioner for the four routes in Shaanxi and participated in state affairs. Known for his forthrightness in governance, he led troops to resist the Western Xia during the reign of Emperor Ren Zong, earning respect in border territories In the third year of the Qingli era (1043), he proposed the "New Policies," which aimed to reform official examinations, reduce redundant staff, lessen burdensome taxes, and enhance military organization. Unfortunately, due to opposition, these policies were never implemented and ultimately failed. Later, Fan Zhongyan fell afoul of Prime Minister Lu Yijian and was exiled to Dengzhou in Henan. In the sixth year of the Qingli era (1046), at the request of his friend Teng Zijing, he penned the famous essay *Record of the Yueyang Tower* for the reconstructed Yueyang Tower, leaving behind the timeless phrase, "Worry before the world worries; rejoice after the world rejoices." He excelled in poetry, lyrics, and prose, compiling a collection titled *the Collected Works of Fan Wenzheng Gong*. He was posthumously honored with the title Wenzheng.

Fan Xiwen, courtesy name Jingwen, was from Qiantang. As a scholar during the Southern Song Dynasty, he submitted a memorial criticizing the official Jia Sidao during the Xianchun period (1265-1274). In the Yuan Dynasty, he recommended capable individuals, including Zhao Fu, to the court, and served as the supervisor of the Hangzhou educational circuit before being appointed as the deputy magistrate of Changxing. He authored *Night Talks by the Pillon*. His son, Fan Gong, was a professor in Wuxi, where he eventually settled and passed away.

Upon approaching the ancestral hall, the first sight to catch the eye is the drum stone at the entrance, embodying a sense of ancient solemnity that seems to narrate the passage of history. Stepping into the Fan Wenzheng Hall feels like traversing a tunnel through time back to a bygone era. The hall consists of three courtyards, each rich with historical traces.

As one enters the main hall, stone tablets inscribed with "Record of the Fan Wenzheng Hall" and "Inscription of the Wuxi Yanqu Bridge Ancestral Hall" stand on either side, chronicling the hall's history and the process of its construction. The walls feature inscriptions detailing Fan Zhongyan's life and the family genealogy chart.

Passing through the main hall, the Dunxu Hall comes into view, with couplets inscribed on the wooden pillars: "The source flows from the virtues of Yao and Shun, spreading their legacy through the ages; may we aspire to the lofty accomplishments of our ancestors, resonating the family's prestige." This hall serves as a meeting place for Fan Zhongyan's descendants. On the main wall, a large portrait of Fan Zhongyan holding a tablet depicts his dignified visage and profound gaze. Above this portrait hangs a plaque reading "Virtue and Family Legacy," flanked by another couplet: "Literary works resound across the realm; loyalty and love number among the great figures." Standing here, one cannot help but recall his famous saying,

"Worry before the world worries; rejoice after the world rejoices," reflecting Fan Wenzheng's sense of responsibility for the nation and its people.

Crossing the stone bridge leads to the Houle Hall, where a plaque reading "Beneficial Minister of the Times" hangs above the main wall, which prominently displays a calligraphy piece of the *Record of the Yueyang Tower* written by the renowned Ming Dynasty calligrapher Wen Zhengming, while the reverse side features a panoramic view of the Yueyang Tower. This piece has also been regarded as a family precept by the Fan clan. This hall serves not only as a study for Fan Zhongyan's descendants but also as a place for self-cultivation. Here, one can experience a tranquil atmosphere and the cultural ambiance of a scholarly lineage.

In the rear garden, a pool of azure water ripples gently, with a winding corridor that resembles a time tunnel, guiding visitors through the ages to appreciate the weight of history. At the corner of the corridor stands a half pavilion named Xianyou Pavilion, which conveys a profound message, reminding individuals to remain attentive to the fate of the country and the nation. Standing in the pavilion and overlooking the beautiful scenery of the rear garden evokes reflections on Fan Zhongyan's deep concern for the nation and its people.

Baoben Hall has the ancestral tablets of the Fan family, showcasing the generational legacy of the family. The calligraphy brick engraving along the eastern wall of the corridor reading "Worry before the world worries; rejoice after the world rejoices" serves as a poignant highlight, reflecting Fan Gong's noble character and global perspective.

To the east of the Baoben Hall is a wellspring, accompanied by a pavilion named Junquan Pavilion. The couplet carved on the columns reads: "Those seeking tall trees must solidify their roots; those wishing for distant streams must clear their springs." Facing the pavilion is a clear pool, vibrant with aquatic plants.

The Junquan Pavilion before you is the smallest existing stage in the Huishan Ancestral Hall Cluster. Similar to the other three, it features a single eave and a gable roof, but is designed to accommodate only one performer for solo singing or playing. Despite its size, this stage serves the same purpose of honoring ancestors and entertaining deities.

The Fan Wenzheng Hall is not only a memorial to the great historical figure Fan Zhongyan but also an essential vehicle for inheriting and promoting the excellent traditional culture of the Chinese nation. Here, one can appreciate Fan Zhongyan's noble qualities and lofty spirit while gaining profound insights into the enduring history and cultural richness of the Chinese nation.

"惠"游祠堂

祠堂群里规格最高的祠堂

规格最高的祠堂纪念的自然是惠山祠堂群里级别最高的人物。那么这位最高级别的人物是谁呢？他就是东岳大帝黄飞虎，纪念东岳大帝的祠堂也就被称为东岳庙，因为黄飞虎还被宋真宗封为天齐仁圣帝，所以祠堂又称圣帝殿。

东岳庙就在惠山直街上，始建于五代后唐同光元年（923年）。现在的东岳庙重建于2010年，庙门前石牌坊巍峨大气，上书"东岳行庙"，当中为什么加了个"行"字呢？这表示此处是黄飞虎在惠山的行宫。匾额上题有"位尊五岳"，五岳之首是泰山，所以黄飞虎又被称为泰山神。大殿正中纪念的是威风凛凛的黄飞虎。

AI语音导览

黄飞虎原本是"国舅",因为他的妹妹是纣王的妃子,但是纣王不但侮辱逼死了他的妻子贾氏,还摔死了他的妹妹,把忠心耿耿的黄飞虎给逼反了。黄飞虎和父亲、二弟、三子、四友带一千家将反出五关,投奔周武王,一起讨伐昏庸暴虐的纣王。之后黄飞虎因兴周灭纣有功,被敕封为五岳之首,泰山元帅。唐玄宗封他为天齐王,宋真宗封他为天齐仁圣帝,后又被封为泰山之神。

东岳庙作为纪念圣帝黄飞虎的行祠,历经数代,长盛不衰。农历三月二十八东岳大帝生日,因此,每年农历三月十四到三月二十八,是惠山最热闹的"八庙朝东岳"庙会,也称惠山香会。

The Highest-Ranked Ancestral Hall in the Cluster

The most prestigious hall within the Huishan Ancestral Hall Cluster is dedicated to the highest-ranking figure, the Eastern Peak Emperor Huang Feihu. The hall honoring the Eastern Peak Emperor is also referred to as the Dongyue Hall, as Huang Feihu was posthumously granted the title of "Heavenly Emperor of Benevolence" by Emperor Zhenzong of the Song Dynasty.

Located on Huishan Zhijie, the Dongyue Hall was originally established in the early Tongguang period of the Later Tang Dynasty (923 AD). The current structure was rebuilt in 2010, featuring a grand stone archway inscribed with "Dongyue Hang Miao." The inclusion of the character "Hang" signifies that this site served as Huang Feihu's palace during his travels in Huishan. The plaque above the entrance declares "Positioned as the Five Peaks," acknowledging that Mount Tai is regarded as the highest among the five sacred mountains, thus earning Huang Feihu the title of "God of Mount Tai." Inside the main hall, a formidable statue of Huang Feihu is prominently displayed.

Huang Feihu was initially the "brother-in-law" of King Zhou, as his sister was one of the king's consorts. However, King Zhou's brutal actions—causing the death of his wife, Jia, and later the death of his sister—led the loyal Huang Feihu to rebel. Accompanied by his father, younger brother, three sons, and four friends, he led a thousand soldiers to break through the five passes and join King Wu of Zhou in a campaign against the tyrannical King Zhou. Following his contributions to the downfall of the tyrant, Huang Feihu was enfeoffed as the leader of the five sacred mountains, known as the "Primordial Master of Mount Tai." Later, he was conferred the title of "Heavenly Qi King" by Emperor Xuanzong of the Tang Dynasty and "Heavenly Emperor of Benevolence" by Emperor Zhenzong of the Song Dynasty, eventually being recognized as the God of Mount Tai.

In society, "life" and "blessing" are paramount pursuits, while "death" and "disaster" are significant taboos. In old Wuxi, people revered the Eastern Peak Emperor Huang Feihu at the Huishan Shengdi Hall to seek blessings for life and prosperity while averting death and calamity, regarding him as the greatest deity worthy of worship.

As a hall dedicated to the venerable Huang Feihu, Dongyue Hall has thrived through several generations. The birthday of the Eastern Peak Emperor falls on the twenty-eighth day of the third lunar month. Thus, from the fourteenth to the twenty-eighth of the third lunar month, Huishan hosts its liveliest event, the "Eight Halls Pilgrimage to Dongyue," also known as the Huishan Fragrant Festival.

肚里能撑船的太平良相

王文正公祠现位于绣嶂街，前身可追溯至南宋绍定三年（1230年）敕建的灵护庙。灵护庙原来是祀王氏西沙四世祖、宋封利济惠民侯王越祖，又名利济惠民侯庙，清乾隆六年（1741年），无锡王氏以该庙祀远祖王旦，遂祠庙合一。灵护庙元代时从城中移复于惠山，清咸丰十年（1860年）毁于兵灾，清同治丁卯（1867年）王氏后裔捐资重建。

王文正公祠建筑风格古朴典雅，具有浓郁的江南水乡特色。整个建筑群由门楼、牌坊、正殿、后殿、配殿等多个建筑组成，构成了一个完整的建筑体系。

王旦出生于后周世宗显德四年（957年），大名府莘县（今山东省聊城市莘县）人，因其生于凌晨，故取名旦，字子明。据传，王旦先天相貌较丑，脸、鼻皆偏，喉部有突起，曾有华山道人预言其有异于他人的面相，说："日后必大贵"。王旦小时候沉默寡言，却好学不倦，颇有文才，深受他父亲兵部侍郎王祐器重。

王祐其实有三个儿子，王旦是二儿子，为了这三个儿子，他在庭院里面亲手种下了三棵槐树，为什么要种槐树呢？这里有个典故，周朝宫廷外种有三棵槐树，周朝三位官职最大的人，太师、太傅、太保，来面朝天子时，就面向三棵槐树站立。因为太师、太傅、太保合称三公，所以三槐就被比作三公。王爸爸种槐树实际上是望子成龙的心态。果然不负王爸爸

厚望，太平兴国五年（980年），王旦进士及第，担任大理评事，后官至同中书门下平章事，也就是宰相。

王旦为相时，举贤荐能，朝政清明，百姓安居，国家太平，史称"太平良相"。王旦深得宋真宗信任，作为真宗的辅佐大臣连任要职18年，其中为相达12年之久。王旦病重后，真宗派内侍探望一天有时达三四次，真宗亲手和药，并同山药粥赐给他。天禧元年（1017年），王旦去世，享年六十一岁。获赠太师、尚书令兼中书令、魏国公，谥"文正"。宋仁宗为其御书"全德元老"之碑，真宗亦有"朕之有文正，如天之有日"御题。欧阳修奉旨为其撰写碑文。

王旦为人低调，最大的特点就是知人善用，在位期间默默举荐了很多人才，并且他雅量过人，尤其是对于和他同年登科的寇准，王旦的雅量体现得淋漓尽致。王寇二人同殿为相，寇准不服王旦，总向真宗打小报告，王旦对此一无所知，还赞美寇准。有一天宋真宗忍不住对王旦说："卿家总说寇准多么多么好，他却专说你的坏话。"王旦说："本来应该这样。我在宰相的位子上时间很久，在处理政事时失误一定很多。寇准对您不隐瞒我的缺点，更加显示出他的忠诚正直，这就是我器重他的原因。"

寇准担任枢密使时，王旦任职中书省，中书省有事需要与枢密院沟通，所拟文书偶尔不合诏书格式，寇准便上奏皇帝，王旦因此受到责问，中书省的堂吏也被责罚了。而不出一月，枢密院送给中书省的文书格式也不对，中书省的官员兴奋地呈给王旦，想借此打击寇准，可王旦却命人将文书送回枢密院，让他们进行修改，并未上奏。

之后寇准准备转任，他私下找到王旦，说想要做"使相"。王旦当时就拒绝了，说"将相的任命，怎么强以求取呢！我不接受私人请托。"寇准也就灰头土脸地回去了。不久，寇准获授武胜军节度使、同中书门下平章事，寇准去宫里谢恩，感恩涕零说还是皇上了解我。但真宗却说这是王旦举荐的，寇准惭愧感叹，认为自己赶不上王旦。

寇准被外放出京也没有消停，过生日建造山棚举办盛大宴会，服装用品奢侈且超过规格，被别人奏报，真宗听说大怒，连服饰都敢僭越，他要造反吗？又是王旦为他辩解："寇准是真的贤德，按理说不致做出这种'呆'事。"真宗听了，叹息一声说："对，这正是呆而已。"于是不过问此事。王旦病重之际，极力荐寇准为相，宋真宗思量良久，终于还是答应了，寇准也得以再次为相。这种雅量令人钦佩，也为后世树立了为官处世的典范。

王旦位极人臣，身居高位，生活却非常俭朴。他的宅第非常简陋，皇帝多次要为他修治，他都以"先人旧庐"为由婉拒。家中被服用具也都是旧物，椅子上的毡垫破得几乎不能再用，家人想用绸布包裹起来，他坚决不同意。临终前留下遗书，要求后代不得向朝廷提出任何要求，并告诫子孙要保持清正廉洁的家风。

高山仰止，景行行止。王文正公祠不仅凝固着无锡王氏家族的记忆，更是中国传统文化中"士大夫精神"的生动注脚，让我们驻足期间，聆听千年的回响，感受这位北宋名相的智慧与气度。

The Upright and Magnanimous Chancellor of Peaceful Times

The Wang Wenzheng Memorial Temple, located on Xiuzhang Street in Wuxi, traces its origins to the Linghu Temple, originally commissioned in the third year of the Shaoding era of the Southern Song dynasty (1230). This temple was initially established to honor Wang Yue, the fourth-generation ancestor of the Wang clan of Xisha, who had been granted the posthumous title of Marquis of Liji and Benefactor of the People by the Song court. In the sixth year of the Qianlong reign (1741), the Wuxi branch of the Wang family began using the Linghu Temple to commemorate their more distant ancestor, Wang Dan, thereby integrating ancestral worship with earlier religious functions. The temple was relocated to Huishan during the Yuan dynasty and was later destroyed in the tenth year of the Xianfeng reign (1860) during wartime. It was rebuilt in 1867 (the Dingmao year of the Tongzhi reign) with funds donated by Wang family descendants.

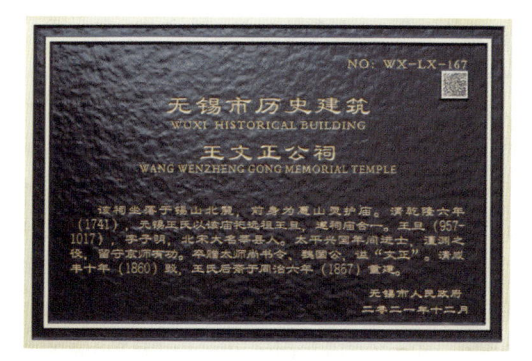

The architectural style of the temple is understated yet refined, representative of the Jiangnan water-town aesthetic. Its layout comprises a comprehensive structure, including a ceremonial gate tower, archways, main and rear halls, and auxiliary buildings.

Wang Dan was born in 957 (the fourth year of the Xiande reign under Emperor Shizong of Later Zhou) in Shen County of Daming Prefecture, today's Shandong province. Named "Dan" because he was born at dawn, he styled himself Ziming. According to legend, his physical appearance was less than striking—his face and nose were asymmetric, and his throat protruded abnormally. A Taoist from Mount Hua once predicted that such unusual features signaled great future honor. Despite his quiet demeanor as a child, Wang Dan displayed a love of learning and remarkable literary talent, earning his father Wang You's deep admiration—Wang You being a Vice Minister of War at the time.

Wang You had three sons and, symbolizing his ambitions for them, personally planted three Chinese scholar trees (huai) in the courtyard—an allusion to the "Three Excellencies" (Grand Preceptor, Grand Tutor, and Grand Guardian) of the Zhou dynasty, whose audience chamber stood before such trees. This act conveyed a father's hope that his sons would achieve the highest offices of state. Wang Dan fulfilled this hope by passing the imperial examination in 980 and subsequently rising to the post of Chancellor (Tong Zhongshu Menxia Pingzhangshi).

As Chancellor, Wang Dan was widely praised for his ability to identify and promote capable individuals, maintaining clarity in governance, societal stability, and peace across the empire—earning him the title of a "Virtuous Chancellor of Tranquil Times." He enjoyed the trust of Emperor Zhenzong of the Song dynasty, serving as his close advisor for 18 years, including 12 years as Chancellor. When Wang Dan fell gravely ill, the emperor dispatched attendants to check on him several times a day and personally prepared medicinal food, including yam porridge, for his ailing minister. Wang Dan passed away in 1017 at the age of 61. He was posthumously honored with the titles of Grand Preceptor, Minister of State, and Duke of Wei, and given the posthumous name "Wenzheng" (Cultured and

Upright). Emperor Renzong commissioned a stele inscribed with the phrase "A Paragon of Complete Virtue," while Zhenzong praised him with the words, "As the heavens have the sun, I have Wenzheng." Ouyang Xiu was appointed to compose the stele inscription.

Wang Dan was known for his humility and remarkable magnanimity. One of the most illustrative examples of his moral character was his relationship with Kou Zhun, a fellow scholar-official who entered office the same year. While both held the post of Chancellor, Kou Zhun frequently reported Wang Dan's supposed shortcomings to Emperor Zhenzong. Unaware of these criticisms, Wang Dan continued to praise Kou Zhun. When the emperor eventually disclosed Kou Zhun's actions, Wang Dan responded serenely: "That is precisely as it should be. I have served as Chancellor for many years and surely made mistakes. His honesty in pointing out my flaws only proves his loyalty—that is why I value him."

This virtue extended even when Wang Dan faced professional tensions. When Kou Zhun, then serving as military commissioner, submitted reports critiquing communications from Wang Dan's ministry, Wang Dan was formally reprimanded. Yet when Kou Zhun's own office later submitted a flawed document, Wang Dan chose not to report it. Instead, he simply returned it for revision, exemplifying forbearance and discretion.

At one point, Kou Zhun approached Wang Dan to request a prestigious appointment. Wang Dan declined, stressing that such offices could not be pursued through private lobbying. Despite Kou Zhun's initial disappointment, he was soon appointed as Military Commissioner of Wusheng and co-Chancellor. When expressing his gratitude, Kou Zhun assumed the credit lay with the emperor—but Zhenzong revealed that it had been Wang Dan's recommendation. Humbled, Kou Zhun confessed he could never match Wang Dan's integrity.

Even when Kou Zhun was later demoted and accused of excessive extravagance during his birthday celebrations, Wang

Dan once again came to his defense. He argued that Kou Zhun's intentions were sincere, not seditious, prompting the emperor to drop the matter. Before his death, Wang Dan went so far as to recommend Kou Zhun for the Chancellorship again, which the emperor reluctantly approved.

Wang Dan lived a life of extreme frugality despite his high office. He declined imperial offers to renovate his home, citing filial respect for his father's "old dwelling." He wore worn-out clothes, used patched furnishings, and insisted on simplicity even in his final days. In his will, he instructed his descendants never to request favors from the court and to uphold a tradition of integrity and moderation.

Wang Wenzheng Memorial Temple today not only embodies the memory of the Wang family of Wuxi but also stands as a monument to the junzi ideal of moral integrity in Confucian scholar-official culture. As visitors stand before its austere halls, they are invited to reflect on the legacy of a Northern Song statesman whose wisdom and tolerance remain a beacon for public service across centuries.

一位年轻的县官，为何在无锡有三座祠堂

惠山直街上，张巡庙西侧有一座松滋王公祠，纪念的是明代嘉靖年间无锡知县王其勤。王其勤出生在湖北松滋，嘉靖三十二年（1553年）进士，来无锡当知县时，不过22岁。有意思的是，除了惠山这座祠堂外，在南门塘泾桥古运河旁有一座南水仙庙，在荡口鹅湖还有一座三公祠，都是用来纪念王其勤的。一位年轻的县官，竟然有三个祠堂，这在无锡历史上是绝无仅有的。那么，到底是怎样的丰功伟绩让他有如此尊崇的地位呢？

这就要从明代倭寇作乱说起了，嘉靖年间，倭寇由东南沿海长驱直入，一路烧杀抢掠，已从吴淞、南汇直逼江阴，无锡告急。王其勤到任第三天，就会同无锡各方人士共商抗倭与筑城事宜。《万历无锡县志》对王其勤筑城有详细记载。嘉靖三十三年（1554年），王其勤用70天时间，将原来土城垣改建成长18里（9千米）、高2丈1尺（约6.3米）的石城墙。据说城墙还没筑好，倭寇就来了。此时东门还有3丈（约10米）宽的一个缺口尚在砌筑中，王其勤急中生智，叫筑城的民夫用大幅青灰绸布画出城墙的样子，拿它遮住缺口。四月二十三日，倭寇从水路窜到了无锡城西，王其勤亲自督战，历时18天，击退倭寇，击毙倭酋四大王，全城数十万人生命、财产得以保全。

据说，筑城抗倭的过程中，还发生了一件"大义灭亲"的

事情。王其勤有一个侄儿，名叫王克宝，随同他一起到无锡，东门有缺口那段城墙正是由他负责的。有一天王其勤来到东门巡视，只见工地上静悄悄的，民夫都在鼾睡，顿时火冒三丈："谁让你们休息的？"民夫们都跪在地上回答说，是因为昼夜施工，劳累过度，要求歇一歇，王克宝开始不同意，经他们苦苦哀求，才勉强同意的，不料因为过度劳累，坐下来便睡着了，这与公子爷无关，请王其勤开恩。但王其勤还是立即命衙役将克宝捆绑，以"忽视敌情，违反军令"的罪名就地斩决。后来无锡百姓为了纪念王其勤大义灭亲，王克宝代人受过，便在处斩王克宝的地方建了一座旱桥，取名"克宝桥"，这座克宝桥经过了400多年的风风雨雨，一直保存在东门城内苏家弄口熙春街上，直到20世纪90年代拓宽人民中路时才被移走。

AI语音导览

无锡学者钱基博把这个故事写成一篇小说《克宝桥》，刊于1916年的《中华小说界》。

明嘉靖年间，倭寇在两年内对无锡发起6次攻城战役，均以失败告终。当然，身为县令，王其勤对无锡的作为，并非筑城抗倭一项，他当政时期，会同前来江南督粮的山东布政使参政翁大立、监察御史孙慎，对全县土地重新丈量，查出漏税无粮田16万亩（约10666公顷），责令补交，免去无田粮7000余石，减轻了农民负担。王其勤也因此得罪了地方势力，受到百般陷害，被无故调离无锡。嘉靖三十六年（1557年）二月，王其勤调升南京户部主事。临行之日，无锡民众夹道相送，队伍绵延数里，无锡士人也纷纷题诗作记，为其饯行，歌颂其德政的诗文汇编成一册《锡山揽袂集》，流传至今。

万历二十四年（1596年），东南再现倭警。当时罢职乡居的高攀龙，想到40年前知县王其勤的抗倭壮举，慨叹王公对无锡百姓恩重如山，无锡却无祠堂纪念，于是倡建报功祠，他认为王其勤事迹与张巡相同，都是保境安民，所以他的祠堂一定要建在张巡庙旁边，同时，又由陈幼学主持修建了祠堂两庑，一并纪念在御倭战斗中殉难的义士何五路等36人。这就是松滋王公祠最早的由来。

后来，清乾隆十六年（1751年）、嘉庆八年（1803年）、道光十八年（1838年），邑绅华希闵、秦瀛及锡金两邑知县曾对松滋王公祠进行过三次修葺，增建益咏堂、遗爱堂等，一并纪念抗倭有功人员苗子白、潘海等于东西夹室。堂右有王公

泉，经疏浚，泉水丰满，水质清澈。祠旧有"仰止先型""捍卫鸿献"匾额。其祠联"筑城垣以御寇氛，感及舆台，卅六人咸知大义；均田赋而恒民业，恩周黎庶，百千载永荐馨香"，正是王其勤在无锡当政期间的真实写照，也表达了无锡百姓对这位县官的敬仰和怀念。

如今，奉祀王其勤的三座祠庙依然屹立于惠山古镇、南长街、荡口古镇三个历史街区，它们见证了那段烽火连天的岁月，也展示了无锡人民英勇抗击外敌的决心和勇气。

Why Does a Young County Official Have Three Ancestral Halls in Wuxi?

In the Huishan district of Wuxi, there stand three halls dedicated to a young county magistrate, Wang Qiqin, who served during the Ming Dynasty. Wang, originally from Songzi, Hubei Province, became a successful jinshi (highest degree in the imperial examination) in the 32nd year of the Jiajing reign (1553) and assumed his post in Wuxi at the age of 22. Remarkably, aside from the Huishan Temple, there are two other halls commemorating him: the Nanshuixian Hall near the ancient Grand Canal by the Nanmeng Tangjing Bridge and the Sangong Hall located by the Ehu in Dangkou. It is unprecedented in Wuxi's history for a single county magistrate to have three halls dedicated to him. What achievement warranted such respect?

To understand this, one must look back to the period when Japanese pirates, known as wako, were rampant along the southeastern coast of China. In the Jiajing era, they advanced relentlessly, causing destruction and looting, having already besieged Wusong and Nanhui, putting Wuxi in imminent danger. Just three days after Wang took office, he convened local leaders to discuss defenses against the pirates and the construction of fortifications. The Ming Dynasty *Wanli Wuxi County Gazetteer* provides detailed accounts of his efforts. In the 33rd year of Jiajing (1554), Wang transformed the existing earthen city walls into a stone fortification stretching 18 li (9 kilometers) long and 2.1 zhang (about 6.3 meters) high over the course of 70 days. According to legend, as the walls neared completion, the pirates arrived. In a moment of ingenuity, Wang instructed laborers to use large gray silk banners to depict the wall's appearance, concealing an unfinished gap (about 10 meters) at the East Gate. On April 23, the pirates approached Wuxi from the western waterway. Wang took personal command of the defense and successfully repelled them after 18 days of combat, killing their leader and saving countless lives and property.

A particularly notable incident occurred during the fortification efforts, exemplifying Wang's commitment to justice. His nephew, Kebao, accompanied him to Wuxi and was tasked with overseeing the section of the wall where the gap existed. One day, while inspecting the East Gate, Wang found the workers asleep due to exhaustion. Enraged, he demanded to know who authorized the break. The laborers explained they had requested rest after working day and night, reluctantly agreed upon by Kebao, who ultimately fell asleep from fatigue. Regardless of their justification, Wang had Kebao arrested and executed on the grounds of negligence and violating military orders. To honor Wang's harsh but principled stance, locals built a bridge at the execution site, naming it Kebao Bridge. This bridge, which has withstood the test of time for over 400 years, was only relocated in the 1990s during the expansion of Renmin Middle Road. The scholar Qian Jibo even fictionalized this tale in a novel titled "Kebao Bridge," published in the *Chinese Novel World* in 1916.

Throughout the Jiajing era, Wuxi faced six attacks by Japanese pirates within two years, all of which were thwarted. However, Wang's contributions extended beyond fortifications; during his tenure, he collaborated with Wang Dali, the administrative commissioner, and Sun Shen, the imperial inspector of Shandong, both of whom came to supervise the grain transport in Jiangnan, to reassess land ownership, discovering 160,000 mu (approximately 10,666 hectares) of untaxed and unplanted land, demanding payment of overdue taxes and alleviating a burden of over 7,000 shi (a unit of measurement for grain) from the peasants. As a result, Wang incurred the wrath of local elites, who conspired against him, leading to his unjust transfer from Wuxi. In the 36th year of Jiajing (1557), he was promoted to a position in the Ministry of Revenue in Nanjing. On the day of his departure, Wuxi's citizens lined the streets to bid him farewell, and local scholars composed poems in his honor, which were later compiled into a collection titled *Xishan Lanwei Ji*.

In the 24th year of Wanli (1596), Japanese piracy resurfaced in the southeast. The retired official Gao Panlong, recalling Wang's heroics from forty years prior, lamented that Wuxi lacked a hall for Wang despite his significant contributions. He advocated for the establishment of a memorial hall, believing Wang's deeds were akin to those of Zhang Xun, who also defended his people. Consequently, the new hall was constructed adjacent to Zhang Xun's hall, with support from Chen Youxue, who also honored 36 martyrs who died fighting the pirates.

Over the years, the Wang Qiqin hall underwent several renovations, notably in the 16th year of the Qianlong era (1751), the 8th year of the Jiaqing era (1803), and the 18th year of the Daoguang era (1838), led by local gentry and officials who expanded its structures and included additional figures who fought against the pirates. The hall features a spring named after Wang, symbolizing the clarity and purity of his legacy. The couplet inscribed at the hall aptly encapsulates Wang's administration: "Constructing fortifications to repel foes, ensuring the populace comprehends the righteousness of 36 martyrs; equitable land distribution assures stable livelihoods, blessing the commoners for generations."

Today, the three halls dedicated to Wang Qiqin remain steadfast in Huishan Ancient Town, Nanchang Street, and Dangkou Ancient Town. They stand as enduring testimonies to a tumultuous era, embodying the spirit and resolve of Wuxi's people in their defense against external threats.

祠堂中的忠靖之士

在惠山直街上，有一座规模颇大的祠堂，就是"张中丞庙"，纪念唐代的忠臣烈士张巡，又称为"忠靖王庙"。俗话说，乱世出英雄，张巡正是遇到了一个成就英雄的乱世，那就是唐代的安史之乱。他本是唐代县令，素有仁心又不畏权贵，所以深得民心，安史之乱期间，他带兵镇守雍丘（今河南杞县），之后又镇守睢阳（今河南商丘），后来提升为河南节度副使和御史中丞，在此过程中，张巡把他的德行和才能发挥得淋漓尽致。

先来说他的才能，张巡的兵法学得相当好，并且不拘书本，运用自如，虚虚实实、变幻莫测，把敌军耍得团团转。诸葛亮草船借箭的故事众所周知，而张巡也创造了草人借箭的神话。在被敌军团团包围、与外界失联的情况下，张巡带兵苦守数月。守城消耗最多的兵器就是箭，面对往城墙上猛冲的敌军，守城士兵就要"嗖嗖"飞射，准备的箭用完了，怎么办？正当大家一筹莫展的时候，张巡想出了妙招，他让大家赶紧扎真人大小的草人，还给草人穿上黑衣，打扮得和夜行客一样，等到天黑，从城墙上方用绳子拴住慢慢放下。因为天黑，敌军看到这一情况，以为张巡趁夜偷袭，于是连连放箭往城头一通乱射，直到天明，敌军才发现上当，原来城上悬着的是穿着黑衣的草人，这时再想把箭拔回来，也来不及了。守城士兵收回草人，回收敌箭，一数竟然有好几万支，一下解决了兵器

视频 张中丞庙

AI语音导览

问题。

如果故事只是到这里就结束，那这也就是草船借箭的翻版，但是，张巡利用了这次事件，继续"以虚化实"，让草人借箭成为连环计中的一环。接下来的几天，张巡继续派人晚上往下放草人，敌军可不上当了。几天后，他让五百勇士身穿黑衣从城墙上往下爬，而敌军由于思维定式，依然以为是来"借箭"的草人，不加防备。等到五百勇士如潮水般冲入敌营，敌军才终于反应过来，混乱中也来不及组织抵抗，溃不成军。凭借这份出众的智慧，张巡在没有外援、条件极度恶劣的情况下守城长达一年十个月，屡次败敌，立下赫赫战功！

再来说说张巡的德行。其实，安史之乱初期，敌军势头相当猛，所以张巡守城的时候，周边已经有不少官员动摇投降了，而张巡并没有从众，而是坚定地选择忠贞报国。守城数月后，外面传来长安失守的消息，当然这个消息是敌军传来的，

目的是让张巡投降。听到这个消息,果然有6位官员立刻想要投降,被张巡斩了,稳住了军心。然而,终因粮草耗尽、士卒死伤殆尽,睢阳城失陷,张巡不幸被俘遇害。据说,张巡督战的时候总是声嘶力竭呼喊,眼眶都崩裂流血,牙齿也被咬碎,敌将对此感到匪夷所思,因此撬开张巡的嘴查看传言是否属实,结果发现张巡的嘴里真的只剩下三四颗牙齿,才真正佩服他的气节。

明代成化九年(1473年),无锡县令李恭建造了张巡庙,之后在清康熙、乾隆、道光年间均有重修,咸丰十年(1860年)张巡庙毁于兵燹,现存建筑为同治八年(1869年)重建。建筑从头门到正殿一共三进。头门有马、马夫,进而有小桥、泉池,可惜现在没有保存下来,围了栅栏充作大门。沿着台阶上去,是面阔三间的仪门,上面悬挂"张中丞庙"竖匾,下面还挂着"锡麓胜境"的大匾,两旁悬挂着一副对联"国士无双双国士;忠臣不二二忠臣"。为什么是"双国士""二忠臣"?除了张巡外还纪念谁?这里先留个悬念。

跨进大门,有好几方遗存的古老石碑,上面的字迹因年代久远而较为模糊,应该都是祭文。二进为戏台、廊楼,戏台平面为凸字形,歇山顶,翼角起翘,如果能站到戏台上抬头看,就能看到屋顶还装饰了穹窿状的藻井。藻井是一种古代建筑天花板的装饰。戏台两边的石柱上有一副楹联"月近云深,遥想孤城横笛;天心风色,共听百世高歌"。这方戏台十分气派,是无锡现存最佳的一处戏台,后面还有供乐队和演员休息的大后台。戏台过去,就是一个广庭,两侧建有长长的歇山顶观楼，以前在张巡诞辰也即农历七月二十五日这一天，会有庆贺戏文演出。庭中有一个宝鼎，两旁种有两棵古银杏，树龄已经有400年了，枝繁叶茂。东边还有一眼六角形的古井，是万历十五年（1587年）凿的，名曰"云泉"。

三进就是正殿，面阔三间，前殿进深六架，带有卷轩，门额上有"风色、天心"的砖刻，和戏台的楹联相呼应，后殿进深八架，也带有卷轩。这座正殿也是祠堂群最雄伟的建筑。张巡的雕像屹立在庙堂之中，是1992年重塑的。只见张巡头戴冲天冠，身穿绿战袍，脸膛呈紫红色，身旁还有一位身穿红袍、头戴乌纱帽的人紧紧倚傍，这就是和张巡志同道合、齐心守城的太守许远。两人紧靠在一起，仿佛正站在睢阳城上同心督战。张巡和许远，正是仪门大匾所书的"双国士""二忠臣"。殿内匾额共有5块，都是年代久远的古匾，有吕耀斗书写的"人伦天道"，廖纶书写的"荫被南天""精忠贯日"，吴念椿书写的"功先李郭"，陆士榕书写的"承天靖寇"。正殿前的石柱上还刻有一副楹联"才兼文武，学希贤圣，英杰天生，忠义素定；同心再造，孤军百胜，一死流芳，千秋显应"，正是对两位国士忠臣，尤其是张巡，以及那段历史恰如其分的评价。

张中丞庙不仅是一个信仰的寄托和历史的印证，更是一个文化符号和精神象征，张巡英勇无畏、精忠报国的精神激励着一代又一代人坚守初心，勇往直前，奋斗不息。

The loyal and Upright Figures in the Amastral Hall

On Zhijie Street in Huishan, there stands a grand hall known as the Zhang Zhongcheng Hall, dedicated to the loyal minister and martyr Zhang Xun of the Tang Dynasty, also referred to as the "Hall of Zhongjing Wang." As the saying goes, "heroes emerge in troubled times," Zhang Xun found himself in such a tumultuous era during the An Lushan Rebellion of the Tang Dynasty. Originally a county magistrate, he was known for his benevolence and courage against tyranny, earning him the people's trust. During the rebellion, he commanded troops to defend Yongqiu (present-day Qixian, Henan) and later Su Yang (present-day Shangqiu), eventually being promoted to Vice Commissioner of the Henan Circuit and Deputy Imperial Censor. Throughout this process, Zhang Xun showcased his exceptional virtues and abilities.

To start with his abilities, Zhang Xun was well-versed in military strategy, employing tactics that transcended traditional doctrines, creating unpredictable maneuvers that left enemy forces disoriented. Most are familiar with Zhuge Liang's legendary tale of borrowing arrows with straw boats; similarly, Zhang Xun spun his own myth of borrowing arrows with straw men. Surrounded by enemy forces and cut off from outside communication, he held his ground for months. It is well-known that the greatest weapon expense in a siege is arrows, and as the enemy surged towards the city walls, the defenders had to shoot arrows rapidly. Eventually, they ran out of arrows. In a moment of desperation, Zhang Xun devised an ingenious plan. He instructed his soldiers to quickly create life-sized straw men, dressing them in black clothing to resemble night travelers, which were then lowered from the walls at night. In the dark, the enemy, seeing this, assumed it was a surprise attack and fired a barrage of arrows at the straw men. Only at dawn did they realize they had been fooled; what hung from the walls were merely straw men, and by the time they attempted to retrieve their arrows, it was too late. The defenders collected the arrows, amounting to tens of thousands, thus solving their weapon shortage.

However, the story does not end here; Zhang Xun skillfully capitalized on this incident, continuing to use deception as a tactic. In the following days, he kept lowering straw men from the walls, but this time the enemy was not easily tricked again, having learned from their previous mistake. As the enemy grew overconfident, even mocking Zhang Xun's intelligence, he executed a clever ruse. Days later, he sent five hundred brave soldiers, dressed in black, to descend from the walls. The enemy, still operating under their previous assumptions, failed to prepare defenses against what they thought were mere straw men "borrowing arrows." When the five hundred soldiers surged into the enemy camp, chaos ensued, and the enemy, unable to organize a proper defense, fled in disarray, only stabilizing their footing several miles away. This display of intelligence is certainly commendable! It was this remarkable wisdom that enabled Zhang Xun to withstand a siege under extremely adverse conditions for one year and ten months, repeatedly defeating the enemy and achieving illustrious military feats.

Now let us discuss Zhang Xun's virtues. At the onset of the An Lushan Rebellion, the enemy forces were exceptionally aggressive, and many officials around him wavered and surrendered. However, Zhang Xun stood firm, choosing loyalty to his country above all else. After several months of defending the city, news finally arrived—albeit from the enemy—intending to persuade him to capitulate, claiming that the capital, Chang'an, had fallen. Upon hearing this, six officials immediately sought to surrender, only to be executed by Zhang Xun, thereby stabilizing troop morale. However, due to dwindling supplies and significant casualties among his troops, Su Yang ultimately fell, leading to Zhang Xun's capture and tragic death. It is said that while he commanded his troops, he shouted so fervently that his throat bled and his teeth shattered. The enemy general, astonished by his resilience, pried open Zhang Xun's mouth to verify the rumors, discovering that he indeed had only three or four teeth left, leading them to genuinely respect his integrity.

In the ninth year of the Ming Dynasty (1473), the county magistrate of Wuxi, Li Gong, constructed the Zhang Xun Hall, which underwent renovations during the reigns of Kangxi, Qianlong, and Daoguang in the Qing Dynasty. It was destroyed during the Xianfeng year (1860) but was rebuilt in the eighth year of the Tongzhi reign (1869). The hall consists of three main sections: from the front gate to the main hall. The front gate features mythical horses and grooms, leading to a small bridge and a spring pool, although these elements have not survived, and a fence now serves as the entrance. Ascending the steps, one encounters the ceremonial gate with three openings, where a vertical plaque inscribed "Zhang Zhongcheng Hall" hangs above, accompanied below by a grand plaque stating "Xilu Shengjing." Flanking these are couplets: "No duality among national heroes, no duality among loyal ministers." Why the mention of "dual heroes" and "dual ministers"? Who, besides Zhang Xun, is also commemorated here? A mystery for now.

Upon entering the main gate, take note of the several ancient stone tablets on both sides. The inscriptions are faded due to age and likely consist of memorial texts. The second section features a stage and corridor; the stage has a protruding rectangular shape and a hip roof, with upward-curving corners. If one stands on the stage and looks up, the roof is adorned with a dome-shaped coffered ceiling—an ancient architectural ceiling decoration that is visually appealing. On the stone columns flanking the stage, there is a couplet: "As the moon nears, clouds deepen, one envisions the lone city playing the transverse flute; with the wind in the heavens, one listens to a thousand years of grand songs." This stage is quite impressive, being the best-preserved stage in Wuxi, with a spacious backstage area for musicians and performers. Beyond the stage lies a vast courtyard, with long pavilions on both sides, where performances used to be held on the anniversary of Zhang Xun's birth, celebrated on the 25th day of the seventh lunar month. In the courtyard stands a precious tripod, flanked by two ancient ginkgo trees, each about four hundred years old, flourishing with lush foliage. To the east is a hexagonal ancient well, dug in the fifteenth year of the Wanli reign, known as "Yunquan."

The third section is the main hall, with three openings. The front hall extends six spans and features a roll-out veranda, with brick inscriptions on the door frame reading "Wind Color, Heavenly Heart," echoing the couplet from the stage. The back hall extends eight spans and also includes a roll-out veranda. This main hall is the most magnificent structure in the hall cluster. A statue of Zhang Xun stands with in the hall, recreated in 1992. Zhang Xun is depicted wearing a crown and a green military robe, his face a reddish-purple hue, and beside him stands a figure in a red robe and black cap—his ally, Governor Xu Yuan, who shared his commitment to defending the city. The two appear united, as if they are monitoring the battlefield of Su Yang together. Zhang Xun and Xu Yuan are indeed the "dual heroes" and "dual ministers" referenced on the grand plaque at the ceremonial gate. Inside the hall, there are five ancient plaques, all significant in age, representing the Chinese government and military. They include: "Human Relations and Heavenly Principles" written by Lü Yaodou, "Shade Covers the Southern Sky" and "Loyalty Pierces the Sun" written by Liao Lun, "Merits Precede Those of Li and Guo" written by Wu Nianchun, "Heaven-Endorsed Quelling of Invaders" written by Lu Shirong. On the stone pillars in front of the main hall, there is a couplet that reads:"Talented in both literature and martial arts, aspiring to the sage's learning, born a hero, inherently loyal and righteous; Rebuilding together with a united heart, a lone army wins a hundred victories, dying with lasting fame, appearing glorious for a thousand autumns." This couplet is an apt evaluation of the two patriotic ministers, especially Zhang Xun, and that period in history.

In conclusion, the Zhang Zhongcheng Hall is a vibrant cultural hub that embodies the spirit of loyalty, righteousness, and the rich history of Wuxi. It stands as a testament to the enduring legacy of Zhang Xun, a figure revered not only for his military prowess but also for his unwavering commitment to his country and people. It is a symbol of the deep-rooted values that continue to inspire generations, reminding us of the importance of loyalty and integrity in our own lives.

出现在《滕王阁序》里面的高士

"落霞与孤鹜齐飞,秋水共长天一色",这是王勃《滕王阁序》的名句。其中还有一句:"人杰地灵,徐孺下陈蕃之榻。"这句话用了一个典故,典故里的主人公就是徐孺子祠的纪念对象。他就是徐稚,"孺子"是他的字。常说"孺子不可教也",但徐稚这位"孺子"却十分可教,他从小就学习两汉时期研究儒家经书的学问——今文经学,此外还精通天文学、历法和算数,是位大才。他不仅学识了得,更兼人品高贵,虽然家里十分贫困,但能够自食其力,不因人穷而志短。他看出来东汉王朝已经病入膏肓,所以绝不愿为了五斗米而折腰事权贵,政府派他去做官,他拒绝了,并说:"大树将颠,非一绳所维。"大树快要倒了,就算用一条绳子拉住它也无济于事。因此,他是有口皆碑的名士,人称"南州高士"。

徐孺子的人品,让另一位品性高洁之士十分仰慕。他就是"一屋不扫,何以扫天下"的陈蕃。陈蕃曾因生性耿直、直言

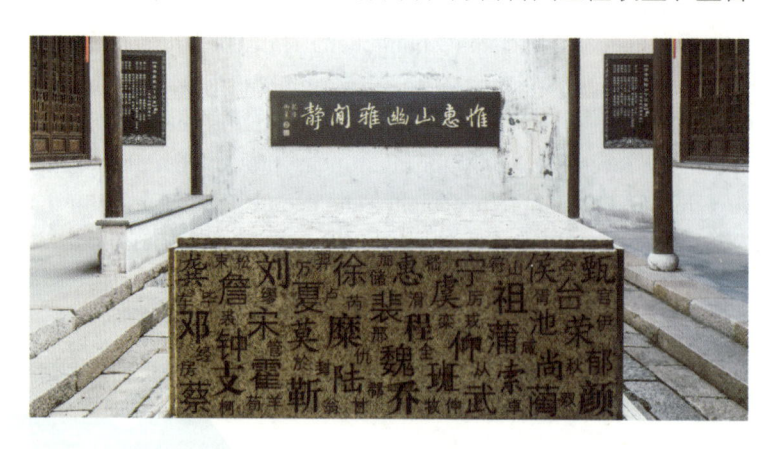

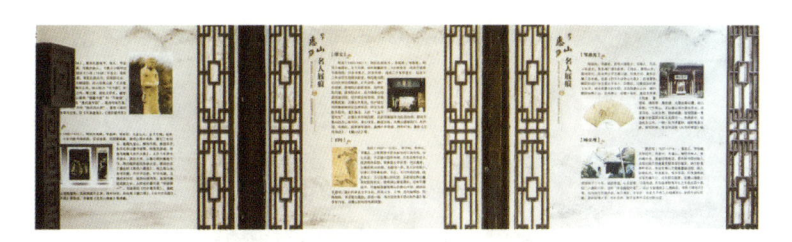

进谏而被外放到豫章（江西一带）当了太守，他一到豫章，不进府休息，就马不停蹄地来拜访徐孺子了，还希望能请徐孺子与他一同当值。徐孺子虽然拒绝了，但还是答应经常去做客。于是，陈蕃为徐孺子定做了一张专供他使用的床，平常就挂在墙上，徐孺子来了，就拿下来用，秉烛夜谈，这就是"徐孺下陈蕃之榻"的典故。

　　为了纪念这位高风亮节的先祖，清代道光七年（1827年），徐氏的后代一起商量，在惠山脚下建造宗祠，作为徐氏在江南的统祠。之后遭遇战乱，一度破败不堪，直到光绪年间，督办金陵机器局的徐建寅回无锡扫墓，看到这个光景，提出重修建议，于是同族中的人出资出力，重新修葺了徐孺子祠。这个祠堂在抗日战争中同样遭到烧毁。直到2011年才再次进行了恢复性重建，使我们今天能够一睹其风采。

　　现在的整个徐孺子祠为三进建筑，布局紧凑，古朴典雅。走进祠堂，首先映入眼帘的是中式的雕花门窗，工艺精湛，透露出浓厚的文化气息。在第一进的门厅里，可以看到关于徐孺子的详细介绍，了解他的一生事迹和卓越贡献。

　　第二进为"惠山文化展示馆"。展示馆内收藏了大量的文物和资料，详细介绍了惠山古镇的历史变迁、民俗文化、庙会文化以及园林文化等。通过这些珍贵的展品和详细的解说，可

以更加深入地了解惠山古镇的文化底蕴和独特魅力。

往里走，第三进展示了"皇帝常来常往的地方"。据史书记载，康熙和乾隆两位皇帝都曾到访过这里，对惠山古镇的美景和文化赞不绝口。因此，这里也被称为"皇帝常来常往的地方"，在这里可以感受到皇家气息与民间文化的完美融合。

值得一提的是，现在的徐孺子祠不仅是纪念徐孺子，展示惠山文化的场所，也是一个经常举办各类展览，开展文化交流的宝地。2024年9月，无锡城市职业技术学院与惠山古镇文化旅游发展有限公司联合主办了"千年回响 敦煌艺术的现代对话——敦煌艺术书画展"，通过艺术展示促进文化传承与创新。10月，无锡城市职业技术学院传媒与艺术设计学院、建筑与环境工程学院毕业设计作品也在此开展，同期展出的还有江南古桥影像，一场场历史与现代的对话在此展开。

徐孺子祠不仅文化内涵极为丰富，环境也十分优美。祠堂周围绿树成荫、彩伞成排，坐在遮阳伞下的桌子边，喝喝咖啡或点一壶茶，河畔轻风吹过，让人倍感惬意。这里不仅是一个文化探索的好去处，也是一个放松身心、享受自然美景的绝佳选择。

The Recluse in the Preface to Pavilion of Prince Teng

The renowned line "The evening glow and solitary ducks fly together; the autumn waters share a color with the vast sky" from Wang Bo's Preface to the Pavilion of Prince Teng also contains another famous reference: "Land ennobled by exceptional figures, where Xu Rusi lay down on Chen Fan's couch." This line pays homage to Xu Ruzi, the object of tribute at the Xu Ruzi Hall. Xu Ruzi, whose given name was Xu Zhi, earned his courtesy name "Ruzi" (literally "promising youth") and proved more than deserving of it. From a young age, he studied the Jinwen classical texts on Confucianism that dated back to the Han Dynasty, excelling also in astronomy, calendrical calculations, and arithmetic. Though impoverished, Xu supported himself through labor, embodying integrity by refusing to compromise his principles for material wealth. When invited to serve as an official, he declined, rejecting offers of special treatment and official transport. His famous words, "A collapsing tree cannot be propped up by a single rope," reflected his foresight regarding the decay of the Eastern Han Dynasty, and his character earned him renown as the "Lofty Scholar of Southern China."

Chen Fan, a highly principled official known for his phrase "If one cannot clean a small room, how can one clean the world?" became an ardent admirer of Xu's character. While exiled to Yuzhang (modern Jiangxi) due to his forthright nature, Chen Fan went directly to visit Xu Ruzi, inviting him to join his administration. Although Xu declined the official role, he often visited Chen, who even prepared a bed for Xu's exclusive use, symbolizing their bond and intellectual exchange. This custom gave rise to the line, "Xu Ruzi lay down on Chen Fan's couch."

To honor this principled forefather, Xu's descendants constructed an ancestral hall at the base of Huishan in 1827, during the Daoguang Emperor's reign. After suffering from conflict and neglect, the hall was restored during the Guangxu era when Xu Jianyin, director of the Jinling Arsenal, proposed reconstruction after visiting the site. The Xu family rallied resources, restoring the hall, although it was destroyed again during the Anti-Japanese War. In 2011, the hall underwent another restoration, allowing future generations to appreciate its legacy.

Today's Xu Ruzi Hall features a three-hall layout with a simple, elegant design that reflects traditional aesthetics. Entering the hall, visitors are greeted by intricate, culturally resonant flower-carved doors and windows. The first hall provides a detailed account of Xu Ruzi's life and achievements. The second hall serves as the Huishan Cultural Exhibition Hall, housing a variety of artifacts and records that illustrate the historical and cultural evolution of Huishan Ancient Town, including folk customs, temple culture, and classical gardens. Through these treasured exhibits and descriptions, visitors gain a profound understanding of the town's cultural essence and unique charm.

As visitors proceed further into the hall, they encounter the third section, known as the "Frequent Imperial Visits Pavilion." Historical records reveal that both Emperors Kangxi and Qianlong visited this location, expressing great admiration for the picturesque scenery and rich culture of Huishan ancient town. For this reason, it has earned its name as a favored royal destination, reflecting a perfect blend of imperial elegance and local cultural heritage.

Notably, today's Xu Ruzi Hall not only honors the esteemed scholar Xu but also serves as a vibrant venue for exhibitions and cultural exchange. In September 2024, Wuxi City Vocational and Technical College collaborated with Huishan Ancient Town Cultural Tourism Development Co., Ltd., to present the "Echoes of the Millennium: Modern Dialogues with Dunhuang Art" exhibition, promoting cultural preservation and innovation through the visual arts. In October, the graduation design works from the college's School of Media and Art Design and School of Architecture and Environmental Engineering were also displayed here, alongside a Jiangnan Ancient Bridge Photography Exhibition. These events foster an ongoing dialogue between history and the present.

The Xu Ruzi Hall is not only a rich cultural site but also a serene and picturesque retreat. Surrounded by verdant trees and colorful parasols, visitors can relax at shaded tables by the riverside, enjoying a cup of tea or coffee as a gentle breeze drifts by. This site offers an exceptional blend of cultural exploration and natural beauty, making it a perfect spot to unwind and appreciate the scenic landscape.

粉身碎骨浑不怕，要留清白在人间

锡山之阴，茂密林木掩映之下，坐落着于忠肃公祠，即于谦祠，祀明代少保于谦，祠内旧有梦神殿，供乡人祈好梦之用。原祠建筑早已塌圮，仅存碑石一方，为清同治八年（1869年）觉安、祥福所立《重建梦神殿碑记》，根据《重建梦神殿碑记》记载，此祠是"万历间邑绅创建，仰荷神灵御灾捍患，功在生民，载明邑志"。

于谦是明朝一位著名官员和将领，他跟岳飞一样，同为民族英雄，曾临危受命出任兵部尚书，力挽狂澜，亲自督战，打胜了关键的京师保卫战，对明朝有再造之功。于谦不仅在军事上有着杰出的贡献，而且在政治上也表现出极高的道德水准。"粉身碎骨浑不怕，要留清白在人间"，这便是于谦一生的信仰与坚守，他清廉正直，以赤子之心，矢志报国，《明史》赞其"忠心义烈，与日月争光"，他的故事广为传颂，他的精神一直激励着后人。万历二十三年（1595年），距离于谦含冤被杀已经过去将近140年了，人们依然没有忘记他，当时，无锡富商吴澄时在建造惠山不二法门之后，深感于谦的忠义精神，建造了于忠肃公祠，康熙年间无锡知县吴兴祚将其列入祀典。

于谦是浙江杭州人，杭州乌龟潭畔就有于谦墓和于谦祠，成化二年（1466年），于谦冤案得以平反昭雪，赐谥"肃愍"，人们在他墓前建起了祠堂，以表达对他的敬仰和怀念之情。一天晚上，浙江巡抚傅盈春在于祠留宿，梦见于谦向他托梦，请

求将谥号"肃愍"改为"忠肃"。他上奏后,朝廷满足了这一请求,以彰显于谦的忠义精神。

在于谦的家乡杭州,他还有另外一个身份——梦神。据《异梦记》和《山窗杂录》等记载,明朝万历年间开始,杭州人就有到于谦祠祈梦的习俗。张岱在《西湖梦寻》中写道:"公祠既盛,而四方之祈梦至者接踵,而答如响。"锡山北麓这座梦神殿与西湖于祠一脉相承,据说祈梦也十分灵验。根据民国时无锡老记者盖绍周的记载,前往梦神殿祈梦的客人,以每年二、八两月为多,便于游山,祠屋也并不宏敞,前后仅有一进,当中三间为大殿,供于忠肃公神位,每晚于六时左右,祈梦者络绎而来,向于谦诉说着他们美好的愿望。今天,虽然古老的祈梦方式已离我们远去,但人们对美好生活的执着追求依然没有改变。

如今,梦神殿已不复存在,仅存《重建梦神殿碑记》。然而,人们始终铭记"粉身碎骨浑不怕,要留清白在人间"的于少保。他清正廉洁、刚正不阿的品格与精神,在现代社会依然具有深远的意义。恢复于谦祠堂,不仅是对这位民族英雄的敬仰与追思,更是对中华民族传统美德的传承与发扬。

Fearless in Death, Resolute in Integrity: The Spirit of Yu Qian

Nestled in the shaded woodlands on the northern slope of Mount Xishan once stood the Shrine of Lord Yu Zongsu, also known as the Shrine of Yu Qian, dedicated to the Ming Dynasty statesman and Grand Guardian, Yu Qian. Within the shrine once existed the Dream Deity Hall, where locals would pray for auspicious dreams. Although the original structure has long since collapsed, a solitary stele remains—an inscription from the eighth year of the Tongzhi reign (1869), erected by monks Jue'an and Xiangfu, commemorating the shrine's reconstruction. According to this stele, the shrine was initially built by local gentry during the Wanli era to honor Yu Qian's spirit, which was believed to offer divine protection. The inscription praises his legacy as beneficial to the people and enshrined in local annals.

Yu Qian stands in Chinese history as both a statesman and military commander of exceptional caliber, his patriotism often compared to that of Yue Fei. Amidst a national crisis, he was appointed Minister of War and led a resolute defense during the crucial battle to protect the Ming capital, securing a decisive victory. His contributions were pivotal in preserving the Ming dynasty at a critical juncture. Yet Yu Qian's legacy is not merely military—he embodied moral integrity of the highest order. His personal creed, "Crush my bones, let my flesh be ground—so long as my virtue remains unstained among men," epitomized his life of loyalty and rectitude. The History of Ming records him as one whose "loyalty and righteousness rival the brilliance of the sun and moon," and his story has been retold for generations, inspiring enduring reverence.

Nearly 140 years after his wrongful execution, in the 23rd year of the Wanli reign (1595), Yu Qian was still honored by the people. The wealthy Wuxi merchant Wu Chengshi, moved by Yu's unyielding patriotism after constructing the Buddhist Famen Temple on Mount Hui, commissioned the Shrine of Lord Yu Zongsu. During the Kangxi reign, Wuxi magistrate Wu Xingzu officially included the shrine in state ritual practice.

Yu Qian was a native of Hangzhou, Zhejiang, where his tomb and a memorial shrine still stand near Turtle Pool. In the second year of the Chenghua reign (1466), his posthumous injustice was redressed, and he was granted the honorary title Sumin. A shrine was later constructed before his tomb to memorialize his loyalty. According to legend, one night during a stay at this shrine, the Zhejiang governor Fu Yingchun dreamt of Yu Qian requesting a change of posthumous title from Sumin to Zongsu (Loyal and Solemn). Upon reporting this to the court, the emperor approved the change, further affirming Yu's embodiment of righteous loyalty.

In his hometown of Hangzhou, Yu Qian holds yet another title—that of the "Dream Deity." According to Records of Strange Dreams and Miscellanies from the Mountain Window, from the Wanli period onward, it became customary for Hangzhou residents to visit Yu Qian's shrine to seek prophetic dreams. Zhang Dai, in Dreams of West Lake, described the shrine as a flourishing center where "wpilgrims came in droves to pray for dreams, and responses followed like echoes." The Dream Deity Hall in Wuxi, situated on the northern slope of Mount Xishan, shared this legacy with its counterpart in West Lake, and was reputedly just as spiritually potent. According to early 20th-century journalist Gai Shaozhou, dream-seekers mostly visited during the second and eighth lunar months, when mountain travel was convenient. The shrine was modest, consisting of a single compound with three main chambers enshrining Yu Qian. Each evening around six o'clock, visitors would arrive in a steady stream, offering their heartfelt hopes to the spirit of Yu Zongsu.

Although the Dream Deity Hall no longer exists—its memory now preserved only in the stele inscription—the legacy of Yu Qian, who pledged to preserve his moral integrity even at the cost of his life, remains undiminished. His unwavering honesty, sense of justice, and incorruptibility continue to resonate in contemporary society. The restoration and remembrance of Yu Qian's shrine is not merely a tribute to a national hero, but also a reaffirmation of the enduring virtues of the Chinese cultural tradition.

祠堂群里最古老的祠堂

AI语音导览

既然是祠堂群里最古老的祠堂，纪念的人物也一定很有年头了。

这位"很有年头"的人物就是春申君黄歇。黄歇是战国时期楚国人，"战国四公子"之一。虽然在很多人的印象中，无锡所在的江南一带不是属于吴国就是属于越国，但其实这一带还曾经归属过楚国。公元前306年，楚威王趁着越国内乱之际，把越国给灭了，这样越国所拥有的吴越之地就并入了楚国版图。因为抗齐战事的需要，加之楚国后期政治中心东移，春申君黄歇后来被封到了吴地，就与江南一带产生了联系。

这种联系至今仍可以从诸多地名上看出来。无锡运河上著名的黄埠墩、惠山的黄公涧、江阴的黄山（君山）、上海的黄浦江，为什么都以"黄"字开头？因为黄歇姓黄，这些地名就以他的姓氏命名了。上海称申城，也是因为春申君的"申"字。足见黄歇在这一带活动频繁，且影响深远。

江南一带多水患，春申君来了以后，治水有功，深得民心。根据《越绝书》记载："无锡历山（惠山），春申君时岁祀以牛"，又有记载"汉时建春申君祠于此，乡民以牛祀黄歇"。可以推断，春申君祠很有可能在汉高祖设立无锡县（公元前202年）后就建立了，按照这个年代推算，距今已有约2200年的历史。另一种算法则可以继续前推至公元前248年，因为这一年开始春申君就从原来的淮北十二县封地转移到了江东封

地，加之在无锡治水有功，是无锡治河第一人，所以百姓极有可能出于爱戴而为他建造生祠，此外春申君在上海治水的时候，百姓就为他建造了生祠。如果这样，那么春申君祠的历史又可以增加数十载。不管哪种算法，春申君祠都是惠山祠堂群最早建立的祠堂，历史年代最为久远。

春申君祠原先建在九龙惠山脚下，到了唐代却被迁移到惠山余脉，旁边的锡山脚下，庙额上写着"忠安大王"四个字，所以春申君祠也俗称"大王庙"。

春申君祠不但继续受到百姓崇拜，还吸引了文人凭吊。唐代诗人张继就曾写诗："春申祠宇空山里，古柏阴阴石泉水。日暮江南无主人，弥令过客思公子。"

惠山还有一处纪念春申君的著名地方，就是惠山头茅峰东坡"白石坞"内蜿蜒流淌的一条山涧，相传黄歇曾带着军队在这里放马饮水。这条山涧也就得了个名字，"春申涧"，也称"黄公涧"。黄公涧在黄梅天的时候，因为雨量充沛，就成了一条天然大瀑布，也是无瀑可赏的无锡难得的时令景观。无锡人黄梅天的独特习俗"游大水"就因此而起，专挑雨水泛滥的时候往惠山黄公涧跑，去观那"势如奔马"，去听那"声如轰雷"。惠山愚公谷主人、明代诗文作家邹迪光还曾写诗赞道："振策春申涧，松风吼乱泉。出云穿众壑，带雨下诸天。"

看来，春申君真是给无锡人民留下了不少文化遗产。

The Oldest Hall in the Ancestral Hall Cluster

As the oldest hall within this cluster, it is inevitable that the person it commemorates has a long-standing history.

This noteworthy individual is Chunshen, Huang Xie, a figure from the State of Chu during the Warring States period and one of the "Four Young Masters of the Warring States." While many might associate the Jiangnan region, where Wuxi is located, with the states of Wu and Yue, this area was once part of Chu. In 306 BC, during the internal turmoil of Yue, King Wei of Chu seized the opportunity to conquer Yue, thereby integrating its territories into the Chu domain. Due to the needs of war against Qi, and with the political center of Chu shifting eastward, Chunshen was later granted land in the Wu region, establishing a connection with the Jiangnan area.

This connection can still be traced through various place names today. For instance, Huangbu Dun along the Wuxi Canal, Huang Gong Stream at Huishan, Mount Huang (Junshan) in Jiangyin, and the Huangpu River in Shanghai all begin with the character "Huang." This is because they are named after Huang Xie, whose surname is Huang. Shanghai is also known as Shencheng, referencing the character "Shen" from Chunshen's name. This illustrates how active and influential Huang Xie was in the region.

The Jiangnan area is prone to flooding, and Chunshen's successful water management endeared him to the people. According to records in the "*Yue Jue Shu*," it is noted that during Huang Xie's time, sacrifices were made using cattle at Lishan (now Huishan), and there are accounts indicating that during the Han Dynasty, a hall was established in his honor, where the locals continued to offer cattle sacrifices to Huang Xie. It can be inferred that the hall was likely established soon after the founding of Wuxi County by Emperor Gaozu of Han in 202 BC, which would date it back approximately 2,200 years. Another calculation can trace its origin back to 248 BC when Chunshen transferred his feudal lands from the Huaibei area to

Jiangdong. Given his contributions to flood management in Wuxi, it is likely that the people constructed a hall in his honor. If this is the case, the history of the Chunshen Hall could be extended by several decades. Regardless of the method of calculation, the Chunshen Hall is recognized as the earliest hall established within the Huishan ancestral hall, boasting the most ancient history.

Originally, the Chunshen Hall was situated at the foot of Huishan, but it was relocated during the Tang Dynasty to the foothills of Xishan. The hall's plaque bears the inscription "Zhong An Da Wang" and it is colloquially referred to as "Da Wang Temple" (Great King Hall).

The surviving Chunshen Hall not only continues to be venerated by the populace but also attracts literary figures who pay homage. The Tang Dynasty poet Zhang Ji wrote a poem that captures this sentiment: "The Chunshen Hall is nestled in the mountain's embrace, ancient cypress shades the stony spring. As twilight descends in Jiangnan, it evokes thoughts of a noble son."

Huishan has another notable site commemorating Chunshen—Bai Shi Wu, a mountain stream that winds through the eastern slope of Mao Peak. Legend has it that Huang Xie led his troops here to water their horses. This stream is known as Chunshen Stream, also referred to as Huang Gong Stream. During the plum rain season, this stream transforms into a spectacular natural waterfall, becoming a rare seasonal sight in Wuxi. The local custom of "touring the great waters" during the plum rain season has emerged, with people flocking to Huang Gong Stream at Huishan to witness the rushing waters and listen to the thunderous sounds of nature. Zou Digang, a Ming Dynasty poet, the master of Yugu Valley in Huishan and literary figure from the area, praised it in verse: "Striking the spring of Chunshen Stream, the pines roar amidst the chaotic waters. Clouds burst through the ravines, bringing rain from the heavens."

Indeed, Chunshen has bequeathed a considerable cultural legacy to the people of Wuxi.

古代的"慈善机构"

在延续千年的惠山祠堂群里,张义庄祠不过才百年芳华,只能算个"年轻的后辈",但它却受万民敬仰,熠熠生辉。张义庄祠是惠山古镇唯一兼具宗祠与义庄功能的祠堂。义庄,便是过去民间的自助慈善机构。

AI语音导览

清末同治初年,无锡张氏族人共同出资,在上河塘兴建祠堂。自建立之初,张义庄祠便开始在纪念祖先的同时,以扶贫济困、造福桑梓为己任,成为民间"慈善机构"。

张义庄祠坐北朝南,面对龙头河,东临薛中丞祠,西接朱乐圃祠,占地面积2400平方米,是上河塘数一数二的大祠堂。作为双联型建筑,张义庄祠左右协调,整体分为东西两部分。

西侧主要作宗祠之用,是一处三开间七进的庭院,前后依次为门厅、明轩、大厅、享堂、隐楼、后堂和住宅。每两座建筑之间,都以天井(明堂)相接。每个天井都种植花卉树木,万年青、天竺、蜡梅、杏树和枇杷树等点缀其间,使祠堂内四季常青,花果飘香。

祠堂门前伫立两座石鼓,显出古朴庄严的气韵。门厅上方高悬"张义庄祠"牌匾,两侧为半阁,中间为起坐室。穿过明轩,迎面参天古柏傲然挺立,寓示着家族吉祥昌瑞、绵长不朽。苍翠掩映下,一座"乐善好施"牌楼巍然耸峙,上有石匾,镌刻"奉旨"二字。清末时期,为表彰张氏义举,朝廷特许建立此牌楼。

大厅与享堂以过厅相连，宏伟宽广，气势非凡，为宗祠的主体。历来族中聚会、议事等活动都在此举行。享堂右侧设一书房，书香翰墨，文气氤氲。享堂后，玉立着一幢江南小楼，透出清新典雅的独特风致，这就是隐楼。若有宾朋来访，便下榻于此。楼前两棵桂花树象征着子孙绵延、金贵满堂。后堂中，安放着张氏祖先牌位。管理这些日常事务的便是整座祠堂的守护者——祠丁。最后面的住宅就是祠丁一家的居所。

东侧主要承担义庄的功能。此处的院落只有一幢建筑，即东厅，俗称新屋。东厅进深8米，宽14米，是收留外来落难

者、纪念女子牌位的地方。以东厅为界，东侧地面分为前后两个区域。厅前是菜园，厅后则为桑园，桃树、石榴树夹杂其间，一泓池水清波荡漾，使祠堂颇能显出和谐精美的田园风光。有此良园，居者便可在此自给自足。

整座祠堂，右庭左院，建筑相谐，花木葱茏，风景殊胜。更令人称奇的是祠堂内还有一条从大门到后宅的通道，全长70米，俗称长弄堂，在惠山祠堂群中独树一帜。

张义庄祠资助族内贫民、惠泽桑梓乡民的义举，传承了中国古老的道德根脉，也源于其族人代代相传的家风。据记载，在无锡，张氏一族造桥铺路、行医济困，开展社会救助，曾捐田千亩建立数座义庄赈济灾民，还于1902年出资创办无锡第一所女子学校，"无锡幼慈女校"。祠堂主之一的张仲涛先生，曾主持创建无锡红十字会，救灾扶贫，抗日战争期间主持义卖，低价供米给平民，抗日战争胜利后创办恒善堂，主持无锡助学活动，对清寒优秀学生提供助学金。

张义庄祠，既是凝聚家族血脉的宗祠，也是延续德行善举的义庄。它让死生皆有奉养的礼义之光，在宗族的开枝散叶中不断延传。

一座祠堂，两重荣光，道德千载，万古流芳。

Charitable Institutions in Ancient Times

Within the centuries-old ancestral hall at Huishan, the Zhang Yizhuang Hall is relatively youthful, having existed for just over a hundred years. However, it commands great respect from the people and shines brightly in its significance. The Zhang Yizhuang Hall is the only hall in Huishan ancient town that combines the functions of both an ancestral hall and a charitable institution, known as a "yi zhuang," which historically served as a self-help charity organization.

In the late Qing Dynasty and early Tongzhi period, the Zhang clan in Wuxi pooled their resources to construct the hall at Shanghetang. From its inception, the Zhang Yizhuang Hall has undertaken the dual mission of honoring ancestors while also alleviating poverty and benefiting the local community, thus functioning as a unique grassroots social welfare institution.

Positioned facing south and overlooking the Longtou River, the hall is flanked by the Xue Zhongcheng Hall to the east and the Zhu Lepu Hall to the west, covering an area of 2,400 square meters, making it one of the largest halls in Shanghetang. As a dual-structure building, the Zhang Yizhuang Hall is symmetrically designed and divided into eastern and western sections.

The western section primarily serves as the ancestral hall, comprising a three-bay and seven-depth courtyard. It features a sequential layout of a hall, a bright corridor, a main hall, a worship hall, an inner building, a rear hall, and living quarters. Each pair of buildings is connected by a courtyard, known as a mingtang, adorned with various plants including wan nian qing (evergreen), Nandina (Chinese tallow tree), la mei (wax plum), apricot trees, and loquat trees, ensuring the hall remains lush and fragrant throughout the seasons.

Two stone drums stand solemnly in front of the hall, exuding an ancient and dignified aura. Above the entrance hall hangs a plaque reading "Zhang Yizhuang Hall," flanked by a half-gable on either side and a sitting area in the center. Passing through the bright corridor, one encounters a majestic ancient cypress tree, symbolizing the family's auspicious fortune and eternal legacy. Beneath the lush greenery stands a towering archway inscribed with "Benevolence and Charity," featuring a stone plaque engraved with the words "By Imperial Decree," established during the late Qing Dynasty to honor the Zhang clan's charitable acts, authorized by the imperial court.

The main hall connects to the worship hall through a grand corridor, notable for its impressive scale and grandeur, serving as the focal point for clan ceremonies, gatherings, and discussions. Adjacent to the worship hall is a study filled with the fragrance of ink and books, emanating a scholarly atmosphere. Behind the worship hall stands a charming Southern-style building known as the Inner Hall, characterized by its elegant and refreshing aesthetic, where guests are welcomed. Two osmanthus trees in front symbolize the continuation of descendants and abundance. The rear hall houses the ancestral tablets of the Zhang family. The daily operations of the hall are overseen by the hall steward, who resides in the residential quarters at the back.

The eastern section primarily fulfills the charitable function of the yi zhuang. This area consists of a single structure known as the East Hall, colloquially referred to as the New House. The East Hall measures 8 meters deep and 14 meters wide, serving as a refuge for outsiders in distress and a place to honor female ancestors. Divided by the East Hall, the ground to the east is segmented into two zones. In front of the hall lies a vegetable garden, while the rear features a mulberry garden, with peach and pomegranate trees interspersed. A tranquil pond ripples nearby, contributing to the harmonious pastoral scenery of the hall. With such a bountiful garden, residents can achieve self-sufficiency.

The hall features a harmonious layout, with lush foliage and picturesque landscapes on either side. Remarkably, there is a passage running from the front gate to the rear hall, extending 70 meters, known as the Long Alley, setting it apart from other halls in the

Huishan area.

The Zhang Yizhuang Hall provides support to impoverished clan members and extends its benefits to the local community, embodying the ancient moral traditions of China, deeply rooted in the family's enduring ethos. Historical records indicate that the Zhang clan in Wuxi contributed to building bridges and roads, practicing medicine to aid the needy, and launching social relief initiatives. They donated thousands of acres of land to establish several charitable institutions for disaster relief and, in 1902, funded Wuxi's first girls' school, the Wuxi Youci Girls'School. One of the hall's founders, Mr. Zhang Zhongtao, played a significant role in establishing the Wuxi Red Cross, facilitating disaster relief efforts, providing affordable rice to civilians during the Anti-Japanese War, and founding the Hengshan Hall after the victory, promoting educational assistance for outstanding underprivileged students.

The Zhang Yizhuang Hall is both a place of familial connection and a center for virtuous deeds. It embodies the principles of benevolence and duty, ensuring that care for both the living and the deceased endures through generations.

A hall that encompasses dual honors, it carries moral significance that transcends time, leaving a legacy that continues to inspire future generations.

祠堂群里的"医国圣手"

无锡市中心学前街上有座薛家花园，挂着光绪皇帝御笔亲题的蓝底金字"钦使第"牌匾，被称为"江南第一豪宅"，在民间又被称为"薛半城"。宅子的主人是清末著名的思想家、外交家、政论家、维新派代表人物薛福成，在无锡可谓家喻户晓，但很多人却不知道他的长兄薛福辰也是清末历史上一位极为重要的无锡籍名人，在惠山古镇祠堂群还有一座祠堂专门来纪念他，这座祠堂就是薛中丞祠。

薛中丞祠，位于惠山上河塘，坐北朝南，面对京杭大运河支流惠山浜，纪念清代名医、无锡人薛福辰，因薛福辰官至都察院副都御史，惯例称其为"中丞"，该祠被称为"薛中丞祠"。

薛福辰，字振美，号抚屏，生于道光十二年（1832年），祖居无锡县西漳寺头，后迁城内前西溪。薛福辰自幼聪慧过人，7岁便能做文章，稍长又博览经史，他为官清廉，既能治理河道，又精通医术，光绪帝称他是"医国圣手"。

薛福辰的一生充满了传奇色彩，但最为人津津乐道的还是他曾为慈禧太后治愈"血蛊"之症的传奇故事。

光绪五年（1879年），慈禧太后患上了一种被称为"血蛊"的重病。经过太医院众多御医诊治，以及名医会诊，慈禧太后的病情却始终未见好转。光绪六年（1880年），朝廷发布上谕，寻求天下名医为慈禧太后治病。朝廷一声令下，各地自

然纷纷响应。大学士、直隶总督李鸿章和湖广总督李翰章、湖北巡抚彭祖贤共同保荐了薛福辰。

薛福辰与其他7位名医一同入宫，入宫后他们先要接受太医院医官的面试，内务府认为"医学、脉理均极精通"，才开始给慈禧治病。他们8位医生和原太医院的一些医生分成几个小组，轮流给慈禧诊脉，各自开出方子。实际上，慈禧并不一定服用他们开的药，主要是对他们进行考察和选择。慈禧的病时轻时重，时好时坏，其间还发生过昏迷，这让薛福辰压力很大，日夜担惊受怕，但好在薛福辰凭借精湛的医术和丰富的经验，逐渐赢得了慈禧太后的信任。

经过两年多的精心治疗，慈禧太后的病情终于得到了控制，并在光绪八年（1882年）十二月完全康复。薛福辰因治

病有功，加赏头品顶戴，调补直隶通永道。这一年除夕，慈禧太后亲书"福"字和"职业修明"匾额赐给薛福辰，同时赐紫蟒袍、玉钩带一副，又赐宴体元殿、长春宫听戏。薛福辰的医名也因此更加驰誉海内。

光绪十年（1884年），薛福辰到通永道履职，在直隶任内，严缉捕，重海防，济民困，政绩卓著，三年后擢升顺天府府尹。一次薛福辰因一件小事被一位姓魏的御史参劾，要求将薛福辰调至太医院，这其实隐含着对薛福辰"因医受宠"的歧视。慈禧太后了解薛福辰为官时同样政绩卓著，看到魏御史的奏章，斥为"大胆妄言"，将魏御史官降三级，反将薛福辰升为宗人府府丞，一年后又迁任都察院左副都御史。不料薛福辰突患中风，半身不遂，于是多次上疏申请，最终才被允许开缺回乡调理。回无锡不久，薛福辰就于七月初二去世，终年57

岁，葬于无锡漆塘大浮山。清廷御赐薛家白银500两用于治丧。薛福辰遗作《素问运气图说》，流传于今。

薛中丞祠始建于清宣统元年（1909年），为大三间三进加备弄布局。1949年后，祠堂收为公产，由政府委托房管部门管理，20世纪50年代起改作民居，住户较多，祠堂被分隔成多处小间。我们现在看到的这座祠堂是2009年2月修复的，经修缮一新的薛中丞祠占地面积861.336平方米，建筑面积472.69平方米，整体布局依然保持原有大三间三进加备弄的格局，共有楼房6间，平房10间，披屋1间，砖木结构。

走进祠门，首先要跨越一座足有50厘米高的门槛。古代设门槛的高低有讲究，门槛体现主人身份和等级。薛福辰因治愈慈禧太后疾病有功被赐为一品官，官职连升三级，所以祠堂门槛就高。

祠屋第一进为"宸翰楼"。楼上三间宽敞明亮，南北窗格，雕花精细，南窗面对锡山龙光塔；楼下中间为祠门，两侧门房与祠门相齐，辟出三间门面的廊道，设廊柱、木栅，庄严肃穆。第二进

为享堂，现布置展示薛福辰生平事迹，陈列薛家古旧物品。第三进为寝堂（后室），在二进和三进中轴位置有工字廊连接，廊轩相连祠屋。备弄位于西侧，有前后通道和散热通风及消防功能。三进后面，附设庭院，花木修竹，环境幽雅。

对联"人游霁月光风表；家在廉泉让水间"，正是慈禧太后所赐。2010年，河北省一位收藏者将此对联电传给惠山古镇办，古镇办按原样复制，悬挂于此。祠堂中陈列的薛家旧物大都由薛福辰后人捐献，薛福辰曾孙女婿顾濂江先生曾先后两次将收藏50多年的薛氏家具、古玩赏件300多件捐出，其中包括薛福辰用过的帽冠顶珠、官服朝珠、腰佩、玻璃碾药器皿、木制捣棒、锡制小药碟、医书《验方新编》以及翁同龢致薛福辰的书信等。2018年，薛福辰的后人又向薛中丞祠无偿捐赠

了一批旧时医疗器械。这批医疗器械的主人是薛福辰的孙子薛育麒。20世纪30年代，薛育麒曾用这些医疗器械救治过难民和抗战伤员。

这些留存于薛中丞祠中的旧物正是薛家世代行医、医者仁心的一种见证与传承，在这里，我们可以感受到这位"医国圣手"的仁心仁术，也可以感受到后人对他的敬仰和怀念。

The "Master Healer of the Nation" in the Ancestral Hall Cluster

In the heart of Wuxi City, along Xueqian Street, stands the Xue Family Garden, bearing a plaque inscribed with the words "Imperial Envoy Residence," personally bestowed by Emperor Guangxu. Referred to as the "First Mansion of Jiangnan," it is colloquially known as "Xue Half-City." The owner of this mansion was Xue Fucheng, a prominent late Qing-era thinker, diplomat, political commentator, and representative figure of the reformist faction. He is a household name in Wuxi. However, many are unaware that his elder brother, Xue Fuchen, is also a significant historical figure from Wuxi. The Xue Zhongcheng Hall, located in the Huishan Ancestral Hall Cluster, is dedicated to him.

The Xue Zhongcheng Hall, situated on Shanghetang in Huishan, faces south and overlooks the Huishan Bank, a tributary of the Grand Canal. It is dedicated to Xue Fuchen, a renowned physician of the Qing Dynasty and a native of Wuxi. Xue Fuchen held the position of Deputy Censor-in-Chief in the Censorate, thus earning the title "Zhongcheng," which is why the hall is named after him.

Born in 1832, Xue Fuchen, styled Zhenmei and nicknamed Fuping, hailed from Xizhang, a village near Wuxi. From an early age, he exhibited extraordinary intelligence, composing essays by the age of seven and later becoming well-versed in classical texts and history. Known for his integrity in governance, Xue was adept not only in managing waterways but also in the medical arts, earning Emperor Guangxu's praise as a "Master Healer of the Nation."

Xue Fuchen's life was filled with remarkable accomplishments, but the most renowned tale is his legendary treatment of Empress Dowager Cixi's "blood poison" illness.

In 1879, during the fifth year of Emperor Guangxu's reign, Empress Dowager Cixi fell gravely ill with a disease described as "blood poison." Despite consultations with numerous imperial physicians and renowned doctors, her condition showed no signs of improvement. The following year, in 1880, an imperial edict was issued, seeking famous doctors from across the empire to treat her. In response, Li Hongzhang, Grand Secretary and Governor-General of Zhili, along with Li Hanzhang, Governor-General of Huguang, and Peng Zuxian, Governor of Hubei, recommended Xue Fuchen.

Xue Fuchen, along with seven other prominent physicians, was summoned to the palace, where they first had to pass an examination conducted by the imperial physicians. The Imperial Household Department, satisfied with Xue's mastery of both medicine and diagnostics, allowed the doctors to proceed with Empress Dowager Cixi's treatment. Divided into teams, they took turns diagnosing her pulse and prescribing treatments. Cixi did not necessarily take their prescriptions, as the process was also a test of their abilities. During the course of her illness, Cixi's condition fluctuated, and she even fell into a coma at one point, placing tremendous pressure on Xue Fuchen. However, through his exceptional medical skills and experience, he gradually gained her trust.

After more than two years of diligent care, Empress Dowager Cixi's condition was brought under control, and by December of 1882, she had fully recovered. In recognition of his service, Xue

Fuchen was awarded the honorary rank of First-Grade Official and transferred to Tongyongdao in Zhili Province. On New Year's Eve that same year, Cixi personally bestowed upon him the character "Fu" (福, meaning fortune) and a plaque inscribed with the words "Zhiye Xiuming" (diligence in one's profession). He was also gifted a purple robe, a jade belt, and honored with a banquet at the Ti Yuan Hall and the opportunity to attend a performance at Changchun Palace. Xue Fuchen's medical reputation grew even more renowned across the empire as a result.

In 1884, Xue Fuchen assumed his post at Tongyongdao. During his tenure in Zhili, he was known for his efforts in strengthening coastal defenses, assisting those in distress, and achieving notable administrative success. Three years later, he was promoted to the role of Prefect of Shuntian Prefecture. However, after a minor dispute involving a censor named Wei, who petitioned for Xue to be transferred to the Imperial Medical Institute—a move laced with disdain for Xue's rise due to his medical expertise—Empress Dowager Cixi intervened. She deemed the petition slanderous and demoted Wei by three ranks, while promoting Xue to the position of Assistant Minister of the Imperial Clan Court. A year later, Xue was further elevated to Vice Minister of the Censorate. Unfortunately, he suffered a stroke and was partially paralyzed, leading him to repeatedly petition for medical leave. Eventually, he was permitted to return to Wuxi for treatment. Not long after returning, he passed away on the second day of the seventh lunar month at the age of 57. He was buried on Dafushan Mountain in Wuxi, and the Qing court granted 500 taels of silver for his funeral expenses. His medical writings, including *Su Wen Yun Qi Tu Shuo* (An Explanation of the Diagrams of the Plain Questions and Five Movements and Six Qi), have been preserved to this day.

The Xue Zhongcheng Hall was originally constructed in the first year of the Xuantong reign. It features a three-bay, three-depth layout with a service alley. After the Liberation, the hall was nationalized and managed by the housing department. By the 1950s, it had been converted into residential housing, with multiple households occupying the subdivided space. The ancestral hall we see today was restored in February 2009, covering a total area of 861.336 square meters, with a building area of 472.69 square meters. The hall retains its original three-bay, three-depth layout, comprising six multi-story building, ten single-story building, and one lean-to structure, all built using brick and wood.

Upon entering the hall, one must step over a threshold that stands about 50 centimeters high. In ancient times, the height of a threshold was symbolic, reflecting the status and rank of the hall's owner. Given that Xue Fuchen was promoted three ranks for curing Empress Dowager Cixi, the threshold of his ancestral hall was raised accordingly.

The first hall is known as the "Chenhan Tower." The upper floor is spacious and well-lit, with intricately carved windows on both the north and south sides. The southern windows face the Longguang Pagoda on Xishan. Below, the central section serves as the main entrance, flanked by rooms with corridors leading to three separate entrances. The atmosphere is solemn and dignified. The second hall is the main sacrificial hall, where exhibits now display Xue Fuchen's life story and personal artifacts from the Xue family. The third hall is the rear hall, connected by corridors to the second hall. To the west lies a service alley, which serves ventilation, cooling, and fire prevention purposes. Behind the third hall is a garden with elegant landscaping and tranquil surroundings.

The couplet inscribed with the words "One lives beyond the serene moonlight and fresh breeze; home lies at the intersection of the well of purity and the stream of humility" was gifted by Empress Dowager Cixi. In 2010, a collector from Hebei Province provided an electronic copy of the original couplet to the Huishan Ancient Town Office, which then had it faithfully replicated and displayed in the hall. Many of the Xue family's artifacts, including furniture, personal belongings, and over 300 antiques, were donated by Xue Fuchen's descendants, including his great-granddaughter's husband, Mr. Gu Lianjiang. These donations include Xue Fuchen's personal items such as official hats, robes, jade waist belts, a glass medicine grinder, wooden pestles, tin medicine dishes, and a copy of *Yan Fang Xin Bian* (Newly Compiled Prescriptions), as well as letters from Weng Tonghe addressed to Xue Fuchen. In 2018, Xue Fuchen's descendants also donated a collection of vintage medical instruments to the Xue Zhongcheng Hall. These instruments once belonged to Xue Fuchen's grandson, Xue Yuqi, who used them to treat refugees and wounded soldiers during the 1930s.

The relics preserved in the Xue Zhongcheng Hall stand as a testament to the Xue family's long-standing medical legacy and their benevolent practice of healing. Here, one can sense the compassionate spirit of this "Master Healer of the Nation," as well as the reverence and remembrance held by his descendants and admirers.

名泉酿名酒

自北宋以来，以二泉水酿造的惠泉酒，美名传遍江南大地。惠泉酒被明清文人誉为至上之品，《红楼梦》中两次提及惠泉酒，《镜花缘》《三言二拍》等古典名著中，也都可以找到惠泉酒的影子。最初酿造惠泉酒的，是南渡后世居于梁溪的蒋家，蒋氏子孙世代承继此造酝之业，号"蒋氏酒（蒋家酒）"，为惠泉酒中名声最著者。宋代米芾曾有《苕溪诗》赞美，诗云"半岁依修竹，三时看好花。懒倾惠泉酒，点尽壑源茶。主席多同好，群峰伴不哗"。此诗作于元祐三年（1088年），此诗的书法作品现收藏于故宫博物院。

明清时期，凭借一手绝佳的酿酒技术，蒋氏酒楼傲立于惠山，文人雅士纷至沓来，尽情陶醉于这里的美酒佳肴之中。明末，浙江王思任在《游慧锡两山记》中赞美道："越人自北归，

望见锡山，如见眷属，其飞青天半，久暍而得浆也。然地下之浆，又慧泉首妙。居人皆蒋姓，市泉酒独佳。有妇折阅，意闲态远，予乐过之。"在这里，他们不仅购买泥塑艺术品、纸质工艺品、木质玩具、兰陵面具、小刀戟等，还在清新的瓷器中品味美酒，畅谈人生百味。沈丘壑更曾言："若让文君坐于此，亦可视相如何也？"入寺礼佛之后，更是揖泉而饮之。清代曹寅当年来无锡，曾写下"买田阳羡应犹过，此处楼居即是仙"的名句。

乾隆皇帝也曾慕名到蒋氏酒楼驻跸喝酒。据《锡山蒋氏宗谱》记载："蒋氏惠山支第二十一世孙麟锦，字大乐，号玉书，国学生，敕授文林郎，秉性敦朴读书明大义，生平行为一以礼法为本，广交游，有刘伶癖，尝以二泉水自置佳酿。会高宗南巡，驻跸公园之吟楼，饮公酿，甘之，有御笔迎翠轩匾额暨其他御品以奖之。"

蒋氏家族与惠山羁绊颇深，蒋氏酒楼持续时间长达四五百年，至民国时期，蒋氏仍持有此酒楼的地契，只不过，酒楼位置几经更迁。

据蒋氏宗谱记载，明洪武至宣德年间，蒋氏族人就在祇园精舍建祠；后因建愚公谷，被置换，愚公谷败落后，原址已无法恢复，蒋氏族人在邹家后人手中购得原址旁地产，重新建家祠；太平天国运动期间，祠堂被烧毁；民国初年，在上河塘蒋氏地基上，蒋氏族人又建造更大规模的宗祠，来祭奠蒋家列祖列宗；抗日战争时期，蒋氏族人把自家的祠堂奉献出来，作为部队的野战医院；2010年，惠山古镇恢复了前面的三间门楼，这就是我们今天看到的蒋氏宗祠。

Famous Springs and Renowned Wines

Since the Northern Song Dynasty, Huiquan Wine (a traditional yellow rice wine from Wuxi), brewed from the water of the Second Spring, has gained renown across the Jiangnan region. It is mentioned twice in *Dream of the Red Chamber* and references to Huiquan Wine can also be found in classic texts such as *Mirror Flower, Water Moon* and *San Yan Er Pai*, where it was celebrated by scholars of the Ming and Qing dynasties as a superior beverage. The brewing of Huiquan Wine began with the Jiang family, who settled in Liangxi after migrating south. The descendants of the Jiang family have carried on this brewing tradition for generations, and their product is known as "Jiangshi wine" (Jiang family wine), recognized as the most esteemed variety of Huiquan Wine . The Song Dynasty poet Mi Fu praised it in his poem *Tiaoxi Poem*, stating, "Half a year amidst the slender bamboos, three seasons watching the beautiful flowers. I am too lazy to pour Huiquan Wine, only indulging in tea from the valley source. Many are my friends of similar taste, and the peaks do not clash." This poem, composed in the third year of Yuan You (1088), is preserved as a calligraphic work in the Palace Museum in Beijing.

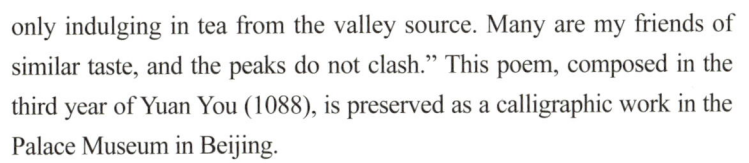

During the Ming and Qing dynasties, the Jiang family's wine house stood proudly at Huishan, drawing in numerous literary figures who reveled in its exquisite wines and delicacies. In the late Ming period, Wang Siren from Zhejiang praised it in *Record of the Two Mountains of Huixu*, stating that the people of Yue, upon returning from the north, felt as if they were meeting their family at the sight of Xishan, as if they had traveled from afar, quenching their thirst with this fine brew. However, among the underground wines, Huiquan Wine is the foremost. The residents, all surnamed Jiang, found their wine reigning supreme in the market. Ladies strolled leisurely through the area, their demeanor graceful, captivating all around. Here, they not only purchased clay sculptures, paper crafts, wooden toys, Lanling masks, and small knives but also savored fine wines in fresh porcelain while discussing the myriad flavors of life. Shen Qiuhe remarked, "If Wenjun were to sit here, how might he appear?" After visiting the hall to pay respects, they would toast with the spring water. Cao Yin from the Qing Dynasty, upon visiting Wuxi, penned the famous line in *Inscription on the Jiang Family Wine House at Xishan*: "To buy land in Yangxian is less important; this place where the tower stands is indeed immortal."

Emperor Qianlong also visited the Jiang family, drinking their wine in admiration. According to the *Jiang Family Genealogy of Xishan*, "Jiang Shi Huishan Branch, twenty-first generation descendant Lin Jin, styled Da Le, with the courtesy name Yu Shu, a student of the National School, granted the title of Wenlin Lang. With a character of simplicity and a profound understanding of great principles, he lived his life in accordance with rituals and laws, cultivating friendships widely. He had a particular affinity for Liu Ling and often brewed fine wine using the water from the Second Spring. During the Southern Tour of the Gaozong Emperor, he stayed at the Yin Pavilion in the park and enjoyed the public brew, finding it delightful, receiving a plaque from the Emperor and other imperial rewards in recognition."

The Jiang family has a deep connection with Huishan, and their wine house has endured for four to five hundred years. Even during the Republic of China, the Jiang family retained the land deed for the establishment, although its location changed multiple times over the years.

According to the Jiang family genealogy, during the Hongwu and Xuande years of the Ming Dynasty, the Jiang family built a hall in the Zhiyuan Jing She; however, it was later replaced due to the construction of the Yugong Valley. After the decline of Yugong Valley, the original site could not be restored. The Jiang family acquired land next to the original site from the descendants of the Zou family and rebuilt their ancestral hall. During the Taiping Rebellion, it was burned down; in the early Republic of China, a larger ancestral hall was constructed on the foundation of the Jiang family in Shanghetang to honor their ancestors. During the Anti-Japanese War, the Jiang family donated their ancestral hall for use as a field hospital; In 2010, the ancient town of Huishan restored the three entrance pavilions, which comprise the Jiang family ancestral hall we see today.

"心与理一"的清正之士

穿过惠山古镇人杰地灵牌坊,漫步下河塘,有一座规模宏大且充满无锡历史记忆的建筑——高忠宪公祠。这座祠堂创建于明崇祯年间,在清代曾两度被毁,却又两度复建,可见其地位的非同一般。2008年,高忠宪公祠再次全面修缮,恢复祠门轩屋,重建戏台、牌坊、花园,这座祠堂重现古镇,面貌一新,目前是古镇4座名列省级文物保护单位的祠堂之一。

祠内纪念的高忠宪公,就是明代的左都御史、兵部尚书,地道的无锡人高攀龙。高攀龙,字云从,又字存之,号景逸,是著名的东林党首领,一生刚正不阿,直言进谏,展现出了非凡的勇气和担当。高攀龙寄情无锡山水,生前就隐居在无锡蠡湖边,还常去鼋头渚湖滩濯足,留下"马鞍山上振衣,鼋头渚下濯足;一任闲来闲往,笑看世人局促"的诗句,借"沧浪之水浊兮,可以濯吾足"之意,嘲讽当时的腐败政治。非常不幸的是,高公日后在腐败的政治环境里遭对手迫害致死。至今鼋头渚有明高忠宪公濯足处,风景殊胜,是游人必到的太湖名胜。

走进祠堂,入目是顾光旭所撰祠联"君子无所争,立纲常,扶名教;大臣不可

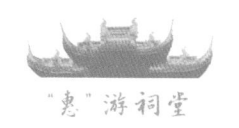

辱，感天地，泣鬼神"。此联通过"君子无所争""大臣不可辱"两句话，表达了对高攀龙高尚品德与气节的高度赞扬，意义深远。"君子无所争"，意为真正的君子不与人争斗，不追求个人利益，而是以道德修养和人格完善为己任。高攀龙曾说："吾立身天地间，只思量做好人，乃第一义，余事都没要紧"，追求的正是君子的宽广胸怀，高贵品性。"大臣不可辱"，则意为高攀龙在面对权力与诱惑时，保持了尊严和原则，宁死不屈，其气节足以感动天地。

祠内还保存着高子遗表石数块，文为"臣虽削夺，旧系大臣。大臣受辱则辱国，故北向叩头，从屈平之遗则。君恩未报，结愿来生。臣高攀龙绝书，乞使者执此报皇上"。一字一句，无不彰显着高攀龙忠诚刚正、舍生取义的"东林风骨"，这种沉着镇静、视死如归的气节，令无数后人佩服敬仰。殊不知面对奸佞追捕迫害，紧急关头能泰然处之的大无畏精神，得益于高攀龙有着半生静坐与读书的功力。关于静坐之法，高攀龙著有《静坐说》，有精辟见解："静坐之法，不用一毫安排，只平平常常，默然静去……以其清净不容一物，故谓之平常。"高攀龙的这种静坐法，并不追求多高的境界，而是静心养性，静中生慧，于平淡朴实中培养意志力和忍耐力。正因如此，高公生死关头心境澄明，神情泰然，笑说："我本视死如归，以清正之心守言官之本分，此生无憾矣"，实践了一生追求的"心与理一"。

史料记载，高攀龙隐居在高子水居"可楼"，澄心养性，静坐韬光，半日读书，半日静坐。可楼四面开窗，因"可以望山、可以观水、可以让清风送爽、可以得阳光普照、可以邀明月相伴"的"五可"而得名，今天的高忠宪公祠门对龙头河，锡惠在望，清风常拂，沐日浴月，正合"五可"之意。

A Person of Integrity Who Unites the Heart With Principle

Passing through the historic archway of Huishan ancient town and strolling down Hetang, one encounters a grand building steeped in the historical memories of Wuxi—the Gao Zhongxian Hall. This hall, established during the Chongzhen period of the Ming Dynasty, has been destroyed and rebuilt twice during the Qing Dynasty, highlighting its significant status. In 2008, the Gao Zhongxian Hall underwent comprehensive renovations, restoring the entrance hall, reconstructing the opera stage, archway, and garden, and thereby revitalizing the hall as one of the four provincial-level cultural heritage sites in the ancient town.

The hall is dedicated to Gao Zhongxian, a native of Wuxi, who served as the Left Chief Councilor and Minister of War during the Ming Dynasty. Gao Panlong, whose courtesy names were Yuncong and Cunzhi, and his style name was Jingyi, was a prominent leader of the Donglin Party. Known for his integrity and forthrightness, he demonstrated remarkable courage and a sense of responsibility throughout his life. He found solace in the scenic landscapes of Wuxi, residing by Lake Li and often visiting the shores of Yuantou Zhu, where he left behind the poem: "On Ma'anshan, I shake my robes; at Yuantou Zhu, I wash my feet. I care little for the mundane world, laughing at the constraints of others." This reflects his disdain for the corruption of his time, as he drew from the phrase "the muddy waters of Canglang can cleanse my feet," unfortunately culminating in his death due to persecution by the eunuchs amid political corruption. Today, Yuantou Zhu features the site where Gao Zhongxian washed his feet, a scenic spot that attracts many tourists visiting the famous Taihu Lake.

Upon entering the hall, one's eyes are immediately drawn to the couplet written by Gu Guangxu: "A gentleman knows no conflict;

he upholds principles and supports education. A minister cannot be dishonored; he moves heaven and earth and weeps for spirits." Through the phrases "a gentleman knows no conflict" and "a minister cannot be dishonored," the couplet expresses profound admiration for Gao Panlong's noble character and steadfast integrity. The phrase "a gentleman knows no conflict" suggests that a true gentleman does not engage in strife for personal gain but instead focuses on moral cultivation and the perfection of his character. Gao Panlong once remarked, "In this world, my only thought is to be a good person; that is my foremost duty, and everything else is secondary," exemplifying the broad-mindedness and noble character of a gentleman. Conversely, "a minister cannot be dishonored" signifies that Gao Panlong maintained his dignity and principles in the face of power and temptation, choosing death over surrender; his integrity was such that it could move heaven and earth, causing even spirits to weep.

The hall also preserves several memorial stones inscribed by Gao Panlong's descendants, with one inscription stating, "Although I have been deprived of my position, I was once a minister. When a minister is humiliated, it is an affront to the country; hence, I bow to the north, following the legacy of Qu Yuan. I have yet to repay the emperor's grace; I vow to do so in the next life. This is a letter from Gao Panlong, requesting that the messenger present this to the emperor." Each word reflects Gao Panlong's loyalty, integrity, and the noble spirit of the Donglin Party, demonstrating a calmness and a readiness to face death that has earned him admiration from countless generations. It is crucial to recognize that his unwavering spirit, especially in the face of treachery and persecution, was likely nurtured by his years of quiet meditation and scholarly pursuits. Regarding the method of meditation, Gao Panlong authored *On Quiet Sitting*, providing insightful perspectives: "The method of quiet sitting requires no arrangements; it is simply ordinary and silent. Its tranquility does not accommodate any distraction, hence it is termed ordinary." Gao Panlong's approach to meditation does not seek lofty states but instead aims at cultivating one's character and nurturing wisdom in simplicity, fostering willpower and patience. Thus, Gao Panlong faced life-and-death moments with clarity and composure, famously stating, "I regard death as a return; with a heart of integrity, I fulfill the responsibilities of a minister; I have no regrets in this life," exemplifying the unity of heart and principle he pursued throughout his life.

Historical records note that Gao Panlong lived in Gaozi Shuiju, known as "Ke Lou," where he cultivated his character and practiced quiet sitting. He dedicated half his day to reading and the other half to meditation. Ke Lou features windows on all sides, as its name suggests—it allows for "viewing mountains, observing water, enjoying the cool breeze, basking in sunlight, and inviting the bright moon as a companion." Today, the Gao Zhongxian Hall faces Longtou River, with views of Xihui in sight, where the cool breeze frequently blows and the sun and moon shine down, aligning perfectly with the "five permissions."

从王武愍公祠看祠堂布局

"庭院深深深几许",古代所谓"深宅"就是包括数进数出若干院落的大户。惠山的众多祠堂,大者能达到几进院落呢?调查显示为四进。四进祠堂在惠山属于规格很高的祠堂,一般都是政府下令建造的官祠。王武愍公祠就是四进祠堂,不但有四重院落,还分了中、西、东三路,沿中路依次设大门、碑亭、享堂、后堂;沿东路设戏台、介福堂及池山;沿西路为其子祠堂,有祠堂与后堂二进。二进、三进与后堂之间以工字廊连接。

准确地说,王武愍公祠是三路四进式祠堂,是惠山祠堂群中规制最为完整、布局最为缜密的祠堂。

从龙头河的门厅进入,就是第一进院落,门墙上方是一方

AI语音导览

砖刻，用篆书写着"王武愍公祠"，由晚清思想家、散文家、吴县人冯桂芬所题。王武愍公祠，又称王恩绶祠，王恩绶，字佩伦，号乐山，武愍是他的谥号，也是政府对他保家卫国、因公殉职的认可。左右院墙分别镶嵌有"勤忠教孝""节义成仁"两方砖雕，也能看出官方对他的高度评价。到底是怎样的功绩能得到如此高度评价，还能让政府下令建造官祠呢？

院落正中的碑亭里面竖着一块"敕建无锡王恩绶祠堂"碑，上有碑文640字。说起来，王恩绶还是著名书法家王羲之的第六十四世孙，祖父和父亲都是儒生，称得上诗书传家。王恩绶从小就很聪慧，而且举止沉静，十一岁的时候就取得了廪生的资格，由县学提供伙食，按现在的说法，就是获得了奖学金。王恩绶不仅读书很努力，还特别讲求道义，拜贤者为老师，在他二十岁成人礼之后，对自己的品德要求就更高了，他喜爱读名臣传，常按照名臣的德行来要求自己。

其实王恩绶的官职并不高，只是湖北武昌知县，而且可能还没正式坐进县衙，就已经因公殉职。所以他得到死后褒奖的重要原因其实是他的精神，一种"明知山有虎，偏向虎

山行"的无畏精神，很明显，这与他平日对自己在品德上的要求是高度一致的。咸丰四年（1854年），正是太平天国运动时期，太平军与清军在湖北地带来回拉锯，因为战事频繁，几乎没人愿意到湖北去做官。王恩绶则表现出了与其他人截然不同的态度，他说了一句话，如果大家都要挑好地方当官，那么太平军什么时候能镇压？于是，他自告奋勇报名到湖北当官。别人好心劝他，说太平军已经深入城池了，索性走慢点，言下之意是不用急着去送死，但是他不同意，反而日夜兼程，快马加鞭。等他到了的时候，原本从太平军手中收复的武昌又被太平军围困，很多人想从城里出来却苦于无门，而城外的王恩绶却想尽办法往城里冲，城外的军队首领看王恩绶是个人才，就劝他留在城外，但他坚决不肯，坚持用绳子缒吊入城。第二天，果然城破。他与武昌知府带着士兵们与太平军进行巷战，最后战死，带去的二儿子和仆人也都一起战死。王恩绶虽然并无保

卫疆土的职责，却能视死如归，与城池共存亡，因此清政府为他在家乡无锡建造祠堂，将他的精神传扬下去。石碑由清末状元、兵部左侍郎洪钧撰文，"无锡自龟山先生讲学东林，真儒蔚起，沿及明季，顾高二公以理学气节扶植名教，伦纪赖以不敝矣。公生于是乡，沐昔贤之余风，志趣学力，涵养素定，用能履险蹈危，不事趣避，忠孝义烈萃于一门。百世而下，过公祠者，以为东林君子后起有人，宜乎俎豆馨香，国家褒忠之典再三至也"。这几句话正是对王公及其家乡无锡的中肯评价。

往前走，有一间横长的硬山顶平屋，就是二门，以前的第二重正门，也称仪门。走进去，就是第二进院落，里面的大殿就是主体建筑——享堂，有王恩绶及先祖诸公的像，也是王氏族人来纪念的地方。砖木结构，装饰讲究，设计精巧，虽然年代有点久远，但是看上去并不显得破旧。院落两侧各有厢房和月洞门通往东、西两路院落，景观极佳。院落内种了四株广玉兰树，树龄已逾百年，长势极好，与古祠相互辉映。东院由月洞门、长廊、水池、厅堂和后花园组成，精美雅致，西院由月洞门、天井、二门和工字殿组成。

王武愍公祠祠门有无锡望族名士秦淡如撰写的楹联"抗志殉危城，如颜常山、张睢阳矢心不二；易名邀旷典，与邹壮节、李刚烈鼎足而三"。这副对联说的是，王恩绶志节高尚，殉身于危亡的武昌，像大唐的颜真卿、张巡那样忠心不二。

The Layout of Ancestral Halls as Seen from the Wang Wumin Hall

The phrase "how deep is the courtyard" captures the essence of what ancient Chinese termed a "deep residence," characterized by numerous courtyards that signify the grandiosity of affluent households. Among the many ancestral halls in Huishan, some are remarkably expansive, extending to four courtyards. Such four-courtyard ancestral halls are considered prestigious in Huishan, typically constructed under government directives. The Wang Wumin Hall exemplifies a four-courtyard structure, featuring not only four distinct courtyards but also three pathways: the central, east, and west routes. The central path includes the main entrance, a stele pavilion, a main hall, and a rear hall. The eastern path features a theater stage, the Jiefu Hall, and a pond, while the western path leads to the hall dedicated to his son, consisting of two additional courtyards connected by a covered walkway.

More precisely, the Wang Wumin Hall is a three-route four-depth design, noted for its complete regulations and meticulous layout within the Huishan Ancestral Hall Cluster. Entering through the entrance hall facing Longtou River leads to the first courtyard, where an inscription in seal script reads "Wang Wumin Hall," penned by the late Qing thinker and essayist Feng Guifen from Wuxian. This hall is also known as the Wang Enshou Hall, named after Wang Enshou, who had the courtesy name Peiren and the posthumous title Wumingong, acknowledging his dedication to safeguarding his country and his sacrifice in the line of duty.

The walls of the courtyard are adorned with two brick carvings inscribed with "Diligence, Loyalty, Education, and Filial Piety" and "Integrity and Sacrifice," reflecting the high regard the authorities held for him. What, then, were the achievements of this gentleman that warranted such commendation and led to the construction of an official ancestral hall?

Central to the courtyard is a stele pavilion housing a tablet inscribed with "Imperially Established Wuxi Wang Enshou Ancestral Hall,"

containing 640 characters. Notably, Wang Enshou was the sixty-fourth descendant of the famed calligrapher Wang Xizhi. Born into a family of scholars, he exhibited exceptional intelligence and poise from an early age, qualifying for the title of "linsheng" at the age of eleven, which is akin to receiving a scholarship today. Wang Enshou was not only diligent in his studies but also emphasized moral integrity, seeking guidance from sages. After his coming-of-age ceremony at twenty, he held himself to even higher ethical standards, often reading biographies of distinguished officials and aspiring to emulate their virtues.

Although Wang Enshou held a modest position as the county magistrate of Wuchang in Hubei, he tragically died in the line of duty before formally assuming his role. His posthumous recognition stems largely from his noble spirit—a willingness to confront danger head-on, embodying the attitude of "knowing there are tigers on the mountain yet still heading towards it." This aligns seamlessly with his rigorous self-expectations regarding morality. In the fourth year of the Xianfeng reign (1854), during the height of the Taiping Rebellion, conflict raged in Hubei, and few were willing to serve in the region. Those selected for government roles often avoided the post. Wang Enshou, however, displayed a starkly different disposition. He famously remarked that if everyone only sought safe positions, how could the Taiping army ever be suppressed? Therefore, he volunteered to serve in Hubei. Others, concerned for his safety, advised him to proceed cautiously since the Taiping army had already infiltrated the city. Nevertheless, he rejected this counsel, choosing instead to hasten his journey.

Upon arrival, Wuchang, which had been retaken from the Taiping army, found itself besieged again. Many sought to escape the city, but Wang Enshou endeavored to enter, despite the peril. The commanders outside recognized his talent and urged him to remain with them, but he insisted on using ropes to lower himself into the city. The following day, the city fell, and he engaged in street fighting alongside the local governor, ultimately dying in battle, along with his second son and servant.

Thus, although Wang Enshou bore no official responsibility for defending the territory, his willingness to face death alongside the city led to the decision to honor him with an ancestral hall in his hometown of Wuxi, ensuring his spirit would endure. The stele was composed by Hong Jun, a top scholar of the late Qing, with lines that articulate a balanced assessment of Wang Enshou and his hometown of Wuxi: "Since the teachings of Mr. Guishan at Donglin, true Confucians have flourished, continuing through the late Ming when Gu and Gao and others upheld the principles of moral integrity. Born in this land, he absorbed the residual virtues of the wise, cultivating his scholarly pursuits, and displayed the capacity to face peril without seeking to avoid danger, embodying loyalty, filial piety, and righteousness."

Continuing forward, one encounters a long, horizontal building with a hipped roof, known as the second gate, previously the second main entrance or ceremonial gate. Upon entering, one arrives at the second courtyard, where the main structure—the Hall of Offering—houses the statues of Wang Enshou and his ancestors, serving as the site for ancestral worship by the Wang clan. The hall, constructed of brick and wood, features exquisite decoration and intricate design, maintaining its elegance despite its age.

Each side of the courtyard contains rooms and moon gate entrances leading to the eastern and western paths, providing splendid views. Within the courtyard, four magnolia trees, over a hundred years old, flourish beautifully, complementing the ancient hall. The eastern courtyard consists of moon gates, long corridors, a pond, a hall, and a rear garden, showcasing refined aesthetics, while the western side comprises moon gates, a courtyard, the second gate, and a T-shaped pavilion.

At the entrance of the Wang Wumin Hall, a couplet composed by the esteemed Wuxi scholar Qin Danru reads: "Brave in spirit, sacrificing for the beleaguered city, like Yan Changshan and Zhang Suiyang, unwavering in loyalty; changing names to invite grandeur, alongside Zou Zhuangjie and Li Ganglie, standing together as equals." This couplet signifies Wang Enshou's noble aspirations and his martyrdom in Wuchang, likening him to the loyal figures of the Tang Dynasty, Yan Zhenqing and Zhang Xun.

宰相祠里大器晚成的宰相

惠山祠堂群中宰相祠堂有8座，纪念的分别是楚相春申君黄歇，唐相李绅、陆贽、张柬之，宋相司马光、王旦、范仲淹、李纲。要论宰相祠里最大器晚成的宰相，那必然是唐相张柬之。

张柬之（625—706），字孟将，襄州襄阳（今湖北襄阳）人。张柬之虽从小熟读经史，也中了进士，但在官场一直是小打小闹，并没有被重用，永昌元年（689年），64岁的张柬之在贤良科策问中得了第一，虽引起了武则天的重视，但还是一直游离在权力边缘，并没有真正得到重用。幸运的是，张柬之得到了狄仁杰和姚崇的赏识。狄仁杰多次在武则天面前推荐张柬之，使之先后迁任洛州司马、司刑少卿、秋官侍郎。后经姚崇举荐，他才以八十高龄坐上了武周朝同凤阁鸾台平章事的官位，也就是宰相，这可真是名副其实的大器晚成。

他当上宰相还不到半年，就发动了著名的神龙政变，对唐代的政治格局产生了深远影响。当时武则天已病，宠臣张昌宗、张易之侍疾在侧，弄权用事，张柬之与另一宰相崔玄暐等人密谋除二张。神龙元年（705年）正月，张柬之、崔玄暐、桓彦范、敬晖等人率领500余名禁军，发动政变。他们首先攻占了玄武门，控制了皇宫的入口，随后，迎太子李显入宫，并直接前往武则天的寝宫。在武则天的寝宫，张柬之等人揭露了张昌宗、张易之兄弟的罪行，并请求武则天退位。武则天在震惊之余，也意识到大势已去，最终同意传位给太子李显。

政变成功后，唐中宗李显复位，改元神龙，大赦天下。张柬之因功被封为汉阳王，并升任天官尚书、中书令，与崔玄暐、桓彦范、敬晖等人一同担任宰相。然而，政变的余波并未平息，武三思等武氏势力仍然活跃，他们勾结韦皇后，对张柬之等人进行排挤和诬陷。同年五月，张柬之被罢相，次年被贬为新州司马，又流放到泷州，忧愤而死，结束了他大器晚成的一生，享年82岁。尽管张柬之在政变后的政治生涯并不顺利，但神龙政变本身仍然是他一生中最辉煌的篇章，也是他作为唐朝名相的重要历史功绩。景云元年（710年），唐睿宗追封张柬之为中书令，谥号文贞。

纪念这位最大器晚成的宰相张柬之的祠堂——张文贞公祠，位于惠山下河塘13号，建于清末民初（约1911年），由裔孙张毅清独资在惠山寺塘泾购地建造。原祠为四间两进形制，第一进为青砖二层结构，门头两侧有砖雕，外侧楼上有木扶栏，砖雕和木栏雕工秀美精细。第二进为江南民居式样，檐下木结构同样雕刻精美。整个祠堂在惠山祠堂群中属较大的一

座。2008年8月至2009年9月，对张文贞公祠进行了修缮，拆除了原封闭于祠门的墙体，恢复原祠门，对二楼木结构进行修缮，基本恢复了祠堂的原有风貌。

施工队伍在对张文贞公祠全面修复时，从该祠堂头进建筑门后右侧厢房内的墙面上发现了一块"无锡县知事公署布告碑"，立于民国十四年（1925年）。石碑为青石材质，由碑身、碑座两部分组成。全碑通宽65厘米，高165厘米，其中碑身高140厘米，碑座高25厘米。碑身上端正中刻有圆形"大吉"两字，两旁分别刻有蝙蝠、祥云图案，寓意吉祥、喜庆。碑文楷书，计330余字。这块石碑记述张文贞公祠是在清末由居锡张氏族人为永思先祖功绩而建的，其中蕴含的报本思源、敬宗睦族的价值观在今天依然有着重要的现实意义，需要大力提倡。

The Late-Blooming Prime Minister in the Ancestral Hall Cluster

Among the nine halls dedicated to prime ministers in the Huishan Ancestral Hall Cluster, the honored figures include Huang Xie, the Prime Minister of Chu; Li Shen, Lu Zhi, and Zhang Jianzhi from the Tang Dynasty; Sima Guang, Wang Dan, Fan Zhongyan, and Li Gang from the Song Dynasty; and Li Hongzhang from the Qing Dynasty. However, when discussing the prime minister who was the epitome of late success, it must be Zhang Jianzhi from the Tang Dynasty.

Zhang Jianzhi (625-706), courtesy name Mengjiang, was a native of Xiangyang in Xiangzhou (modern-day Xiangyang, Hubei). Despite his early proficiency in the classics and history and passing the imperial examination as a jinshi, his career initially stagnated, and he remained in minor positions for many years. It wasn't until the first year of Yongchang (689), at the age of 64, that he excelled in the "Exemplary Virtue Examination," which attracted the attention of Empress Wu Zetian. However, despite this recognition, he continued to be marginalized in the political sphere. Fortunately, he earned the favor of notable officials Di Renjie and Yao Chong. Di Renjie recommended him several times to Wu Zetian, which led to his appointments as Sima of Luozhou, Shaoqing of the Court of Judicial Review, and Minister of the Autumn Office. It was only through Yao Chong's further recommendation that Zhang Jianzhi, at the remarkable age of 80, finally rose to the position of "Tong Fengge Luantai Pingzhangshi" in the Wu Zhou Dynasty, effectively becoming prime minister—truly a case of "late success."

Merely half a year after his promotion to prime minister, Zhang Jianzhi spearheaded the famous Shenlong Coup, which had a profound impact on the political landscape of the Tang Dynasty. At the time, Empress Wu Zetian was ill, and her favored ministers,

Zhang Changzong and Zhang Yizhi, were controlling court affairs. Zhang Jianzhi conspired with another prime minister, Cui Xuanwei, to eliminate the two. In the first month of the first year of Shenlong (705), Zhang Jianzhi, Cui Xuanwei, Huan Yanfan, Jing Hui, and others led over 500 palace guards in a coup. They first seized the Xuanwu Gate, securing control of the palace entrance. They then escorted Crown Prince Li Xian into the palace and confronted Empress Wu Zetian in her chambers, exposing the crimes of Zhang Changzong and Zhang Yizhi. Faced with the undeniable accusations and the deteriorating situation, Wu Zetian had no choice but to abdicate in favor of the crown prince, Li Xian.

Following the coup, Li Xian was restored to the throne as Emperor Zhongzong, initiating the Shenlong era and granting amnesty across the empire. Zhang Jianzhi was rewarded for his role in the coup with the title of Prince of Hanyang and was promoted to Minister of State and Grand Chancellor, sharing power with Cui Xuanwei, Huan Yanfan, and Jing Hui. However, the political aftershocks of the coup persisted, and the Wu clan, including Wu Sansi, remained active. They conspired with Empress Wei to undermine Zhang Jianzhi and his allies. In May of the same year, Zhang Jianzhi was dismissed from his position and subsequently demoted to Assistant Prefect of Xinzhou. The following year, he was further exiled to Longzhou, where he died in grief and indignation at the age of 82, marking the end of his extraordinary life. Despite the difficulties he faced after the coup, the Shenlong Coup remains his most remarkable achievement, cementing his legacy as a distinguished prime minister of the Tang Dynasty. In the first year of Jingyun (710), Emperor Ruizong posthumously honored Zhang Jianzhi with the title of Chancellor and gave him the posthumous name of "Wenzhen."

The hall dedicated to this illustrious late-blooming prime minister, Zhang Wenzhen Hall, is located at 13 Xiahetang, Huishan. It was constructed in the early Republic of China (around 1911) by his descendant Zhang Yiqing, who purchased land at the Huishan

Temple for its construction. The original structure had four rooms with two courtyards, featuring a two-story brick facade in the first courtyard with exquisite brick carvings and wooden railings on the upper floor. The second courtyard resembled traditional Jiangnan-style residences, with intricately carved woodwork under the eaves. The hall, one of the largest in the Huishan Ancestral Hall Cluster, underwent extensive renovations between August 2008 and September 2009, restoring the original appearance of the hall by removing a wall that had sealed off the entrance and repairing the wooden structures on the second floor.

During the restoration process, a stone stele was discovered in the right annex of the first courtyard. The stele, titled "Wuxi County Government Office Proclamation Stele," was erected in the 14th year of the Republic of China. Made of blue stone, the stele consists of a main body and a base, measuring 65 centimeters wide and 165 centimeters tall, with the main body standing 140 centimeters high and the base 25 centimeters high. The upper part of the stele is inscribed with the characters "Great Fortune" in a circular emblem, flanked by carvings of bats and auspicious clouds, symbolizing good fortune and celebration. The stele's text, written in regular script and containing over 330 characters, records that the Zhang clan of Wuxi built the hall in the late Qing Dynasty to honor their ancestor Zhang Wenzhen for his meritorious deeds. The values of reverence for one's ancestors and solidarity within the clan, as expressed in the stele, remain relevant today and serve as a valuable cultural legacy.

祠堂群里最"潮"的祠堂

祠堂群里有座很"潮"的祠堂，那就是坐落在龙头河边上的杨藕芳祠。祠堂建成两层楼房的式样，采用清水砖砌墙，围成口字院落，呈现出一派西洋风范，在周边的祠堂中甚是显眼。

那么，杨藕芳祠怎么会选用如此"潮"的西方款式呢？这是因为，杨藕芳祠建于民国时期，正值无锡民族工商业蓬勃兴起之时，西方文化不断融入中国。杨藕芳祠享堂中还有两根巴洛克圆柱，楼廊柱和檐框式也充分体现出巴洛克风格凹凸有致的曲线立面，室内的门楼门罩也采用了大块的西方图案。

但是这座西方风格的祠堂却又处处隐含中式元素。西式的二层楼全部采用中国传统的清水砖砌造，巴洛克圆柱用的也是特制的中式青砖，东西两侧山墙全部采用无锡最古老最传统的"观音兜"封火山墙，精美的筑瓦正脊，室内西式图案中还隐嵌着中国传统的"暗八仙"图案。

从祠堂的建筑风格，可以感受到主人杨藕芳的个性。一方面，他力主洋务、锐意改革。1885—1889年到中国台湾任台北道员的四年中，他修建了台湾第一条铁路，创办了台北邮政和电报，修建了马路，开辟了海运，建造了学校、民政、警所和药局。1895年回到家乡无锡后，又和兄长杨宗濂创办了无锡近代第一家纺织厂——业勤纱厂。另一方面，他又不忘祖宗、不丢传统。虽然他在台北从政期间搞了很多洋务，但依然

坚持传教农桑，不忘农本。

　　正是这种兼容并蓄的情怀才造就了如此之"潮"的祠堂特例。2006年，杨藕芳祠作为惠山古镇祠堂群的核心祠堂被列入全国重点文物保护单位。

　　杨藕芳祠不仅是纪念杨藕芳个人功绩的场所，更是无锡乃至整个中国近现代民族工商业发展历程的见证。如今，杨藕芳祠还成了社区文化交流的活跃平台，经常举办各种文化活动和社会活动，如艺术展览、社区聚会等，传统文化与现代生活找到了巧妙的结合点。

The Most "Trendy" Ancestral Hall in the Ancestral Hall Cluster

Among the ancestral halls in the cluster, there is one that stands out for being particularly "trendy," it is the Yang Oufang Hall located by the Longtou River. The building features a two-story structure constructed with exposed brick walls, forming a courtyard in the shape of a square, exuding a distinct Western style that is quite eye-catching amidst the surrounding ancestral halls.

So, why did the Yang Oufang Hall adopt such a "trendy" Western architectural style? The answer lies in its construction during the Republican era, a time when the national industry and commerce in Wuxi were flourishing, with Western culture increasingly merging into China.

The two-story structure of the Yang Oufang Hall showcases Western style, with Baroque columns inside the hall and architectural features that highlight the characteristic curves of Baroque design. The interior doorways also incorporate large Western motifs.

However, this Western-style ancestral hall subtly incorporates Chinese elements at every turn. The entire two-story structure is built with traditional Chinese exposed brick walls, and the Baroque columns are crafted from specially made Chinese blue bricks. The gable walls on the east and west sides are adorned with Wuxi's oldest traditional "Guanyin Dou" fireproof walls, showcasing exquisite ridge tiles. Furthermore, within the Western designs, traditional "hidden Eight Immortals" motifs are also intricately embedded.

The architectural style of the ancestral hall also reflects the personality of its owner, Yang Oufang. On the one hand, he was a proponent of modernization and eager for reform. During his tenure as the governor of Taipei of China from 1885 to 1889, he accomplished significant feats, such as establishing Taiwan's first railway, founding Taipei's postal and telegraph services, developing roads and maritime transportation, and building schools, civil administration offices, police stations, and pharmacies. After returning to his hometown of Wuxi in 1895, he, alongside his brother Yang Zonglian, founded the first modern textile factory in Wuxi—Yeqin Textile Factory. On the other hand, he remained devoted to his ancestral roots and did not forsake tradition. Despite his many Western ventures during his political career in Taipei, he continued to advocate for agricultural education and the importance of farming.

This spirit of embracing both tradition and modernity resulted in such a unique and "trendy" ancestral hall. In 2006, the Yang Oufang Hall was designated as a key national cultural relic protection unit, being recognized as the core ancestral hall of the Huishan ancient town.

The Yang Oufang Hall serves not only as a memorial to the personal achievements of Yang Oufang but also as a testament to the development of national industry and commerce in Wuxi and throughout China in the modern era. Today, it has evolved into an active platform for community cultural exchange, frequently hosting various cultural and social events, such as art exhibitions and community gatherings, cleverly merging traditional culture with modern life.

让乾隆皇帝青睐有加的祠堂

在中国历史上，皇帝的青睐往往意味着被赋予无上的荣耀。众所周知，乾隆皇帝对无锡惠山情有独钟，六下江南每次必到惠山，他钟爱惠山的"幽雅闲静"，留下了诸多佳话。有这样一座祠堂，乾隆皇帝六下江南四次到访，作诗、题祠名、书写匾额赐赠，这在古镇一百多座祠堂里是绝无仅有的。那么，这究竟是一座怎样的祠堂呢？

光霁祠，又称"濂溪周夫子祠"，是为了纪念北宋时期的大儒周敦颐而建。周敦颐，字茂叔，世称"濂溪先生"，宋、明理学的奠基人，被尊为孔孟以来的第三位圣人。这座祠堂建于乾隆七年（1742年），由周敦颐二十三世孙周汝远筹资督建，自宅基乡移建惠山下河塘，乾隆十三年（1748年），获批列入官祭。濂溪公传世名作《爱莲说》脍炙人口，几百年来一直是蒙学经典。据记载，乾隆皇帝少时就能背诵讲解《爱莲说》，曾得康熙皇帝嘉许，对他日后特别垂爱光霁祠不无影响。

乾隆二十二年（1757年），乾隆皇帝第二次下江南来到惠山，周汝远头顶周敦颐小像跪迎，叩请皇帝为祠堂赐祠额，乾隆皇帝欣然应允，取《宋史·周敦颐传》中黄庭坚赞周敦颐人品的"光风霁月"之"光霁"两字为祠名，并赐五言诗一首："锡麓祀先贤，孙支世守旃。开程朱道学，继孔孟心传。水碧山青处，松蕤竹秀边。千秋光霁在，底复藉龙眠。"乾隆以"光霁"二字高度褒奖周敦颐的理学思想和品德，御书匾额，御诗赞颂，成就周

家门楣高光时刻。2009年祠堂修复时，有关部门专设两组泥人雕塑，再现"迎接圣驾""祭祀仪典"的场面。今天，光霁祠的镇馆之宝：乾隆御书"光霁祠额碑""乾隆御诗碑""濂溪夫子惠山祠祀碑"等6块珍贵古石碑默默伫立，仍在诉说这段往事，诉说着祠堂的兴衰荣辱，诉说着时代的风云变迁。

这座被皇帝眷顾的光霁祠，坐南朝北、采用了传统的三开间、两进深的设计，边厢为两层过楼。前有门廊、石兽，有旗杆石八条，门头有蓝底金字"光霁祠"御题竖匾。楼上楼下共二十四间，设仪厅、享堂、太极阁、知乐处等。楼上是著名的光霁楼，拥有观赏龙头河两岸风景的绝佳视角。

从乾隆御诗"水碧山青处，松藨竹秀边"就能看出光霁祠所在是个山清水秀的好地方，更妙的是光霁祠的周遭环境、景

物与周敦颐故里祠堂非常类似，都是前有流水潺潺，后有青山葱茏，且都是两条水路在祠前会合，东方一桥飞架两岸。那龙头河上的宝善桥，桥形上下浑然一体，俨然一个太极图形，就像在演绎濂溪公的《太极图说》。

与其他祠堂相比，光霁祠祠楼虽小，却别有洞天，美不胜言，《光霁祠置造规略》中记述了280多年前的祠堂景致，春雨冬雪，四时佳景。后拥锡山宝塔，左牵九龙山脉，两山寺院上下错综，朱扇楼阁，掩隐重林，犹如天然图画，只需闲坐祠楼几席之上，透过阁窗即可一览无余，当年站在光霁阁上远眺，可观看到寺塘春晓、石门云起、香浜罗带、善桥太极、夕岭画屏、龙山翠嶂、西郊香市、北塘舟骑等祠楼八景。

如今，这座让乾隆皇帝青睐有加的祠堂，已成为惠山古镇一处重要的旅游景点，川流不息的八方游客走进这座充满故事的祠堂，登上光霁阁，眺望河塘两岸，虽然随着城市的变迁，当年的八景之美已成追忆，但雨过天晴时，风清月明处，凭窗远眺，还是能感悟一下"光霁"的境界，体验先人襟怀坦荡的感觉！

The Hall Favored by Emperor Qianlong

In Chinese history, the favor of an emperor often signified unparalleled honor for a place. It is well known that Emperor Qianlong was particularly fond of Wuxi's Huishan, visiting it every time he made his six southern tours. He admired the peaceful elegance of Huishan and left behind many memorable stories. Among the numerous ancestral halls in the ancient town, there is one hall that received Qianlong's special attention. He visited it four times during his six southern tours, wrote poems, bestowed names, and personally inscribed plaques, a distinction unmatched among the over 100 ancestral halls in the area. So, what makes this hall so exceptional?

Guangji hall, also known as "Lianxi Zhou's Hall," was built to honor Zhou Dunyi, a renowned Confucian scholar of the Northern Song Dynasty. Zhou Dunyi, styled Maoshu and commonly referred to as "Master Lianxi," was the founder of Song-Ming Neo-Confucianism and revered as the third sage after Confucius and Mencius. The hall was constructed in 1742, during the seventh year of Qianlong's reign, under the supervision of Zhou Dunyi's 23rd-generation descendant, Zhou Ruyuan. It was relocated from Zhou's ancestral home to Huishan's Xiahetang. In 1748, it was officially listed as an imperial hall. Zhou Dunyi's renowned essay *Ode to the Lotus* has been a classic of elementary education for centuries. It is recorded that Qianlong, even in his youth, could recite and interpret *Ode to the Lotus*, which earned him praise from Emperor Kangxi and may explain his particular fondness for Guangji Hall.

In 1757, during his second southern tour, Qianlong arrived at Huishan, where Zhou Ruyuan, carrying a portrait of Zhou Dunyi, knelt to greet him and requested the emperor to bestow a name upon the hall. Qianlong gladly agreed, drawing from Huang Tingjian's praise of Zhou Dunyi's character in *the History of the Song Dynasty* and selecting the characters "光霁" (Guangji), meaning "clear and bright after the storm," to name the hall. Qianlong also composed a five-character poem for the hall, praising Zhou Dunyi's philosophical contributions and moral integrity. The emperor's personal inscription and poetry marked a moment of high honor for the Zhou family. In 2009, during the hall's restoration, lifelike clay figures were added to recreate the scene of the emperor's arrival and the sacrificial rituals. Today, the hall houses several treasures, including Qianlong's personally inscribed "Guangji Hall" plaque, the "Qianlong Imperial Poem" stele, and the "Lianxi Master Huishan Hall Sacrificial Stele." These ancient stone steles, though silent, continue to narrate the hall's history and the ebb and flow of the ages.

The Guangji Hall, favored by the emperor, is designed in the traditional three-bay, two-hall layout, facing south with auxiliary two-story wings. Its front features a porch, stone beasts, and eight flagstones. Above the entrance is a vertical plaque inscribed with "Guangji

Hall" in blue and gold characters by Qianlong. The building contains ceremonial halls, the main hall, the Guangji Tower, the Taiji Pavilion, and the Zhile Chamber, The famous Guangji Tower on the upper floor offers a stunning view of both banks of the Longtou River.

Qianlong's poem, "In the place where the water is clear and the mountains are green, beneath the luxuriant pines and bamboo," describes the serene and picturesque setting of Guangji Hall. Even more remarkable is the hall's location, which bears a striking resemblance to Zhou Dunyi's ancestral hall in his hometown, with its flowing streams, lush mountains, and two converging waterways. The Baoshan Bridge on the Longtou River, with its perfect integration of form, resembles a Taiji symbol, as if illustrating Zhou Dunyi's *Explanation of the Taiji Diagram*.

Compared to other halls, Guangji Hall may be small, but it offers an exquisite experience. Historical records from over 280 years ago describe its enchanting scenery through the seasons. Overlooking the pagoda on Xishan, surrounded by interwoven halls and lush forests, the scene resembled a natural painting. Sitting in the hall and gazing out through its lattice windows, one could view the "Eight Views of the Hall": the Spring Dawn at the Temple Pond, Clouds Rising from Stone Gate, Fragrant Shore of the Baoxiang Stream, the Taiji Bridge, Evening Peaks, the Verdant Dragon Mountains, the Fragrance of the Western Suburbs, and the Boats and Horses of Beitang.

Today, Guangji Hall, once favored by Qianlong, has become an important tourist attraction in Huishan Ancient Town. Although the beauty of the "Eight Views" has faded with the passage of time, visitors can still ascend the Guangji Tower, gaze upon the riversides, and, in moments of clear weather, feel a connection to the tranquil and open spirit embodied in the name "Guangji," experiencing the serene and virtuous character of the ancestors.

祠中古树寄情怀

AI语音导览

视频 顾洞阳先生祠

说起惠山的古树，年代大抵都可追溯到明代，这也是惠山被称为无锡"露天历史博物馆"的原因之一。除了前文提到过的惠山寺明代古银杏，还有一棵明代的古银杏就在顾洞阳祠中。

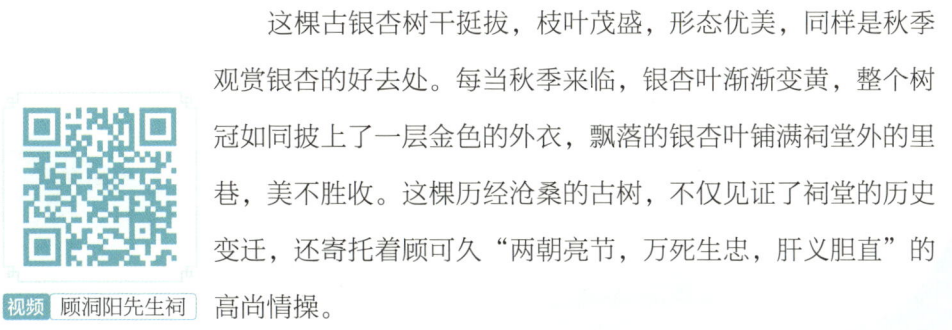

这棵古银杏树干挺拔，枝叶茂盛，形态优美，同样是秋季观赏银杏的好去处。每当秋季来临，银杏叶渐渐变黄，整个树冠如同披上了一层金色的外衣，飘落的银杏叶铺满祠堂外的里巷，美不胜收。这棵历经沧桑的古树，不仅见证了祠堂的历史变迁，还寄托着顾可久"两朝亮节，万死生忠，肝义胆直"的高尚情操。

那么这棵树当年是谁栽下的呢？史料上并没有直接记载，但是根据间接的史料信息，可以推测建造顾洞阳祠的海瑞最有可能。

海瑞为什么会建造顾洞阳祠呢？原因很简单，顾洞阳是海瑞的恩师。顾洞阳在琼州（今海南省）期间积极提倡教育，亲自主持课试，以非凡的洞察力，录取了琼山（今海口市）人海瑞。明隆庆三年（1569年），时任应天巡抚的海瑞来到无锡访师，当时洞阳公已经去世九年，海瑞大为悲恸，为追念恩师，海瑞立即奏请朝廷，并捐俸建顾洞阳祠于惠山寺塘泾。明万历元年（1573年），海瑞辞职回海南时，再次来无锡，挥毫写下那首著名的《谒先师顾洞阳公祠》："两朝崇祀庙谟新，抗疏名传骨鲠臣。志矢回天曾扣马，功同浴日再批鳞。三生不改冰霜操，万死仍留社稷身。世德尚馀清白在，承家还见有麒麟。"该诗的碑刻现存于无锡市碑刻馆。

顾洞阳，本名是顾可久，号洞阳。他出任过福建泉州知府、江西赣州知府，之后升到正四品的广东按察副使，主管广东省司法事务，同时兼管海南岛的军防事务。他在海南岛做了很多实事，一是到处访查，了解民情；二是勘察地形，将关隘、险阻、冲要、海港、山川等地理元素绘制成图，加上说明文字，编制了2卷《琼州府山海图说》；三是多次主持海南省人才选拔，海瑞就是这样被选出来的。

顾可久是明朝著名的谏官，秉性耿直、直言敢谏。他不但不揣度圣意，而且明明知道了皇帝的意思，还要和皇帝对着干，正因如此，两度惹恼皇帝，受了廷杖。因此他被称为"骨鲠之臣"，家乡人把他和杨淮、张选、黄正色同称为"锡谷四谏""嘉靖四忠"。联想到海瑞也是"直言敢谏"的牛脾气，所以顾可久以非凡的洞察力相中海瑞，也在情理之中。

顾可久在第二次廷杖之后，没过多久就得到了皇帝的宽恕，还升了官，之后就到福建、江西、广东、海南一带去任职了。不过这种耿直刚强的性子肯定不讨地方黑势力和权臣的喜欢，顾可久也因此遭到这些人的恶意中伤而最终被迫辞职。

现在，惠山还有一个无锡人很爱去的场所——碧山吟社，特别是每年中秋时节，去碧山吟社赏桂的人络绎不绝。很多人可能并不知道，这里就是顾可久辞职隐退故乡后经常待的地方，他和同乡人张选、王问、华察等在这里重振诗会，每日吟诗作文、美酒相伴。这些诗作并未失传，而是合成了20卷的《洞阳诗集》流传于世。他还写了6卷《唐王右丞诗集注说》和《李杜诗体略》。他还写得一笔小楷好字，深得王羲之、钟繇笔法精髓。秉性刚正、爱民如子、学问又如此之大的顾可久先生，着实让人景仰！

"惠"游祠堂

惠山古镇记忆馆

硕洞阳先生祠

现在的顾洞阳祠也是一处非常有看头的祠堂。从大门进去就是前庭院，门边就是著名的"无顶亭"四面牌坊，牌坊的四根花岗石角柱还是以前的旧物。牌坊下本来还有一对石狮子，20世纪80年代已经移去了惠山寺。大门西侧就是那棵明代古银杏，故人已去，古木犹在，高大挺拔的身姿似乎在诉说着对直言敢谏的顾可久的怀思。东边本来有一处浴日泉，泉水在阳光的沐浴下晶莹剔透的样子一定很可爱，可惜现在已经看不到了，只留下墙角的"浴日泉"石碑，这块碑是顾可久的八世孙顾光旭写的。

来到跨院，正中就是主体建筑享堂，硬山顶，面阔三间，进深七架。

穿过享堂，就是后庭院，是顾洞阳祠重修时添建的。院子里有一座两层的祠楼，也是硬山顶，面阔四间，进深七架，靠东的一间屋子里面有楼梯，登楼可以"穷千里之目"，赏四时美景。

祠楼的西北是拜石山房，墙上嵌着一块诗碑，上面是顾可久写的《西斋雨中》《溪上避暑》，还有顾光旭的两块"诗冢碑"。拜石山房以前还有"忠君爱国"的匾额，两旁有顾光旭撰写的楹联"教成于家，溯三国六朝，光昭世德；慎追乎远，本一门双义，佑启后人"。

2006年，顾洞阳祠作为惠山镇核心祠堂被列入全国重点文物保护单位。

The Sentiments Reflected in the Ancient Trees of the Ancestral Hall

When discussing the ancient trees of Huishan, most can trace their origins back to the Ming Dynasty, contributing to Huishan's reputation as Wuxi's "Open-Air History Museum." In addition to the ancient ginkgo tree from the Ming Dynasty mentioned earlier at Huishan Temple, another such tree resides in the Gu Dongyang Hall.

This ancient ginkgo boasts a tall trunk and lush foliage, making it a beautiful spot for autumn leaf-viewing. As autumn approaches, the leaves gradually turn yellow, cloaking the tree in a golden mantle. The fallen ginkgo leaves blanket the alley outside the ancestral hall, creating a picturesque scene. This venerable tree has not only witnessed the historical changes of the ancestral hall but also embodies the noble spirit of Gu Kejiu, who exemplified loyalty and integrity during turbulent times.

So, who planted this tree? Historical records do not provide a direct answer, but indirect evidence suggests that it was most likely Hai Rui, the builder of the Gu Dongyang Hall. Yes, that Hai Rui, known as "Qing Guan" in folk tales.

Why did Hai Rui construct the Gu Dongyang Hall? The reason is simple: Gu Dongyang was Hai Rui's mentor. During his time in Qiongzhou (modern-day Hainan Province), Gu Dongyang actively promoted education and personally oversaw examinations. With exceptional insight, he selected Hai Rui, a local from Qiongshan (present-day Haikou). In the third year of Longqing reign (1569), when Hai Rui visited Wuxi as the Governor of Yangzhou, he mourned the passing of Gu Dongyang, who had died nine years prior. In memory of his mentor, Hai Rui promptly petitioned the imperial court and donated part of his salary to establish the ancestral hall at Huishan Temple's Tangjing. In the first year of wanli reign (1573), when Hai Rui resigned and returned to Hainan, he visited Wuxi once more to pay his respects, penning the renowned poem "Visiting the Ancestral Hall of Gu Dongyang":

"Two dynasties revere the hall's new laws,
Defending justice, his name endures through time.
Determined to turn fate, he once urged the horse,
His deeds, like scales, reborn in daylight shine.
Three lifetimes unchanged in his icy integrity,
Ten thousand deaths remain loyal to the nation.
His worldly virtue shines bright in purity,
Generations hence will still witness the qilin."

This poem is inscribed on a stone tablet that currently resides in Wuxi's Stele Museum.

Gu Dongyang, whose birth name was Gu Kejiu. He served as the Prefect of Quanzhou in Fujian and Ganzhou in Jiangxi. He later ascended to the position of Deputy Inspector of Guangdong, overseeing judicial matters in the province while also managing military affairs in Hainan. Gu Kejiu accomplished much during his time in Hainan: he traveled extensively to understand local conditions, surveyed the geography to document strategic locations, and conducted provincial examinations to select talents, one of whom was Hai Rui.

Gu Kejiu renowned for his integrity and frankness, he was not afraid to challenge the emperor, often opposing his wishes. As a result, he twice drew the emperor's ire and faced punishment. Gu Kejiu's unwavering loyalty earned him the title of "the Loyal and Straightforward Minister," and he, alongside Yang Huai, Zhang Xuan, and Huang Zhengse, was honored as one of the "Four Rectifiers of Xigu." Given that Hai Rui also had a reputation for candor and forthrightness, it is understandable that Gu Kejiu would identify him as a potential protégé.

After his second punishment, Gu Kejiu soon received imperial pardon and was promoted, subsequently serving in various roles in Fujian, Jiangxi, Guangdong, and Hainan. However, his unwavering character did not endear him to local factions or corrupt officials, leading to slander and, ultimately, his resignation.

Today, Huishan boasts a beloved spot for Wuxi locals—the Banshan Yinshe. Particularly during the Mid-Autumn Festival in August, visitors flock to this site to appreciate the osmanthus blossoms. Many may be unaware that this was where Gu Kejiu often retreated after his resignation, where he and fellow townsman Zhang Xuan (one of the "Four Rectifiers"), along with Wang Wen and Hua Cha, revived poetry gatherings, composing verses accompanied by fine wine. Fortunately, these poems have not been lost to time; they were compiled into a twenty-volume collection titled *Dongyang Poetry Collection*. He also wrote a six-volume commentary on the Poems of Wang Wei and Li Bai, showcasing his admiration for these renowned poets, reflecting his own literary talents.

It is worth noting that he also excelled in small script calligraphy, mastering the styles of Wang Xizhi and Zhong Yao—a remarkable individual indeed! Gu Kejiu, with his principled character, love for the people, and extensive scholarship, is truly admirable!

Currently, the Gu Dongyang Hall is an intriguing site to visit. Entering through the main gate, one finds the front courtyard, featuring the famous "Wuding Pavilion," with its four-sided archway, the original granite columns of which still remain. Originally, a pair of stone lions stood at the archway, but they were relocated to Huishan Temple in the 1980s. To the west of the main gate stands the ancient ginkgo from the Ming Dynasty, a tall and stately tree that seems to evoke memories of the forthright Gu Kejiu. To the east, there once was the Yuri spring, whose crystalline waters must have been delightful, but it has since disappeared, leaving only a stone tablet marking its location, inscribed by Gu Kejiu's eighth-generation descendant, Gu Guangxu.

Crossing the courtyard, the central structure is the main hall for worship, featuring a hard roof with three bays and a depth of seven brackets. Beyond the main hall lies the rear courtyard, which was added during the restoration of the Gu Dongyang Hall. Within this courtyard stands a two-story ancestral tower, also featuring a hard roof, with four bays and a depth of seven brackets. The easternmost room contains a staircase leading to an elevated area where one can take in breathtaking views throughout the seasons.

To the northwest of the ancestral tower is the Baishi Mountain. The walls of the Baishi Mountain House feature a poetic tablet, including Gu Kejiu's works *Rain in the West Studio* and *Summer Retreat by the Stream*, alongside two tablets from Gu Guangxu's "Poetry Mound." Previously, a plaque inscribed with "Loyalty to the Emperor, Love for the Nation" hung in the Baishi Mountain House, flanked by couplets written by Gu Guangxu:

"Devotion to family and country, nurturing virtues,

Holding steadfast to morals, honoring ancestors."

This ancestral hall remains a remarkable site of cultural significance.

谁创办了无锡第一所中学

无锡市第一中学、辅仁中学、天一中学和江苏省锡山高级中学等都是无锡著名中学。那么这几所名校里面有没有无锡历史上第一所中学呢？答案是有的，那就是辅仁中学。

辅仁中学的创办是应了某位先生的倡议，因为当时无锡还没有中学，学子们只能半途辍学，或者跑到外地辛苦求学，所以这位毕业于上海圣约翰大学的无锡学子就在上海圣约翰大学无锡同乡会中发出倡议，募集资金，创办辅仁中学。这位先生就是唐鋆（yíng）镇，也称唐纪云，纪云是唐先生的字。正因如此，在辅仁中学创立前期设置的董事部中，唐纪云一直担任董事部部长。在辅仁中学创立初期外国校长回国探亲期间，唐

纪云还兼任校长，所以他也是辅仁中学的第三任校长。现在辅仁中学里面还有一座纪云亭，就是为了纪念唐纪云先生造福乡里的功德，纪念他为无锡教育史翻开的重要一页。

那么，唐纪云先生为什么会首先提出呢？这其实和唐纪云先生接受的宗规家训直接相关。

唐纪云先生的爷爷是唐懋勋，咸丰年间，他为了躲避战乱，举家搬到了无锡羊尖的严家桥。咸丰年间严家桥交通不便，但唐懋勋却看中了严家桥这块地方物产丰富、民风淳朴、四乡殷实、市集繁荣，因此下决心在这里定居下来，并继续从事老本行，也就是开布庄。他开了春源布庄，之后又多业态经营，做起了典当、养蚕和木材等生意，还进驻地产业，购买了6000亩田地，成为富甲无锡东北的名人。这不是说明人家经商特别厉害吗，和热衷教育事业有什么关系呢？热衷教育本非一句空话，既要有情怀，还要有经济实力。可以说，唐氏家族从唐懋勋开始就特别擅长经商，为唐氏子孙用实际行动支持教育事业奠定了坚实的经济基础。

这份情怀可以追溯到唐氏的明代祖辈们，例如明代万历年间，唐泰徵就捐出300亩田地和600两金银盖"希望小学"，资助赶考学子路费，给予优秀学子奖学金。当了官的子孙后代要拿出一部分薪酬放入家族的"慈善基金会"，以保证经费来源稳定。这一切都不是单纯依靠子孙后代个人的情怀和信仰，而是写入"唐氏宗规"，作为家族规范代代传承。这是唐氏家族十分重视和大力赞助教育事业的核心原因，也是其教育情怀的渊源。

唐纪云和他的叔伯们、兄弟们、子侄后辈都严守宗规家训，为家乡以及其他地区的教育事业做出了重要的贡献。无锡严家桥小学从创办到两度复校，都是唐家出资出力；无锡国学专修学校是唐家出钱资助并长期担任经济校董；无锡崇安寺小学建造新教学楼也是唐家出资……在境外发展的唐家子孙还捐助过香港理工大学、香港中文大学、美国麻省理工学院、美国斯坦福大学、美国加州大学伯克莱分校等名校，这些大学都有以唐家子孙名字命名的礼堂、图书馆、宿舍楼等建筑。

说了这么多，您一定猜到了唐懋勋及其子孙后辈和唐襄文公祠之间的关系。没错，唐襄文公祠纪念的唐顺之就是唐家的祖先。唐懋勋在清代光绪三年（1877年）修建了这座单路多进祠堂来祭祖，里面有比较大的祠堂花园。祠堂门楣上有清同

治十三年（1874年）的状元陆润庠为唐顺之写的文联，"义理事功两派，山中静坐，海上陈师，史笔赞洸洋，岂仅文章留正则；左右儒稗六编，絜戟承家，楹诗裕后，风诗歌硕大，长将庙貌肃明禋"。

唐顺之其实并非无锡人，而是常州武进人，史称荆川先生。从小就聪明过人，在会试中取得第一名。他本来还可以在殿试中获得第一名，却因为得罪考官而被降到了二甲第一名。这份知识分子的铮铮傲骨使得唐顺之在仕途中又得罪了权臣张璁而被"开除公职"。唐顺之回乡后并未自暴自弃，而是潜心治学，天文、地理、乐律、兵法无不涉猎，并将所学融会贯通，从诸家之言中节选精华编成了《左》《右》《文》《武》《儒》《稗》六编传世，正是对联中"左右儒稗六编"所指。本来想要终老林岩的唐顺之后来因为倭寇的横行掳掠而再度出山，在倭难最为厉害的嘉靖年间立下了抗倭的赫赫战功，尤其是嘉靖三十八年（1559年）的崇明一战，战绩卓著，留名千古，也就是对联中所说"海上陈师，史笔赞洸洋，岂仅文章留正则"。

从荆川先生到纪云先生，从唐襄文公祠到辅仁中学，这个家族不一般！

Who Founded the First Middle School in Wuxi?

Wuxi boasts several prestigious middle schools, including Wuxi No. 1 Middle School, Furen Middle School, Tianyi Middle School, and the Jiangsu Xishan Senior High School. Among these renowned institutions, Furen Middle School holds the distinction of being the first middle school in Wuxi's history.

The establishment of Furen Middle School stemmed from the initiative of a certain gentleman, as there were no middle schools in Wuxi at the time. Students either had to drop out or travel far and wide to pursue their studies. This individual, a graduate of St. John's University in Shanghai, proposed the establishment of Furen Middle School through the Wuxi Alumni Association of St. John's University, raising funds for its creation. This gentleman was Tang Jiyun, also known as Tang Yingzhen, with "Jiyun" being his courtesy name. Consequently, he served as the head of the board of directors during the early years of Furen Middle School. Additionally, during the absence of the foreign principal who returned home to visit family, Tang also acted as principal, thus becoming the school's third headmaster. Today, within the campus of Furen Middle School stands the Jiyun Pavilion, commemorating Tang Jiyun's contributions to his hometown and the educational history of Wuxi.

What motivated Tang Jiyun to champion this noble cause? This endeavor is directly related to the family traditions and teachings he received.

Tang Jiyun's grandfather, Tang Maoxun, relocated his family to Yanjiaqiao in Wuxi during the Xianfeng era to escape the turmoil of war. Despite Yanjiaqiao was remote and lacked public transportation, Tang Maoxun recognized the area's abundance of resources and simple folkways, as well as its prosperous markets. Thus, he resolved to settle there and continue his family trade in textiles. He opened a fabric shop named Chunyuan, and subsequently diversified into pawn broking, sericulture, timber, and real estate, acquiring 6,000 mu of farmland and becoming a notable figure in northeast Wuxi. One might wonder what this business acumen has to do with his passion for education. The answer lies in the idea that supporting education is not just an empty phrase; it requires both passion and the capability to take action when necessary. The Tang family's long-standing business expertise laid a solid economic foundation for supporting educational initiatives.

  Moreover, the family possessed both financial strength and a commitment to education. This educational ethos can be traced back to the Tang family's ancestors from the Ming Dynasty. For instance, during the Wanli period, Tang Taizheng donated 300 mu of land and 600 taels of silver to establish a "Hope Primary School," assisted students with travel expenses for exams, and provided scholarships for academic achievements. Descendants who became officials were expected to contribute a portion of their salary to the family's "charity foundation" to ensure a stable source of funding. Importantly, this commitment was not solely dependent on individual goodwill serving as a standard for successive generations and instilling these values into the family's legacy. This is the core reason the Tang family places such great emphasis on and support for educational endeavors, as well as the source of their educational dedication.

Consequently, Tang Jiyun, along with his relatives and descendants, adhered strictly to their family codes, significantly contributing to educational initiatives in both their hometown and beyond. The establishment and revival of Wuxi Yanjiaqiao Primary School were both funded and supported by the Tang family. They also financed and maintained long-term economic governance at Wuxi National Studies Specialized School, and contributed to the construction of new buildings for Wuxi Chong'an Temple Primary School. Furthermore, descendants of the Tang family who developed overseas have made donations to prestigious institutions such as The Hong Kong Polytechnic University, The Chinese University of Hong Kong, Massachusetts Institute of Technology, Stanford University, and the University of California, Berkeley, where buildings like halls, libraries, and dormitories bear the names of Tang family members.

From all this, one can easily infer the connection between Tang Maoxun, his descendants, and the Tang Xiangwen Memorial Hall. Indeed, Tang Shunzhi, honored at the hall, is an ancestor of the Tang family. In the third year of the Guangxu reign (1877), Tang Maoxun constructed this ancestral hall with multiple entrances to honor his ancestors, complete with a spacious garden. The hall features a couplet written by the top scholar Lu Runshang during the 13th year of the Tongzhi reign, which reads:

"Righteousness and merit are two paths;

In the mountains, sit quietly; on the sea, Chen Shi.

The historian's pen praises the broad ocean,

Not merely leaving the prose to abide by standards."

Tang Shunzhi, originally from Wujin, Changzhou, was historically known as Mr. Jingchuan. Gifted with remarkable intelligence from a young age, he achieved first place in the national examination. He could have secured first place in the highest-level imperial examination if not for offending an examiner, which led to his demotion to the first place in the second class. His steadfast intellectual integrity caused him to clash with the powerful minister Zhang Cong, resulting in his dismissal from office. After returning to his hometown, Tang Shunzhi did not succumb to despair but devoted himself to scholarship, mastering various subjects including astronomy, music theory, geography, and military strategy. He synthesized his learning, omitting what he disagreed with from various schools, and produced the six-volume *Zuo, You, Wen, Wu, Ru, and Bai*, which is referenced in the couplet's mention of "the six volumes of Ru and Bai." Although he intended to spend his later years in Lin Yan, the incursion of Japanese pirates compelled him to re-enter public life. During the notorious Jiajing era, he achieved significant military success against these invaders, particularly noted for his impressive accomplishments in the battle of Chongming in the thirty-eighth year of Jiajing, which ensured his place in history, as noted in the couplet's lines: "On the sea, Chen Shi; the historian's pen praises the broad ocean, not merely leaving the prose to abide by standards."

From Mr. Jingchuan to Mr. Jiyun, from the Tang Xiangwen Memorial Hall to Furen Middle School, this family is truly extraordinary!

保留下来的三大影壁

影壁，起源于中国，也称作照壁、影墙、照墙，是古代宫殿、官府衙门、寺庙和深宅大院前的一种建筑，即门外正对大门以作屏障的墙壁，曹雪芹在《红楼梦》中就描写了"北边立着一个粉油大影壁"。

影壁的功用是作为建筑组群前面的屏障，以别内外，并增加威严和肃静的气氛，有装饰的意义。影壁往往把宫殿、王府或寺庙大门前围成一个广场或庭院，成为人们进大门之前的停歇和活动场所，也是停放车轿上下回转之地。

现惠山祠堂群中，多数影壁已毁改殆尽，保留下来的共三处，有李鹤章祠前的隔河影壁，顾可久祠、张巡庙前的隔街影

壁。李鹤章祠纪念的是清末名臣李鸿章的弟弟李鹤章，李鸿章在中国近代史上留下了浓墨重彩的一笔，弟弟李鹤章是清朝战功卓著的勇猛武将，官至三品知府，曾国藩曾高度评价其"战争之才超越时贤"。他曾转战于苏州、常熟、无锡、常州，无锡是其立功之地，于此建专祠。

祠堂采用李鹤章故乡安徽的"四水归堂"形式，在天井中心摆放着两门大炮，主厅的梁上悬挂着"戎马纵横"匾额。李鹤章祠前就有一块富有历史价值的隔河影壁。

影壁作为中国建筑中重要的单元，与房屋、院落建筑相辅相成，组合成一个不可分割的整体。雕刻精美的影壁具有建筑学和人文学的重要意义，有很高的建筑与审美价值。

The Three Preserved Shadow Walls

Originating in China, shadow walls—also referred to as zhaobi, yingqiang, or zhaoqiang—are traditional constructions found in front of ancient palaces, government offices, temples and grand residences. These walls act as barriers directly opposite the main gates, as illustrated in Cao Xueqin's *Dream of the Red Chamber*, where he describes "a large pink shadow wall standing to the north."

The primary function of a shadow wall is to serve as a barrier in front of a group of buildings, delineating the boundary between the interior and exterior while enhancing an atmosphere of solemnity and grandeur. Shadow walls often enclose a square or courtyard in front of palaces, princely residences, or temples, providing a space for visitors to pause and engage in activities before entering the main gate. They also serve as areas for vehicles to maneuver and turn around.

Currently, there are three known shadow walls within the Huishan Ancestral Hall Cluster, although most have been destroyed or significantly altered. These include the river-facing wall in front of the Li Hezhang Hall, as well as street-facing walls in front of the Gu Kejiu Hall, and the Zhang Xun Hall. The Li Hezhang Hall honors Li Hezhang, the brother of the prominent late Qing Dynasty statesman Li Hongzhang, who left a significant mark on modern Chinese history. Li Hezhang was an accomplished and valiant general with significant military achievements, eventually holding the official title of third-grade governor. His performance in battles around Suzhou, Changshu, Wuxi, and Changzhou earned him recognition, leading to the establishment of his ancestral hall in Wuxi.

The architecture of the Li Hezhang Hall adopts the "Four Rivers Return to the Hall" style from Li Hezhang's hometown in Anhui, featuring two cannons. The ancestral hall also boasts a historically significant river-facing shadow wall.

As an important element of Chinese architecture, shadow walls complement residential and courtyard structures, forming an inseparable whole. The intricately carved shadow walls possess substantial architectural and cultural significance, alongside considerable architectural and aesthetic value.

亭子为什么没有顶

没有顶的亭子您听说过吗？在惠山古镇上就有这样的亭子。古镇上的无顶亭其实说的是华孝子祠和顾洞阳祠中的四面牌坊。

这种四面牌坊并不是四块牌坊一字排开，做镇静威武状，而是亲密地围合成一个口字形。为什么围成口字形的牌坊会被人误以为是无顶亭呢？这是因为，一块牌坊的下部为左右两根柱子，往上还有层层的斗拱，顶部是一个翼角起翘的大屋顶。四块这样的牌坊围在一起，从任意一面的前方望过去，就像是有四根柱子、四个坡面的方形攒尖顶亭，只有进入这个"亭子"，才会发现，这里不像普通亭子一般设有美人靠等座栏，更主要的是，抬头就看到一方蓝天，自然产生"无顶之亭"的联想。也难怪民间会把四面牌坊称为"无顶亭"，这也是四面

牌坊的奇妙之处。

顾洞阳祠的四柱四面牌坊为明代最高级别的牌坊，底下为四根花岗岩柱，顶部为木质结构，顶部中心有一个方孔，寓意"上不封顶"。

朱宇辉博士赞誉"其建筑艺术价值可与徽州歙县许国石牌坊相辉映，在整个江南地区也不多见"。

华孝子祠的四面牌坊同为木石结构，藻饰精美，牌坊围合的正中央建有一个有青石雕花栏杆的水池，名叫"承雨池"，落雨天，檐间雨水就会汇聚到这个水池之中，表示"承接甘露"的意思。大家可能没想到，这里原来还是华家的"陈列室"。陈列什么呢？牌坊内的四面原先都挂着匾额，用来标榜华氏宗族中的科第成名之辈。明清时期，无锡华氏共出进士37名，其中榜眼2名。民间就流传着华氏宗族"未出状元，所以亭不结顶"的说法，只有出了状元，才能风风光光地结顶，画上圆满句号。当然，匾额现在早已没有了，不过，这样的坊间传说倒为这肃正的牌坊增添了一些趣味。

Why does the pavilion have no roof?

Have you heard of pavilions without roofs? In Huishan Ancient Town, there are indeed such structures. The so-called "roofless pavilions" refer to the four-sided archways found in the Hua Xiaozi Hall and the Gu Dongyang Halls.

These four-sided archways do not stand rigidly in a straight line like four blocks but are instead closely arranged in a square formation. So, why do these archways, arranged in a square, lead people to mistakenly perceive them as roofless pavilions? This is because each archway consists of two vertical columns at the bottom, topped with layers of dougong (bracket sets), culminating in a large roof that protrudes at the corners. When viewed from the front of any of these four archways, they naturally resemble a square pavilion with four columns and four sloping roofs. However, once you enter this "pavilion," you quickly notice that, unlike ordinary pavilions, it lacks features such as beautiful benches. Most importantly, when you look up, you see an expansive blue sky, which evokes the notion of a "roofless pavilion." It's no wonder that the local populace refers to these four-sided archways as "roofless pavilions." This is one of the intriguing aspects of these structures.

The four-column archway at the Gu Dongyang Hall represents the highest level of archway construction from the Ming Dynasty. It features four granite columns at the base and a wooden structure at the top, with a square hole in the center, symbolizing "an open top." Dr. Zhu Yuhui praises its architectural artistry, stating that it can be compared to the stone archways of Xu Guo Stone Archway in She County, Huizhou, and is quite rare throughout the Jiangnan region. The four-sided archway at the Huxiaozicai Hall is also built from wood and stone, adorned with exquisite decorations. At the center of the enclosed archway is a water pool with intricately carved balustrades made of blue stone, named "Chengyu Pool." During rainy days, water collects in this pool, symbolizing the reception of sweet dew. You may not have realized that this space once served as a "showroom" for the Hua family, showcasing the accomplishments of their notable members. In simpler terms, the four archways used to display plaques inscribed with the names and exam scores of descendants who excelled in the imperial examinations. During the Ming and Qing Dynasties, the Wuxi Hua family produced 37 successful candidates, including two second-place scholars. A popular saying among the locals goes, "No top scholar has emerged, so the pavilion remains unfinished." It implies that only when a top scholar is produced will the pavilion be completed, marking a glorious conclusion. Of course, the plaques are no longer there. Nevertheless, such local legends add an element of charm to these solemn archways.

第二篇 惠风祠话

回响在祠堂群里的世界名曲

AI语音导览

　　说到世界名曲，或许你首先想到的是贝多芬的《命运交响曲》，那激荡人心的旋律仿佛诉说着命运的跌宕起伏。那么，你是否知道中国也出了一首东方的"命运交响曲"？这首曲子就是著名的《二泉映月》，由中国传统乐器二胡奏来，如怨如慕，如泣如诉，深情地演绎着人生的酸甜苦辣。

　　这首被日本指挥家小泽征尔认为"此曲只应跪着听"的"命运交响曲"是无锡音乐家华彦钧一生坎坷命运的写照和对生命体验的拷问。

　　华彦钧，无锡人习惯称他为"瞎子阿炳"，阿炳并非天生眼盲，他是过了而立之年后才看不见的。早年的阿炳生活在道

"惠"游祠堂

观中,因为他的父亲是雷尊殿的观主,所以阿炳原先也是个小道士。那么小道士出身的阿炳为什么有如此高的音乐修养呢?这是因为道教在举行斋醮仪式时,都要演奏道教音乐,这个传统早在南北朝时期就有史料记载,之后无锡道教音乐经过不断发展,日益成熟,现已成为省级非遗项目了。随着时间的推移,演奏道教音乐的乐器也日益丰富,在早期的钟、磬等打击乐器基础上,逐步引入了吹管乐器、弓弦乐器和弹拨乐器等。演奏乐器的并不是外请的音乐班子,而是道观内的道士们,也就是说,道观内藏着很多民间音乐家。阿炳在这样的环境中成长,从小就对各种乐器和道教音乐耳濡目染,加之父亲严格的培养,阿炳不仅喜爱音乐,而且精通音乐。他十六七岁便学会了结构繁复、技法多变的梵音,吹、拉、弹、打、唱、念样样精通,并能正式参加道教音乐的演奏活动。

但是顺风顺水的生活在阿炳过了30岁之后发生了巨大的转变,他因为染上恶习而导致生活贫困,雪上加霜的是他的双目还因病失明了,最终只能街头卖艺,过着穷困潦倒的日子。贫盲交加,让他遍尝生活的苦楚,历尽人世的艰辛。这样的生活经历对于当事人来说,无疑是沉重的打击,然而,正是这种磨难,却无形中为音乐注入了深沉厚重的力量和源源不断的灵感。阿炳,在这样的生活背景下,积累了丰富而深刻的情感体验,他通过手中的二胡,将这些情感如实地倾诉出来,每一弓、每一弦都饱含着他的喜怒哀乐。《二泉映月》就这样诞生了。

现在苏教版五年级下册语文书中收录了一篇文章《二泉

映月》，里面说到，眼盲的阿炳经历了生活的颠沛流离，再次来到二泉的时候，听着耳畔淙淙流水声，想起了自己坎坷的经历，原先简单的流水声渐渐变作"深沉的叹息，伤心的哭泣，激愤的倾诉，倔强的呐喊"，于是阿炳拿起二胡，通过琴声把积淀已久的情怀倾吐给二泉的茫茫月夜。久而久之，就形成了后来的《二泉映月》。

这首曲子本来可能会随着阿炳生命的结束而消逝在无锡的街头巷尾，但是因为一个偶然的机会，这首曲子得遇春天，最终成为世界名曲。一天，在南京艺术学院的校园里，著名的音乐史学家杨荫浏教授听到了一阵让他心尖一颤、过耳难忘的乐音，他循声而去，看见一位学生正在投入地拉二胡，那乐音正从琴弦中倾泻而出，杨教授听得如痴如醉。这首乐曲正是《二泉映月》，当然拉二胡的人并非阿炳。那么，这个学生怎么也会演奏阿炳这首曲子呢？原来，这位学生名叫黎松寿，也是无锡人，更巧的是，他正好住在阿炳隔壁。因为从小酷爱二胡，被阿炳发掘，于是阿炳萌生怜才之心，经常倾囊相授。黎松寿也是因为这份机遇，长大后考上南京艺术学院，最终还成为南京师范大学音乐系的教授。这首曲子让杨教授无比激动，因为他当时受到中央音乐学院委托要对地方民乐进行抢救性保护，这样的乐曲无疑应该优先纳入保护范畴。就这样，杨教授为阿炳一共录制了六首曲子，分别是三首二胡曲《二泉映月》《听松》《寒春风曲》和三首琵琶曲《大浪淘沙》《龙船》《昭君出塞》。

不过那时的《二泉映月》还不叫"二泉映月"，事实上连

名字也没有。那后来怎么取名"二泉映月"了呢？这是因为阿炳经常在二泉附近拉这首曲子，于是，杨教授就以此为灵感，取名"二泉映月"。

不料，没过几个月，1950年12月，阿炳就因病去世，葬于无锡西郊璨山脚下"一和山房"道士墓地。1979年5月，墓遭破坏，于1983年迁葬惠山东篱、二泉之南现址。墓地面积742平方米，主体由幕墙和翼墙组成，状如音乐台；旧墓碑现藏市博物馆，新墓碑由中国音乐研究所、无锡市文联立，杨荫浏书。墓前立阿炳铜像，由钱绍武雕塑。墓东南，有一状如道士斜卧的天然石，惟妙惟肖，引人遐想。每年来墓地悼念阿炳的游客数以万计，络绎不绝。时常有人在墓旁演奏他的作品，如泣如诉，如怨如慕。

"二泉映月"已然是世界知名文化IP，音乐本就是惠山古镇的底色，如今，矗立在惠山映月里广场上的巨型赛博朋克风的阿炳雕塑，仿佛正向来来往往的游客诉说着作为中国民族音乐重要发源地的无锡"激活民乐之城，打造音乐之都"的新目标。

Echoes of World Renowned Music in the Ancestral Halls

When discussing world-renowned music, one might first think of Beethoven's *Symphony No. 5*, whose stirring melody seems to narrate the ebbs and flows of fate. However, are you aware that China also has its own "Symphony of Fate," known as *the Moon Reflected in the Second Spring*? This piece, performed on the traditional Chinese instrument the erhu, conveys emotions of longing and sorrow, eloquently portraying the bittersweet experiences of life.

This "Symphony of Fate," which Japanese conductor Seiji Ozawa said "should only be listened to on one's knees," is a reflection of Wuxi musician Hua Yanjun's rough life and his interrogation of life experience.

Hua Yanjun, referred to affectionately as "Blind A Bing" by the locals, did not inherit his blindness at birth; he lost his sight only after reaching adulthood. In his early years, A Bing lived in a Daoist temple, as his father was the temple's abbot, which meant he started life as a young Daoist. How did a young man of such a background develop remarkable musical talents? This is due to the tradition of performing Daoist music during religious rituals, a practice documented since the Southern and Northern Dynasties. Over time, Wuxi's Daoist music evolved into a mature art form and has now been recognized as an intangible cultural heritage at the provincial level. As the years passed, the instruments used in Daoist music diversified, expanding from percussion instruments like bells and stone chimes to include woodwinds, strings, and plucked instruments. The musicians were not hired professionals but the temple's Daoist priests, indicating that the temple was a sanctuary for many folk musicians. Growing up in such an environment, A Bing was immersed in various instruments and Daoist music from an early age. Coupled with his father's rigorous training, he not only developed a love for music but also mastered it. By the age of sixteen or seventeen, he had become proficient in cluster and varied Buddhist chants, mastering various instruments and participating in Daoist musical performances.

However, after turning thirty, A Bing's life took a dramatic turn. He fell into vice, leading to poverty, and tragically lost his sight due to illness.

He ultimately resorted to street performing, living a life of destitution. This dual hardship of poverty and blindness subjected him to immense suffering, yet it was precisely these trials that infused his music with profound depth and continuous inspiration. Against this backdrop, A Bing amassed rich and intense emotional experiences, which he conveyed through his erhu. Every stroke of the bow and every plucked string encapsulated his joys and sorrows. Thus, *the Moon Reflected in the Second Spring* was born.

Today, a textbook for fifth-grade students published by Jiangsu Education includes a lesson on *the Moon Reflected in the Second Spring*. It describes how the blind A Bing, having endured the tumult of life, returned to the Second Spring, listening to the soothing sounds of water. Reflecting on his tumultuous experiences, the simple sound of flowing water transformed into "deep sighs, sorrowful cries, impassioned confessions, and resolute shouts." A Bing then picked up his erhu and, spontaneously playing, poured forth his long-held emotions, which eventually evolved into the piece *the Moon Reflected in the Second Spring.*

This piece might have faded away along with A Bing's life, lost in the streets of Wuxi. Yet, by a stroke of luck, it blossomed into a world-renowned composition. One day, on the campus of Nanjing Arts Institute, the esteemed musicologist Professor Yang Yinliu was captivated by an unforgettable melody. Following the sound, he discovered a student immersed in playing the erhu; the music was flowing from the strings. Professor Yang was enthralled. The piece was *the Moon Reflected in the Second Spring*, though the player was not A Bing. How did this student from Nanjing Arts Institute come to play A Bing's unique composition? The student, named Li Songshou, was also from Wuxi and coincidentally lived next door to A Bing. Fascinated by the erhu from a young age, Li was discovered by A Bing, who recognized his talent and often mentored him. This opportunity allowed Li to pursue his studies at Nanjing Arts Institute and later become a professor in the music department at Nanjing Normal University. Professor Yang was profoundly moved by the piece, as he had been commissioned by the Central Conservatory of Music to undertake the urgent protection of local folk music; clearly, this composition warranted prioritization for preservation. Subsequently, he recorded six pieces from A Bing: three erhu compositions, *the Moon Reflected in the Second Spring*, *Tingsong*, and *Han Chun Feng Qu*, as well as three pipa pieces, *Da Lang Tao Sha*, *Long Chuan*, and *Zhao Jun Chu Sai*.

At that time, *the Moon Reflected in the Second Spring* did not yet bear its title, as it had no name at all. The title was inspired by A Bing's frequent performances near the Second Spring, leading Professor Yang to name it *the Moon Reflected in the Second Spring*.

However, just a few months later, in December 1950, A Bing passed away due to illness and was buried in the Daoist cemetery at the foot of Can Mountain in Wuxi. In May 1979, his grave was vandalized, and the remains reburied in 1983 at the current site south of the Second Spring. The burial area covers 742 square meters, with a main structure consisting of a wall and side walls resembling a music platform. The original gravestone is housed in the municipal museum, while a new gravestone was erected by the Chinese Music Research Institute and the Wuxi Federation of Literary and Art Circles, inscribed by Yang Yinliu. In front of the grave stands a bronze statue of A Bing sculpted by Qian Shaowu. To the southeast of the grave is a natural stone that resembles a Daoist lying down, evoking imagination. Each year, tens of thousands of visitors come to pay their respects to A Bing, often performing his works nearby, echoing with emotion and longing.

"*the Moon Reflected in the Second Spring*" has already become a world-renowned cultural IP. Music has always been the essence of Huishan Ancient Town. Today, the massive cyberpunk-style statue of Abing standing in Huishan Yingyue Square seems to be telling the coming and going tourists about Wuxi's new goal as an important birthplace of Chinese ethnic music: "Revitalizing the City of Folk Music and Building a City of Music."

第二篇"惠风祠话"图片来源：惠山古镇、陈鸣谦、肖慧、金石声、邵映红、刘楠、上海冷空气、松花江、浅笑、Abby、小宇、潘攀

第三篇 诗画梁溪

本篇邀请您一起欣赏关于无锡、惠山以及祠堂的诗词,穿越时空的隧道,跟随古人的足迹,聆听他们的低吟浅唱,让我们一同沉浸在这诗与画的世界里,品味时光的韵味,感受岁月的沧桑。

无锡篇

无锡县历山集

南北朝·江淹❶

愁生白露❷日，怨起秋风年。
窃悲杜蘅❸暮，揽涕❹吊空山❺。
落叶下楚水❻，别鹤噪吴田。
瘴气❼阴不极❽，日色❾半亏天。
酒至情萧瑟❿，凭樽还惘然⓫。
一闻清琴⓬奏，歔泣⓭方留连。
况乃⓮客子⓯念，直视⓰丝竹⓱间。

❶ 江淹（444—505），字文通，宋州济阳考城（今河南省商丘市民权县）人，南朝著名文学家、散文家，历仕三朝。传世名篇有《恨赋》《别赋》，今存《江文通集》辑本。
❷ 白露：秋天的露水。
❸ 杜蘅：即杜若，多年生草本植物，花紫色，根状茎可入药。文学作品中常用以比喻君子、贤人。
❹ 揽涕：挥泪。
❺ 空山：幽深少人的山林。
❻ 楚水：兴化的别称，相传春秋时兴化属吴，战国时属楚，为楚将昭阳的食邑，也泛指古楚地的江河湖泽。
❼ 瘴气：山林间因湿热蒸郁而成的毒气，这里指山中的雾气。一作"岚气"。
❽ 不极：无穷，无限。
❾ 日色：指阳光，也借指时间。
❿ 萧瑟：凋零，冷落，凄凉。
⓫ 惘然：失意貌，忧思貌，迷糊不清貌。
⓬ 清琴：音调清雅的琴。
⓭ 歔（xū）泣：叹息哭泣。
⓮ 况乃：何况，况且。
⓯ 客子：离家在外的人。
⓰ 直视：一作"直置"。
⓱ 丝竹：弦乐器与竹管乐器总称，也泛指音乐。

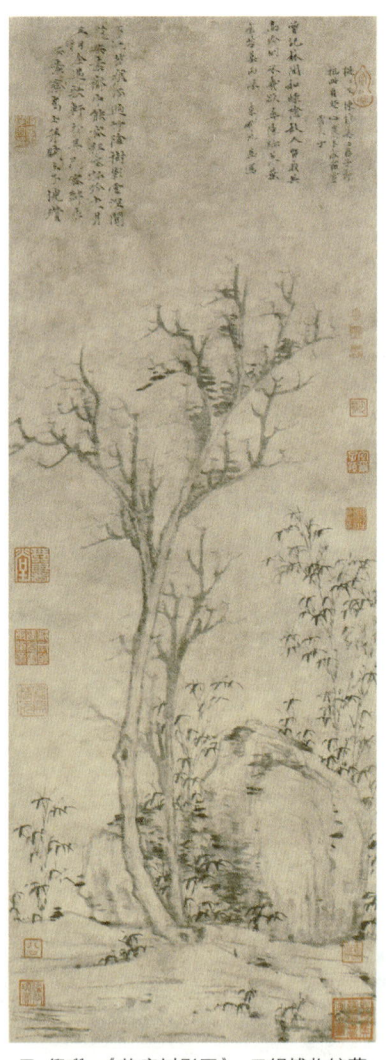

元 倪瓒 《苔痕树影图》 无锡博物馆藏

悯农❶二首·其二
唐·李绅❷

锄禾日当午，汗滴禾下土。
谁知盘中餐，粒粒皆辛苦。

❶ 一作"古风"。此诗作于何时何地历来有多种说法。其中一说为李绅惠山读书时，见烈日之下老伯艰辛耕作，联想起书中关于大灾之年，饿殍遍野的记载有感而发所作。李绅曾在惠山寺读书十几年，几次科举失利和官场受挫后，他都回到惠山，闭门苦读。元代王仁辅《无锡县志》载，惠山曾有李绅读书遗迹"李相书堂"。

❷ 李绅（772—846），字公垂，亳州（今属安徽）人，生于乌程（今浙江湖州），长于润州无锡（今属江苏），唐代著名诗人。元和元年（806年）进士，历任御史中丞、户部侍郎、滁州刺史、河南尹、宣武节度使等。武宗时得到重用，先拜相，后出任淮南节度使。会昌六年（846年）病卒。

别无锡南禅莲老
宋·曹勋❶

仆❷昔困众难，老来始一欣。
得履方外❸趣，不涉券❹内闻。
留锡憩福境，禅悦志所勤。
日款❺乡关❻旧，俱叹鸿鹄分。
偶同一窗雨，永怀九仙❼云。
好持洞下香，法界❽期普薰。

❶ 曹勋（1098？—1174），字公显，一作功显，号松隐，阳翟（今河南禹州）人。宋代文学家、词人、大臣，曾出使金国。遗著由子曹耜辑为《松隐集》，《宋史·艺文志》著录为四十卷。
❷ 仆：旧时男子谦称，指自己。
❸ 方外：尘世之外。
❹ 券：同"倦"，疲累。
❺ 款：缓慢。
❻ 乡关：家乡，故乡。
❼ 九仙：泛指众仙。
❽ 法界：佛教用语，意指众生所在的境界。

青山寺❶

宋·尤袤❷

峥嵘楼阁插天开，门外湖山翠作堆。
荡漾烟波迷泽国，空蒙云气认蓬莱。
香销龙象辉金碧，雨过麒麟剥翠苔。
二十九年❸三到此，一生知有几回来。

❶ 青山寺：古代无锡有两个青山寺，一是惠山南产山北的青山寺，另一是梅园西十八湾的华藏寺。清光绪《无锡金匮县志》："华藏禅寺在县西三十五里。华藏山亦名青山寺。"诗中有"烟波迷泽国，云气认蓬莱"，惠山南青山寺无此景，皆为华藏寺原青山寺所见。尤袤写《青山寺》同时作《云海亭》诗：亭前山色绕危栏，亭下波涛直浸山。波上渔舟亭上客，相看浑在画图间。诗中言太湖之水直浸山下，则成《青山寺》为今华藏寺注脚。

❷ 尤袤（1127—1194），字延之，小字季长，号遂初居士，晚号乐溪、木石老逸民，常州无锡（今江苏省无锡市）人，南宋著名诗人。绍兴十八年（1148年）进士，官至礼部尚书兼侍读。尤袤与杨万里、范成大、陆游并称为"南宋四大诗人"。原有《梁溪集》五十卷，早佚。清人尤侗辑有《梁溪遗稿》两卷，刊行于时。

❸ 二十九年：应为尤袤时为29岁，即绍兴二十五年（1155）。

元 倪瓒 《秋亭嘉树图》 北京故宫博物院藏

无锡县春日
宋·高翥❶

吴楚❷新岐路❸，江湖旧散人❹。
放船❺来古县，沽酒❻供闲身❼。
花卸一村雨，鸟啼千树春。
野塘❽风卷地，无复❾见芳尘❿。

❶ 高翥（1170—1241），初名公弼，后改名翥，字九万，号菊磵，余姚（今属浙江）人。游荡江湖，布衣终身，是江南诗派中的重要人物，有"江湖游士"之称。晚年居西湖，有《菊磵集》二十卷，已佚。
❷ 吴楚：泛指春秋吴楚之故地，即今长江中下游一带。
❸ 岐路：由大道分岔出去的小路。
❹ 散人：不为世用的人，闲散自在的人。诗人自称是江湖闲散之人。
❺ 放船：开船，行船。
❻ 沽酒：从市上买来的酒，买酒。
❼ 闲身：古代指没有官职的人。
❽ 野塘：野外的池塘或湖泊。
❾ 无复：不再。
❿ 芳尘：指落花。

无锡❶
宋·文天祥❷

金山❸冉冉❹波涛雨，锡水泯泯❺草木春。
二十年前曾去路，三千里外作行人。
英雄未死心为碎，父老相逢鼻欲辛。
夜读程婴存赵❻事，一回惆怅一沾巾。

❶ 德祐二年（1276年），文天祥被派往元营中谈判，遭元军扣留，并沿大运河押解北上，路过无锡，泊于黄埠墩。文天祥回想多年前和弟弟文璧一起赴京城廷对，也曾经过这里。时事迁易，他"感今怀昔，悲不自胜"，写下了这首名篇。
❷ 文天祥（1236—1283），初名云孙，字宋瑞，又字履善，自号文山、浮休道人。吉州庐陵（今江西吉安县）人，南宋政治家、文学家、抗元英雄。宝祐四年（1256年）进士，官至右丞相兼枢密使。
❸ 金山：这里指黄埠墩，黄埠墩旧名小金山。
❹ 冉冉：形容迷离的样子。
❺ 泯泯：形容水的清澈。
❻ 程婴存赵：春秋时，晋国义士程婴为保全赵氏孤儿，将自己的儿子交出，将赵氏孤儿养大，终于报得家仇。

朗诵　无锡

夜泊伯渎[1]
元·赵孟頫[2]

秋满梁溪伯渎川,尽人游处独悠然。
平墟[3]境里寻吴事,梅里河边载酒船。
桥畔柳摇灯影乱,河心波漾月光悬。
晓来莫遣催归棹[4],爱听渔歌处处传。

[1] 伯渎:即伯渎河,原名泰伯渎,商朝末年,泰伯在梅里建立勾吴国后,为了灌溉、排洪,开凿的中国历史上第一条人工河流,已有3200年历史。

[2] 赵孟頫(1254—1322),字子昂,号松雪、松雪道人,又号水精宫道人、鸥波,中年曾作孟俯,吴兴(今浙江湖州)人。元代著名书画家,楷书四大家之一。赵孟頫博学多才,能诗善文,懂经济,工书法,精绘艺,擅金石,通律吕,解鉴赏。特别是书法和绘画成就最高,开创元代新画风,被称为"元人冠冕"。他也善篆、隶、真、行、草书,尤以楷、行书著称于世。

[3] 平墟:古地名,在今无锡梅里古镇。梅里是商末周初吴国之都。东汉《吴越春秋》记载:"泰伯祖卒葬于梅里平墟",唐《史记正义》也有记载:"泰伯居梅里平墟,在无锡东南三十里是也"。

[4] 棹:船桨。

太湖
明·文徵明[1]

岛屿纵横一镜中,湿银[2]盘紫[3]浸芙蓉。
谁能胸贮三万顷,我欲身游七十峰。
天远洪涛翻日月,春寒泽国隐鱼龙[4]。
中流仿佛闻鸡犬,何处堪追范蠡[5]踪。

[1] 文徵明(1470—1559),原名壁,字徵明。长洲(今江苏苏州)人。因先世为衡山人,故号衡山居士,世称"文衡山"。文徵明的书画造诣极为全面,诗、文、书、画无一不精,人称"四绝"全才。在诗文上,与祝允明、唐寅、徐祯卿并称"吴中四才子"。在画史上,与沈周、唐寅、仇英合称"吴门四家"。

[2] 湿银:指月下水波。

[3] 盘紫:是对万紫千红的湖岸的形象描绘。

[4] 鱼龙:泛指水族生物。

[5] 范蠡:春秋末期越国大夫,是中国历史上著名的政治家、军事家、谋略家、经济学家,被史学界称为治国良臣、兵家奇才、经营之神,商家鼻祖,被中国民间供奉为"文财神"。相传,在帮助越王勾践灭吴雪耻后,范蠡认为勾践"可与同患,难于处安",因此弃官而去,变名易姓,携西施隐居太湖一带

朗诵 太湖

和韵
明·王问①

莲蓉湖上锡城东，旧是先生讲学宫②。
性善已闻推孟子，道明端为阐中庸。
春生绛帷③横经④坐，寒压桥门⑤立雪⑥从。
遗址久芜今复振，令人千载仰高风。

① 王问（1497—1576），字子裕，人称仲山先生，常州府无锡（今江苏无锡）人，明代画家。嘉靖十七年（1538年）进士，历任户部主事、车驾司郎中、广东按察佥事。后弃官归乡，长期隐居于湖滨宝界山。工诗文，能书法，山水画近南宋院体，别具面貌，亦擅人物、花鸟。

② 讲学宫：指东林书院，位于江苏省无锡市梁溪区，又称"龟山书院"，由杨时创建于北宋政和元年（1111年），后废弃。明万历三十二年（1604年），顾宪成等人重建书院并在此讲学。

③ 绛帷：红色帷幕，喻指授业师长或授课处所，是对师门、讲席之敬称。

④ 横经：横陈经籍，指受业或读书。

⑤ 桥门：古代太学周围环水，设有四门，以桥相通，因此得名"桥门"。此处指代就学之所。

⑥ 立雪：出自《宋史·道学传二·杨时》程门立雪的典故："杨时见程颐于洛。时盖年四十矣。一日见颐，颐偶瞑坐，时与游酢侍立不去。颐既觉，则门外雪深一尺矣。"指学生恭敬求教，比喻尊师重教、虔诚求学。

鼋头渚游眺同蒋文学王茂才
明·孙继皋①

渚②势欲吞湖，湖流归旧吴。
天浮一鼋出，山挟万龙趋。
浪急悬厓③动，风颠系艇孤。
持竿堪此地，渔钓本吾徒④。

① 孙继皋（1550—1610），字以德，号柏潭，常州府无锡县（今江苏省无锡市）人，万历二年（1574年）进士第一（状元）。官至吏部侍郎，晚年讲学于东林书院。有《宗伯集》《柏潭集》。

② 渚：水中小块陆地，此处指鼋头渚。鼋头渚为太湖西北岸无锡境内的一个半岛，因有巨石突入湖中，状如浮鼋翘首而得名，是太湖风景名胜区的主景点之一。鼋头渚现为国家5A级景区，有充山隐秀、鹿顶迎晖、鼋渚春涛、万浪卷雪、湖山真意、十里芳径、太湖仙岛、江南兰苑及中犊晨雾、广福古寺、樱花谷等10余处景点。

③ 悬厓（yá）：厓，同"崖"。悬厓，即悬崖。

④ 吾徒：我辈。

"惠"游祠堂

水居❶

明·高攀龙❷

到此情偏适，安居兴日新。
闲来观物妙，静后见人亲。
啼鸟当清昼，飞花❸正莒春。
呼童数新笋，好护碧窗筠❹。

❶ 水居：明万历二十六年（1598年），辞官归乡的高攀龙在蠡湖边的鱼池头水中构筑一处居室，名为水居，作为隐居读书之所。其中又有一座小楼，四面开窗，可以望山，可以观水，可以清风送爽，可以阳光普照，可以明月作伴，因而高攀龙题名为"可楼"，并作《可楼记》。后，水居被毁。如今，当地在金城湾建高子水居，融入环蠡湖风景区。
❷ 高攀龙（1562—1626），字存之，又字云从，江苏无锡人，世称"景逸先生"。明代政治家、思想家、东林党领袖，"东林八君子"之一。著有《高子遗书》12卷等。万历十七年（1589年）中进士。后遇父丧归家守孝。天启六年（1626年）三月，高攀龙不堪屈辱，投水自尽，时年六十四岁。崇祯初年（1628年），朝廷为高攀龙平反，赠太子太保、兵部尚书，谥"忠宪"。
❸ 飞花：飘飞的落花。
❹ 筠：竹皮，借指竹子。

元 倪瓒 《水竹居图》 中国国家博物馆藏

梦江南·其五
清·纳兰性德❶

江南好,真个❷到梁溪。
一幅云林❸高士画,
数行泉石故人❹题。
还似梦游非。

❶ 纳兰性德(1655—1685),叶赫那拉氏,字容若,号楞伽山人,清代著名词人。原名成德,避讳太子保成,改名性德,满洲正黄旗人。清康熙十五年(1676年)进士,官三等侍卫,随康熙出巡南北。纳兰性德工文章,善骑射,词作尤被时人称道。他主张作诗须有才学,填词须有比兴,反对模仿。其词委婉传情,凄恻动人,也有慷慨雄浑之作,王国维赞谓"北宋以来,一人而已"。著有《通志堂集》。
❷ 真个:的确,果真。
❸ 云林:元代画家倪瓒,字元镇,号云林子,善绘山水。
❹ 故人:泛指友人,性德友人多为江浙名士。此处写性德在无锡见到的多处风景都有故人的题咏。

元 倪瓒 《梧竹秀石图》 北京故宫博物院藏

"惠"游祠堂

惠山篇

过历山湛长史❶草堂❷
南朝·刘铄❸

兹岳蕴虚诡,凭览❹趣亦赡。

九峰相接连,五渚❺逆萦❻浸。

层阿❼疲且引❽,绝岩❾畅方禁。

溜❿众夏更寒,林交昼常荫。

伊余⓫久缁涅⓬,复得味恬淡。

愿遂安期生⓭,于焉惬高枕。

---

❶ 湛长史:湛挺(生卒年不详),字茂之,南朝时期刘宋人,诗人,官任司徒右长史。后隐居在无锡的惠山,筑草堂在里面读书,与南平王刘铄友善,更以诗章唱酬留刻于石。

❷ 草堂:《无锡金匮县志·卷三十二·艺文》记载,唐人邱丹曾言:"无锡县西郊五里,有惠山寺,即宋司徒右长史湛茂之之别墅也,旧名历山。故南平王刘铄有《过湛长史历山草堂》诗,湛有酬和。"湛长史所建历山草堂即是惠山寺前身。

❸ 刘铄(431—453),南朝宋宗室。彭城人,字休玄。宋文帝第四子。九岁封南平王,后为豫州刺史。刘劭杀宋文帝,以为中军将军。柳元景军至,劭挟铄同战。及平,宋孝武帝迎铄入军营。毒杀之。谥穆。

❹ 凭览:登高远望。

❺ 五渚:五湖,即太湖。

❻ 萦:缠绕,环绕。

❼ 层阿:重叠的或高耸的山冈。

❽ 引:伸长,延长。

❾ 绝岩:指极其陡峭的山崖。

❿ 溜:水流。

⓫ 伊余:自称,指我。

⓬ 缁涅:比喻身处浊世而不污。

⓭ 安期生:秦代齐地琅琊人,传说他曾从河上丈人习黄帝、老子之说,卖药东海边,人称"千岁翁"。后之方士、道家因谓其为居海上之神仙。事见《史记·乐毅列传》、汉刘向《列仙传》等。

送陆鸿渐山人❶采茶回

唐·皇甫曾❷

千峰待逋客❸,香茗复丛生。
采摘知深处,烟霞羡独行。
幽期山寺远,野饭石泉清。
寂寂燃灯夜,相思一磬声。

❶ 陆鸿渐山人:陆羽(733—约804),名疾,字鸿渐,又字季疵,自号竟陵子,复州竟陵(今湖北天门)人。工诗,嗜茶,创煎茶法,著《茶经》三卷,旧时称为茶神、茶圣、茶仙。
❷ 皇甫曾(?—785),字孝常,润州丹阳(今属江苏)人,唐代诗人。天宝十二年(753年)登进士第,历官侍御史、舒州司马、阳翟令等。皇甫曾工于诗,与兄冉齐名。
❸ 逋客:逃亡的人,后指避世的隐者。

重到惠山

唐·李绅

再到石泉寺内,有禅师鉴玄影堂,在寺南峰下。顷年与此僧同在惠山十年,鉴玄在寿春相访,因追旧欢。

碧峰依旧松筠❶老,重得经过已白头。
俱是海天❷黄叶信,两逢霜节菊花秋。
望中❸白鹤怜归翼,行处青苔恨昔游。
还向窗间名姓下,数行添记别离愁。

❶ 松筠:指松与竹。
❷ 海天:形容浩渺无垠的空间。
❸ 望中:视野之中。

朗诵 重到惠山

元 倪瓒 《容膝斋图》 台北故宫博物院藏

题惠山泉·其一
唐·皮日休❶

丞相❷长思煮泉时，郡侯❸催发只忧迟。
吴关❹去国❺三千里，莫笑杨妃❻爱荔枝。

---

❶ 皮日休（约838—约883），字袭美，一字逸少，曾居住在鹿门山，自号鹿门子，又号间气布衣、醉吟先生。复州竟陵（今湖北天门）人，晚唐文学家、散文家，与陆龟蒙齐名，世称"皮陆"。咸通八年（867年）进士及第，在唐时历任苏州刺史从事、著作局校书郎、太常博士、毗陵副使。后参加黄巢起义，或言"陷巢贼中"（《唐才子传》），任翰林学士，起义失败后不知所踪。诗文兼有奇朴二态，且多为同情民间疾苦之作。
❷ 丞相：指李德裕，唐武宗时宰相。他为了用惠山泉水煮茶，命令地方官吏从三千里外的江苏无锡惠山把泉水送到京城里来。
❸ 郡侯：指常州刺史，当时无锡隶属常州。当地刺史为了及时地将惠泉运达长安，必须催促驿使赶快启程，只担心耽搁了时间。
❹ 吴关：指昭关，在安徽境内，春秋战国时作为吴、楚分界。诗中泛指吴地。
❺ 去国：去，距离。国，指当时京城长安。
❻ 杨妃：杨贵妃，唐玄宗李隆基宠妃，名玉环。因她爱吃鲜荔枝，朝廷让驿使从岭南飞速运往长安。其奢侈生活劳民伤财，广受谴责。

惠山谒钱道人烹小龙团登绝顶望太湖
宋·苏轼❶

踏遍江南南岸山，逢山未免更留连。
独携天上小团月❷，来试人间第二泉。
石路萦回九龙❸脊，水光翻动五湖❹天。
孙登无语❺空归去，半岭松声❻万壑传。

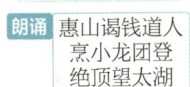

❶ 苏轼（1037—1101），字子瞻，号"东坡居士"，世称"苏东坡"，眉山（今四川眉山）人。宋嘉祐二年（1057年）中进士，历任于杭州、徐州、湖州等地，之后屡遭贬谪，宋徽宗时获大赦北还，途中于常州病逝。苏轼博学多才，诗文书画皆精，对后世有很大的影响，是有宋一代的天才文人。其诗清新豪健，个性鲜明，与黄庭坚并称"苏黄"；其词开豪放之风，与辛弃疾并称"苏辛"；其文晓畅明达，意趣横生，与欧阳修并称"欧苏"，为"唐宋八大家"之一；其书丰腴跌宕，天真烂漫，与黄庭坚、米芾、蔡襄并称"宋四家"；其画风格独异，写意不羁。有《东坡七集》和《东坡乐府》等传世。

❷ 小团月：即小龙团茶，又叫龙凤团茶，是宋代贡茶。宋代时饮茶之风盛行，茶叶多做成团饼状。北宋王辟之《渑水燕谈录》："建茶盛于江南，近岁制作尤精，龙、凤团茶最为上品，一斤八饼。庆历中，蔡君谟为福陆运使，始造小团以充岁贡，一斤二十饼，所谓上品龙茶者也。仁宗尤所珍惜，虽宰臣未尝辄赐，惟郊礼致斋之夕，两府各四人，共赐一饼。宫人剪金为龙、凤花，贴其上，八人分蓄之，以为奇玩，不敢自试，有嘉客，出而传玩。欧阳文忠公云：'茶为物之至精，而小团又其精者也。'"此是苏轼双关之语，以团茶喻圆月。

❸ 九龙：惠山，又称西神山、历山、九龙山、龙山、华山。据《蠡溪笔记》所载：晋西域僧慧照来此主持，名声远播，遂名慧山（"慧""惠"相通）。相传舜帝曾躬耕于此山。山有九陇，俗谓九龙山。

❹ 五湖：此处指太湖，其名古称震泽、笠泽、具区等，又称五湖。《国语·越语下》韦昭注："五湖，今太湖。"《文选·江赋》李善注引张勃《吴录》："五湖者，太湖之别名也。"

❺ 孙登无语：《三国志·魏书·王粲传》："南朝宋·裴松之注引晋·孙盛〈晋阳秋〉：'康见孙登，登对之长啸，逾时不言。'康辞还，曰：'先生竟无言乎？'登曰：'惜哉'！"《晋书·阮籍列传》："至半岭，闻有声若鸾凤之音，响乎岩谷，乃登之啸也。"

❻ 松声：松涛声。

焦千之[1]求惠山泉诗
宋·苏轼

兹山[2]定空中,乳水满其腹。
遇隙[3]则发见[4],臭味实一族[5]。
　浅深各有值,方圆随所蓄。
　或为云汹涌,或作线断续。
　或鸣空洞中,杂佩[6]间琴筑[7]。
　或流苍石缝,宛转龙鸾[8]蹙[9]。
　瓶罂[10]走四海,真伪半相渎[11]。
　贵人高宴[12]罢,醉眼乱红绿。
　赤泥[13]开方印,紫饼[14]截圆玉[15]。
　倾瓯[16]共叹赏,窃语笑僮仆。
　岂如泉上僧,盥洒自挹掬[17]。
　故人怜我病,蒻笼[18]寄新馥。
　欠伸北窗下,昼睡美方熟。
　精品厌凡泉,愿子致一斛[19]。

元 倪瓒 《江亭山色图》 台北故宫博物院藏

[1] 焦千之:字伯强,时任无锡县令。
[2] 兹山:这座山,诗中指惠山。
[3] 遇隙:逮着间隙,遇见间隙处。
[4] 发见:亦作"发现",显现,出现。
[5] 一族:一个宗族、家族。
[6] 杂佩:亦作"杂珮",总称连缀在一起的各种佩玉。
[7] 琴筑:琴和筑,皆为古琴。
[8] 龙鸾:龙与凤。
[9] 蹙:皱,收缩。
[10] 瓶罂:泛指小口大腹的陶瓷容器。
[11] 渎:水沟,小渠。
[12] 高宴:盛大的宴会。
[13] 赤泥:封口所用的红色泥土。
[14] 紫饼:茶名,指团茶茶饼。
[15] 圆玉:似圆形碧玉的茶饼。
[16] 倾瓯:指将茶汤全部喝下。
[17] 挹掬:捧取。
[18] 蒻笼:用蒲草编成的笼子。蔡襄《茶录》:"茶不入焙者,宜密封裹,以蒻笼盛之,置高处,不近湿气。"
[19] 斛(hú):容量单位,旧时,十升等于一斗,十斗即一百升,等于一斛。

游惠山（并叙）·其一[1]

宋·苏轼

梦里五年过，觉来双鬓苍。
还将尘土足，一步漪澜堂[2]。
俯窥松桂影，仰见鸿鹤翔。
炯然[3]肝肺间，已作冰玉光。
虚明[4]中有色，清净自生香。
还徒世俗去，永与世俗忘。

[1] 本诗作于宋元丰二年（1079年），这年苏轼乘船至无锡，游惠山。
[2] 漪澜堂：位于天下第二泉庭院，始建于宋代，现存为清代重建的敞轩，歇山顶。
[3] 炯然：明亮的样子。
[4] 虚明：空明，清澈明亮。

谢黄从善司业[1]寄惠山泉

宋·黄庭坚[2]

锡谷寒泉椭[3]石俱，并得新诗虿尾[4]书。
急呼烹鼎供茗事，晴江急雨看跳珠[5]。
是功与世涤膻腴[6]，令我屡空[7]常晏如[8]。
安得左轓[9]清颍尾[10]，风炉[11]煮茗卧西湖。

[1] 黄从善司业：黄隐，原名降，字从善，福建莆田人。宋治平四年（1067年）进士，先后担任过国子监司业和殿中侍御史。黄隐与黄庭坚交厚。著有《黄从善集》四卷。
[2] 黄庭坚（1045—1105），字鲁直，号山谷道人，晚号涪翁，洪州分宁（今江西省九江市修水县）人，北宋著名文学家、书法家，为盛极一时的江西诗派开山之祖，与杜甫、陈师道和陈与义素有"一祖三宗"（黄为其中一宗）之称。与张耒、晁补之、秦观都游学于苏轼门下，合称为"苏门四学士"。生前与苏轼齐名，世称"苏黄"，著有《山谷词》。黄庭坚书法独树一帜，为"宋四家"之一。
[3] 椭（tuǒ）：小而狭长。

[4] 虿（chài）尾：虿尾，蝎子的尾巴。形容书法笔画劲挺，遒劲有力，好像蝎子尾巴。
[5] 跳珠：喻指溅起来的水珠或雨点。
[6] 膻腴：肥美的羊肉，这里指油脂肥腻。
[7] 屡空：一无所有，空乏的样子。
[8] 晏如：悠闲安适的样子。
[9] 左轓（fān）：古代车厢两旁反出如耳的部分，用以障蔽尘泥。汉时以朱色涂障蔽来表示官阶，凡俸禄在六百至一千石者都以朱涂左轓。
[10] 颍尾：即颍口。指今安徽省颍上县东南、颍水入淮之处。此地土壤肥沃，物产丰饶，旧时即为繁华之地。宋代诗人张耒赞叹："美哉洋洋清颍尾，西通天邑无千里。舸舠大舩起危樯，淮颍耕田岁收米。"
[11] 风炉：一种炉灶，旁边附有风箱，拉动时可以鼓风使火更旺。

"惠"游祠堂

同子瞻赋游惠山三首·其一
宋·秦观[1]

辍棹[2]纵幽讨[3]，篮舆[4]入青苍[5]。
圆顶相邀迓[6]，旃檀[7]燎深堂。
层峦淡如洗，杰阁[8]森欲翔。
林芳[9]含雨滋，岫日[10]隔林光。
涓涓续清溜[11]，靡靡传幽香。
俯仰佳览眺，悠哉身世忘。

泊舟无锡雨止遂游惠山
宋·杨万里[1]

天教老子[2]不空回，船泊山根雨顿开。
归去江西人问我，也曾一到惠山来。

---

[1] 秦观（1049—1100），字太虚，又字少游，别号邗沟居士，世称淮海先生，高邮（今江苏省高邮市）人，北宋词人。元丰八年（1085年）进士，官至太学博士、国史馆编修。秦观一生坎坷，所写诗词，高古沉重，寄托身世，感人至深。秦观墓位于无锡惠山二茅峰南坡，原建于其故乡高邮，南宋绍兴初，其子秦湛任常州通判时，将棺柩自高邮迁葬于无锡。清嘉庆年间，其远孙秦瀛于墓前重立青石墓碑，上刻"秦龙图墓"。惠山秦观墓至今已有900多年历史。

[2] 辍棹：辍，表示中途停止。辍棹，指的是放下舟楫。

[3] 幽讨：寻访幽隐的地方。

[4] 篮舆：古代供人乘坐的交通工具，形制不一，一般以人力抬着行走，类似后世的轿子。

[5] 青苍：借指山林。

[6] 邀迓：邀请，迎请。

[7] 旃檀：即檀香。

[8] 杰阁：高阁。

[9] 林芳：林中的花。

[10] 岫日：岫，其本义是山穴或山洞，岫日指山中的阳光。

[11] 清溜：指水流清澈顺滑。

[1] 杨万里（1127—1206），字廷秀，号诚斋，吉州吉水（今江西省吉水县）人。南宋著名诗人、大臣，与陆游、尤袤、范成大并称为"中兴四大诗人"。因宋光宗曾为其亲书"诚斋"二字，故学者称其为"诚斋先生"。杨万里一生作诗20000多首，传世作品有4200首，被誉为一代诗宗。他创造了语言浅近明白、清新自然，富有幽默情趣的"诚斋体"。杨万里的诗歌大多描写自然景物，且以此见长。他也有不少反映民间疾苦、抒发爱国感情的作品。著有《诚斋集》等。

[2] 老子："老夫"的自称。

惠山云开复合

宋·杨万里

二年常州不识山，惠山一见开心颜。
只嫌雨里不子细❶，仿佛隔帘青玉鬟。
天风忽吹白云坼❷，翡翠屏开倚南极❸。
政缘❹一雨染山色，未必雨前如此碧。
看山未了云复还，云与诗人偏作难。
我船自向苏州去，白云稳向山头住。

❶子细：谨慎，小心。
❷坼（chè）：指裂开，分裂。
❸南极：南方极远之地。
❹政缘：政，通"正"，正好，恰好。缘，因为。

雪后陪使客游惠山，寄怀尤延之❶

宋·杨万里

已到苏州未到常，惠山孤秀蔚苍苍。
一峰飞下如奔马，万木深围古道场❷。
锡骨中空都是乳❸，玉泉致远久偏香。
眠云❹跂石❺梁溪叟，恨杀风烟隔草堂。

❶尤延之：尤袤，字延之，与杨万里、范成大、陆游并称为"南宋四大诗人"。
❷道场：修炼的场所。
❸乳：乳泉，甘美而清洌的泉水。
❹眠云：比喻山居。
❺跂石：指垂足而坐于石上。

陆子泉[1]
明·秦璠[2]

达人[3]不作千年计，志士长怀万物情。
陆子自能耽此水，二泉吾得濯其清。
明明夜月亭间竹，日日秋风谷底铛[4]。
头白[5]一瓢知冷暖，抱琴高卧听松声。

[1] 陆子泉：即天下第二泉，因唐代陆羽品评天下泉水，以无锡惠山泉为第二始名，故又名陆子泉。
[2] 秦璠（1428—1493），字景美，号东皋，明代无锡人。著有《东皋集》。
[3] 达人：通达事理的人。
[4] 铛（chēng）：泛指金属制作的物品。
[5] 头白：指年老的时候。

题碧山吟社[1]图
明·吴宽[2]

诗坛高筑壬寅[3]岁，胜事遥传大历[4]年。
买地有资酬野衲[5]，品泉无谱问茶仙。
树藏亭子清风里，路绕云根小洞边。
赓[6]和愿随诸老后，结盟迟我赋归田。

[1] 碧山吟社：位于天下第二泉之南，垂虹廊终点处，春申涧以北。吟社始建于明成化十八年（1482年），由秦旭等无锡十位诗坛耆英结庐龙缝泉侧，构十老堂、捻须亭、濯缨亭、流馨亭、借山亭，凿涵碧池，开芙蓉径，辟古木坡。诗酒唱和，吊古怀今，觞咏其中。名家沈周绘《碧山吟社图》，吴门状元吴宽吟诗致贺，邵宝等名宦题跋。1959年，无锡市人民政府修复碧山吟社景点。
[2] 吴宽（1435—1504），字原博，号匏庵、玉亭主，世称匏庵先生或匏翁，直隶长洲县（今江苏省苏州市）人，因后谥"文定"，后世称为吴文定。成化八年（1472年）状元，官至礼部尚书。明代著名诗人、散文家、书法家。有《匏庵集》。
[3] 壬寅：指碧山吟社始建于明成化十八年（1482年），天干地支纪年法为壬寅年。
[4] 大历：唐代宗李豫的年号。大历年间，文学上出现了"大历十才子"这一诗歌流派。吴宽将碧山吟社十位成员，比作"大历十才子"。
[5] 野衲：山野中的僧徒。
[6] 赓：继续，连续。

山中访王校书·其二

明·邵宝❶

连阴晓为北风开,春入山中第一回。
亭上远天须卷幔❷,槛前新水欲浮杯❸。
校书❹客避参军辟,问字❺人传别驾来。
明日更邀朱趣玉,黄公涧❻畔踏苍苔。

❶ 邵宝(1460—1527),字国贤,号二泉,人称"二泉先生",直隶无锡县(今江苏无锡)人。明代学者、藏书家。成化二十年(1484年)进士,历任户部员外郎、江西提学副使、浙江右布政使、湖广左布政使、都察院右副都御史、户部侍郎等。工诗文,善书法,有《漕政举要》《容春堂集》等。
❷ 卷幔:将帘子卷起。
❸ 浮杯:古代每逢三月上旬的巳日集会,人们在水渠旁,于上流放置酒杯,任其飘浮,停在谁的面前,谁即取饮,称为"浮杯",也叫"流觞"。此处指饮酒。
❹ 校书:与参军、别驾同为官职名。
❺ 问字:比喻向人请教学问。
❻ 黄公涧:在今无锡惠山古镇景区内,位于天下第二泉以南百米许之惠山东麓,相传战国末年春申君黄歇于此涧饮马而名,又名春申涧,是无锡观瀑的著名胜景。

游惠山

明·文徵明

几度扁舟过惠山,空瞻紫翠❶负跻攀❷。
今日坐探龙头水,身在前番紫翠间。

❶ 紫翠:指惠山的美丽景色。
❷ 跻(jī)攀:指攀登。

煮茶

明·文徵明

绢封阳羡月❶，瓦缶❷惠山泉。
至味心难忘，闲情手自煎。
地炉❸残雪后，禅榻❹晚风前。
为问❺贫陶谷❻，何如❼病玉川❽。

❶ 阳羡月：阳羡，今宜兴。阳羡月，指阳羡茶，是唐代贡茶，茶饼形状如明月。
❷ 瓦缶：小口大腹的瓦器，盛水用。
❸ 地炉：烧火的黑色土台子，用于温茶或温酒。
❹ 禅榻：坐禅时的席位，也称禅床。
❺ 为问：借问，请问。
❻ 陶谷：北宋大臣，宋初曾任礼部尚书、户部尚书等。其人善文章，善隶书，嗜茶，著有《清异录》二卷。《通鉴长编》载："宋陶谷得党太尉家姬，遇雪，谷取雪水烹茶，谓姬曰：'党家有此风味否？'对曰：'彼粗人，安有此？但能于销金帐下，浅斟低唱，饮羊羔儿酒耳。'"
❼ 何如：如何，怎么样。
❽ 玉川：唐代诗人卢仝，自号玉川子，喜爱饮茶。

元 倪瓒 《六君子图》 上海博物馆藏

祠堂篇

1. 春申君祠

春申君❶祠

唐·张继❷

春申祠宇❸空山里,古柏阴阴❹石泉水。
日暮江南无主人,弥令过客思公子。
萧条❺寒景傍山村,寂寞谁知楚相❻尊。
当时珠履三千客,赵使怀惭不敢言❼。

---

❶ 春申君:春秋战国时期楚国大臣黄歇的封号。黄歇(?—前238),楚国人,游学博闻,擅长辞辩。楚考烈王元年(前262年),以黄歇为相,赐其淮河以北十二县,封为春申君。黄歇明智忠信,宽厚爱人,以礼贤下士、招致宾客、辅佐治国而闻名于世,与魏国信陵君魏无忌、赵国平原君赵胜、齐国孟尝君田文并称为"战国四公子"。

❷ 张继(约715—约779),字懿孙,襄州(今湖北襄阳)人,唐代诗人。天宝十二年(753年)进士。大历中,以检校祠部员外郎为洪州(今江西省南昌市)盐铁判官。诗多登临纪行之作,清远自然,不事雕琢。

❸ 祠宇:祠堂。

❹ 阴阴:幽暗深邃的样子。

❺ 萧条:寂寞冷落,凋零。

❻ 楚相:春申君曾为楚相。

❼ 当时珠履二句:珠履,以珍珠装饰的鞋子,比喻幕僚生活奢华。《史记·春申君列传》载:"赵平原君使人於春申君,春申君舍之於上舍。赵使欲夸楚,为玳瑁簪,刀剑室以珠玉饰之,请命春申君客。春申君客三千馀人,其上客皆蹑珠履以见赵使,赵使大惭。"

朗诵 春申君祠

"惠"游祠堂

2. 陆子祠

题陆子泉上祠堂
宋·杨万里

先生吃茶不吃肉,先生饮泉不饮酒。
饥寒祇❶忍七十年,万岁千秋名不朽。
惠泉遂名陆子泉,泉与陆子名俱传。
一瓣佛香炷遗像,几多衲子❷拜茶仙。
麒麟图画冷似铁,凌烟冠剑❸消如雪。
惠山成尘惠泉竭,陆子祠堂始应歇,
山上泉中一轮月。

❶ 祇(zhī):表示恭敬。
❷ 衲子:指僧侣。
❸ 冠剑:古代官员戴冠佩剑,后指官员或官职。

3. 李忠定公祠

新晴出郊之❶惠山
明·邵宝

步出西郊见暮春,树头红尽绿初匀。
上方❷下界❸无游女,北坞南冈有逸人。
山色倍增今雨碧,泉声转入近池真。
竹根处处惊雷动,忠定祠❹前数箨鳞❺。

❶ 之:到,至,去。
❷ 上方:天界。
❸ 下界:指人间。
❹ 忠定祠:即李忠定公祠,在无锡市惠山寺日月池旁,为纪念宋代抗金名臣李纲而建。李纲(1083—1140),字伯纪,号梁溪先生,祖籍福建邵武,出生于江苏无锡。宋代官员、抗金名臣、学者。徽宗政和二年(1112年)进士。历任太常少卿、兵部侍郎、东京留守、亲征行营使、尚书左仆射兼门下侍郎等。力主抗金,扶掖宗泽等名将。卒谥"忠定"。工诗文,亦能词,有《梁溪全集》。
❺ 箨(tuò)鳞:箨,竹皮、笋壳。箨鳞,指竹笋的外皮。

朗诵 新晴出郊之惠山

4.顾洞阳公祠

谒先师顾洞阳公祠①
明·海瑞②

两朝③崇祀④庙谟⑤新，抗疏⑥名传骨鲠臣⑦。
志矢回天曾扣马⑧，功同浴日再批鳞⑨。
三生不改冰霜操，万死仍留社稷身。
世德⑩尚馀清白在，承家⑪还见有麒麟。

朗诵 谒先师顾洞阳公祠

① 顾可久（1482—1561），字舆新，号前山，别号洞阳，南直隶无锡（今江苏无锡）人。明正德九年（1514年）进士，官至广东按察司副使。为官耿直敢谏，曾两遭廷杖，是明代有名的刚直之臣。隆庆三年（1569年），应天巡抚海瑞奏请朝廷并捐俸，于无锡惠山寺塘泾建造顾可久祠，次年落成。万历元年（1573年），海瑞亲临无锡谒祠，并作《谒先师顾洞阳公祠》诗，此诗后由顾可久的后裔、清代官吏、书法家顾光旭书写并刻成石碑。

② 海瑞（1514—1587），字汝贤，号刚峰，海南琼山（今海口市）人。明代著名清官。海瑞一生，经历了正德、嘉靖、隆庆、万历四朝。他打击豪强，疏浚河道，修筑水利工程，力主严惩贪官污吏，禁止徇私受贿，并推行一条鞭法，强令贪官污吏退田还民，遂有"海青天"之誉。万历十五年（1587年），海瑞病死于南京官邸。赠太子太保，谥"忠介"。海瑞死后，关于他的传说故事，民间广为流传。

③ 两朝：顾可久曾历仕明正德、嘉靖两朝。
④ 崇祀：尊崇祭祀。
⑤ 庙谟：朝廷的重大决策和谋略。
⑥ 抗疏：上奏章直言其事。
⑦ 骨鲠臣：骨鲠，比喻有骨气、刚直。骨鲠之臣，指刚正忠直的官员。
⑧ 扣马：拉住马不使行进，以"扣马"为直谏之典。
⑨ 批鳞：古人以龙比喻君主，传说龙喉下有逆鳞径尺，触之必怒而杀人。后遂以"批鳞"指敢于直言犯上。
⑩ 世德：祖宗世代的德行。
⑪ 承家：承继家业。

5. 华宝祠

华宝①祠

明·秦瀿

周孔②去来人道③弱，悠然见子表南齐④。
终身父命难违背，万古天心岂缪迷⑤。
青简⑥孝名垂宇宙，白头遗像照山溪。
舜之不告⑦缘无后，若解行权⑧也可妻。

① 华宝：古代著名孝子。《南史》立传说："晋陵无锡人也。父豪，晋义熙末，戍长安，宝年八岁。临行谓宝曰：'须我还，当为汝上头。'长安陷，宝年至七十不婚冠。或问之，宝辄号恸弥日，不忍答也。"
② 周孔：中国古代两位圣人周公和孔子的合称。
③ 人道：人伦，指社会的伦理关系。
④ 南齐：南北朝时期南朝的第二个朝代。
⑤ 缪迷：缪，错误；迷，迷惑。
⑥ 青简：竹简，古代用以书写的狭长竹片。借指青史、史书。
⑦ 舜之不告：引用了舜帝不告而娶的故事，说明了在特定情况下，适当的变通也是可以接受的，但前提是不能违背根本的原则。
⑧ 行权：改变常规，权宜行事。

元 倪瓒 《疏林图》 日本大阪市立美术馆藏

6. 张中丞庙

明月逐人来❶·惠山山麓谒睢阳祠❷
清·陈维崧❸

坏廊径仄，哀湍响激。

松杉外、层层夜色。

悲歌南八❹，箭着浮图甓❺。

铁像❻贺兰苔涩。

斟得一杯，黛沈❼几瓯❽茗汁。

依稀见、云旗下食。

恰逢泓底，龙啸潭风急。

又认戍楼❾闻笛❿。

❶ 词牌名，宋代词人李持正所创。
❷ 睢阳祠：即张中丞庙，在今无锡惠山古镇内惠山直街120号，民间俗称"大老爷殿"，是祀唐"安史之乱"时，死守睢阳而献身的御史中丞张巡而建。现建筑为清同治八年（1869年）邑人集资修建。庙貌庄严，为无锡市保存较完整的古建筑之一。
❸ 陈维崧（1625—1682），字其年，号迦陵，南直隶常州府宜兴县（今江苏宜兴）人，明末清初词人、骈文家，"江左三凤凰"之一。少负文名，明亡后，科举不第。康熙十八年（1679年），举博学鸿词科，授官翰林院检讨，任《明史》纂修官。工骈文，最工词，负盛名，为阳羡词派宗主，与浙派词首领朱彝尊并称。著有《两晋南北史集珍》《湖海楼诗文词全集》《陈迦陵文集》《迦陵词》。
❹ 南八：南霁云，唐代名将。因其行八，故称南八。安史之乱时，作为张巡的部将，协助守卫睢阳。至德二年（757年），睢阳被安庆绪部将尹子奇包围，南霁云到临淮求救。河南节度使贺兰进明认为睢阳必失，出兵无益，拒绝出兵。南霁云怒断一指，然后离去。由于寡不敌众，睢阳城破，诸将被俘，南霁云等人宁死不降，壮烈牺牲。
❺ 箭着浮图甓（pì）：浮图，佛塔。甓，砖。韩愈《张中丞传后叙》："云知贺兰终无为云出师意，即驰去；将出城，抽矢射佛寺浮图，矢着其上砖半箭。曰：'吾归破贼，必灭贺兰！此矢所以志也。'"
❻ 铁像：张中丞庙殿外原有贺兰进明跪像，供民众鞭笞，后致该跪像被推倒损坏。现有清同治年间铸造的贺兰进明两只铁脚，作长跪状，供人们践踏。
❼ 沈：沉。
❽ 瓯（ōu）：碗，杯。
❾ 戍楼：瞭望台，古时军士用来远望的高楼。
❿ 闻笛：古人常用笛声意象来表现戍边时凄婉思念之意。张巡守睢阳时，作有《闻笛》一诗。

7. 惠山寺

忆题惠山寺书堂
唐·李绅

故山一别光阴改，秋露清风岁月多。
松下壮心❶年少去，池边衰影老人过。
白云生灭❷依岩岫❸，青桂❹荣枯托薜萝❺。
惟有此身长是客，又驱旌旆❻寄烟波。

❶ 壮心：豪壮的志愿，壮志。
❷ 生灭：这里指云的起灭。
❸ 岩岫：峰峦。
❹ 青桂：桂树。桂树常绿，所以称青桂。
❺ 薜萝：薜荔和女萝，都是野生植物，常常攀缘于山野林木或屋壁之上。
❻ 旌旆（pèi）：旗帜。

题惠山寺
*唐·张祜*❶

旧宅人何在，空门客自过。
泉声到池尽，山❷色上楼多。
小洞生❸斜竹，重阶❹夹细❺莎。
殷勤❻望❼城市，云水暮钟和。

❶ 张祜（约792—约853），字承吉，清河（今属河北邢台）人，一说南阳（今属河南）人。初寓居苏州。元和、长庆中，漫游大河南北及江南各地，后至长安。有《张承吉文集》十卷行世。
❷ 山：一作"月"。
❸ 生：一作"穿"。
❹ 重阶：层层台阶。
❺ 细：一作"瘦"。
❻ 殷勤：频繁；反复。
❼ 望：一作"入"。

朗诵 题惠山寺

惠山听松庵

唐·皮日休

千叶莲花❶旧有香，半山金刹❷照方塘❸。
殿❹前日暮高风❺起，松子声声打石床❻。

无锡惠山寺

宋·苏舜钦❶

寺古名传唐相❷诗，三伏奔迸❸予何之❹。
　云山相照翠会合，殿阁对走凉参差。
　清泉绝无一尘染，长松自是拔俗姿。
二边羌胡❺日斗格❻，释子❼宴坐❽殊不知。

---

❶ 千叶莲花：神话传说中的一种多瓣莲花。相传南朝高僧僧显在惠山栽植，后来僧显服食了金莲，坐化成仙。唐代陆羽《游惠山寺记》载："惠山，古华山也……华山上有方池，池中生千叶莲花，服之羽化。"

❷ 金刹：庙宇，指惠山寺。

❸ 方塘：指开凿于南朝的金莲池。

❹ 殿：指惠山寺大同殿。陆羽《游惠山寺记》称："池上有大同殿，以梁大同年置因名之"。

❺ 高风：此处指高空之风，即天风。

❻ 石床：全称"听松石床"，一名"听松石"。原在惠山寺大殿月台东北，今公园古银杏树旁听松亭内。

---

❶ 苏舜钦（1008—1048），字子美，开封（今属河南）人，曾祖父由梓州铜山（今四川中江）迁至开封。景祐元年（1034年）进士及第，曾任县令、大理评事、集贤校理等职。北宋著名文学家，工诗文，善书法。他与梅尧臣齐名，人称"苏梅"。有《苏舜钦集》存世。

❷ 唐相：指中唐诗人李绅，他曾任尚书右仆射，早年曾在惠山读书。他的《悯农》诗家喻户晓。元代学者王仁辅在《无锡县志》中说："李相书堂在惠山，小径紫纤，有堂三楹，中绘唐李绅像。绅未遇时，常读书惠山。"

❸ 奔迸：奔涌。

❹ 何之：往哪里去。

❺ 羌胡：指胡人和羌人。泛指古代西北地区的游牧民族。

❻ 斗格：格斗，搏斗。指边疆烽火不熄，战斗不止。

❼ 释子：指僧徒。因出家人均舍本姓，随佛祖释迦姓，故称释子。

❽ 宴坐：安坐，闲坐。

"惠"游祠堂

惠山诗
元·王仁辅[1]

红杜[2]溪边舣[3]小舟，青莲宇内作清游。
土花绣碧淡如画，岚翠泼云浓欲流。
短李[4]清风存古意，大苏团月[5]洗春愁。
摩挲泉石舒长啸，未羡神仙十二楼[6]。

[1] 王仁辅，字文友，巩昌（今甘肃省陇西县）人。两娶皆吴人，故多知吴中山水人物，作《无锡县志》二十八卷，侨居无锡梅里乡衹陀村（今属江苏省无锡市）。无子，门人倪瓒赡之终其身，死为之服址丧而葬。
[2] 红杜：一种攀援灌木。
[3] 舣：停船靠岸。
[4] 短李：指唐代诗人李绅，因其诗短小精悍，便有个"短李"的外号。
[5] 大苏团月：大苏，指苏轼。大苏团月，指苏轼曾有诗云"独携天上小团月，来试人间第二泉"。
[6] 十二楼：指神话传说中的仙人居处。

吴门[1]归入惠山寺
明·邹迪光[2]

胜游不惜屡，余兴尚淋漓。
竹路青相借，花宫翠乱披。
酒阑[3]留月住，曲半受风吹。
为问梁溪夜，何如吴苑[4]时。

[1] 吴门：指苏州。
[2] 邹迪光（1550—1626），字彦吉，号愚谷，直隶常州府无锡县（今江苏无锡）人。万历二年（1574年）进士，官至湖广提学副使。万历十七年（1589年），罢官归里，在惠山下筑愚公谷，多与文士觞咏其间，极园亭歌舞之胜。工诗画，有《郁仪楼集》《调象庵集》《石语斋集》《文府滑稽》等。
[3] 酒阑：宴饮过半，即将结束之时。
[4] 吴苑：吴地的苑囿，借指苏州。

8.寄畅园

寄畅园二十咏·其一（嘉树堂）

明·秦燿❶

嘉木❷围清流，草堂置其上。
周遭林樾❸深，倒影池中漾。

❶ 秦燿（1544—1604），字道明，号舜峰，直隶无锡县（江苏无锡）人。明隆庆五年（1571年）进士，累官至都察院右副都御史，巡抚湖广，人称"秦中丞"。后被诬解职归家。遂重修族内转传下来的别墅园林"凤谷行窝"，以王羲之诗"寄畅山水阴"句中的"寄畅"二字命名，改名"寄畅园"，优游其间十三年。秦燿为所改建的寄畅园，构列二十景，他逐景赋诗，以诗言志，总称《寄畅园二十咏》。
❷ 嘉木：美好的树木。
❸ 林樾（yuè）：林木。

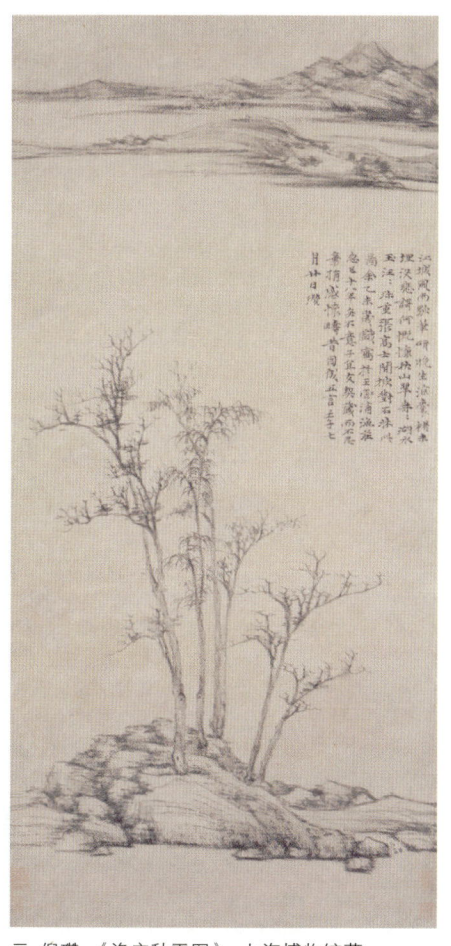

元 倪瓒 《渔庄秋霁图》 上海博物馆藏

寄畅园二十咏·其九（卧云堂）
明·秦燿

白云❶已出岫，复此还山谷。
幽人卧其间，常抱白云宿。

❶ 白云：以白云喻园主寄情山水。卧云堂系寄畅园的主体建筑，始建于明万历年间，坐西朝东，前后两造，中隔天井。其得名源于所处位置东枕锡山，西倚惠山，有白云生山中，"苍生望为霖雨者乎"之意。该堂是康熙、乾隆巡幸寄畅园时的接驾处，因皇帝赐额，又名御书碑厅。曹雪芹祖父曹寅也在该堂题过诗，后毁于咸丰十年（1860年）兵火。2000年重建第一进。

秦留仙❶寄畅园三咏·其一❷
清·吴伟业❸

黛色常疑雨，溪堂正早秋。
乱山来众响，倒景漾中流。
似有一帆至，何因半塔❹留。
眼前通妙理，斜日在峰头。

❶ 秦留仙：秦松龄（1637—1714），字汉石，又字次椒，号留仙，又号对岩。无锡人。顺治十二年（1655年）进士。工诗，有《苍岘山人集》。

❷ 又题作：山池塔影。

❸ 吴伟业（1609—1672），字骏公，号梅村，别署鹿樵生、灌隐主人、大云道人，江苏太仓人。明崇祯四年（1631年）进士，曾任翰林院编修、左庶子等职。后仕清，曾任国子监祭酒等职。顺治十三年（1656年），因母丧南归，隐居于乡，不再出仕。吴伟业善诗词，其诗多写哀时伤事的题材，情致悠然，内容深婉，尤以七言歌行为著，后人称为"梅村体"。与钱谦益、龚鼎孳并称"江左三大家"，为娄东诗派开创者。著有《梅村家藏稿》《梅村诗馀》等。

❹ 塔：指龙光塔，位于江苏省无锡市惠山古镇景区锡惠名胜区内，处于锡山山顶，始建于明万历二年（1574年），几经修葺。龙光塔是无锡古代科举兴旺的象征，被无锡人奉为无锡文风"风水塔"，是独特的城市地理标志。

第三篇　诗画梁溪

秦园
清·赵翼[1]

看竹何须主，林扃[2]曲折通。
人行山翠里，秋在水声中。
邱壑[3]因天巧，松杉有古风。
我无书可卖，敢问尔家东。

[1] 赵翼（1729—1814），字耘崧，一字云崧，号瓯北，别号三半老人，常州府阳湖县(今江苏常州)人，清代著名史学家、诗人、文学家。乾隆二十六年（1761年）进士，授编修，历任广西镇安知府、广东广州知府等职，官至贵州贵西兵备道。后辞官，主讲于安定书院。诗与袁枚、蒋士铨齐名，并称为"乾隆三大家"。有《廿二史札记》《陔余丛考》《瓯北诗话》《檐曝杂记》《皇朝武功纪盛》等。

[2] 扃（jiōng）：门，门户。

[3] 邱壑：深山与幽壑，借指风景幽美之地。

惠山秦氏园
清·魏源[1]

屋借惠山屏[2]，径随惠山转。
谁道园中湖[3]，却涵园外巘[4]。

元　倪瓒　《紫芝山房图》　台北故宫博物院藏

[1] 魏源（1794—1857），原名远达，字汉士，后字默深（又作墨生），号良图，湖南邵阳人，清末思想家、政治家、文学家。道光二十五年（1845年）进士，官至高邮知州。治学以经世致用为宗旨，与龚自珍齐名。魏源是近代中国"睁眼看世界"的文人之一。鸦片战争后作《海国图志》，倡"师夷长技以制夷"说。晚年弃官潜心著述，有《古微堂诗文集》《圣武记》《元史新编》《老子本义》等。

[2] 屋借惠山屏：指寄畅园的造园手法，其借惠山景入园。

[3] 园中湖：指园中的人工湖锦汇漪，位于寄畅园的中心，山影、塔影、亭影、树影、树影、花影、鸟影，尽汇池中。池北土山，乔柯灌木，与惠山山峰连成一气；而在嘉树堂向东看，又见"山池塔影"，将锡山龙光塔借入园中，成为借景的楷模。

[4] 巘（yǎn）：指山。

寄畅园
清·爱新觉罗·弘历

轻棹[1]沿寻曲水湾，秦园寄畅暂偷闲。
无多[2]台榭[3]乔柯[4]古，不尽烟霞飞瀑潺。
近族[5]九人年六百，耆英[6]高会[7]胜香山。
松风水月[8]垂宸藻[9]，昔日卷阿[10]想像间。

[1] 轻棹：指小船。
[2] 无多：没有多少。
[3] 台榭：台和榭，泛指楼台等建筑物。
[4] 乔柯：高枝。
[5] 近族：血统关系较近的宗族。秦氏族人迎驾时，几位代表年龄合为600余岁，故有此句。
[6] 耆英：年老德高之人。
[7] 高会：盛大的聚会。
[8] 松风水月：像松风那样清朗，似水月那样明洁。喻人品高洁。
[9] 宸藻：指帝王的诗文。
[10] 卷阿：《大雅·卷阿》是中国古代第一部诗歌总集《诗经》中的一首诗。

再题寄畅园
清·爱新觉罗·弘历

雨余[1]山滴翠，春暮卉争芳。
搴薜[2]盘云径，披松渡石梁[3]。
鸣湍[4]空尘意，列岫[5]澹烟光。
更许传佳话，遮留诗债偿。

[1] 雨余：即雨后。
[2] 搴（qiān）薜：搴，拔取，采摘；薜，指薜荔。
[3] 石梁：石桥。
[4] 鸣湍：指急流。
[5] 列岫：指排列耸立的山峦。

游寄畅园题句
清·爱新觉罗·弘历

烟溪又复泛梁鸿，路侧名园曲折通。
新景林岚六尘[1]表，昔游岁月寸心中。
清泉白石自仙境，玉竹冰梅总化工[2]。
小憩便当移跸[3]去，一声定磬下花宫[4]。

[1] 六尘：佛教称色、声、香、味、触、法六境为六尘。
[2] 化工：自然造化而成。
[3] 移跸：即移驾。
[4] 花宫：指佛寺。

介如峰

清 · 爱新觉罗 · 弘历

寄畅园中一峰亭亭独立，旧名美人石，以其弗称，因易之，而系以诗。

一峰卓立殊昂藏❶，恰有古桧森其旁。
视之颇具丈夫气，谁欤❷号以巾帼行。
设❸云妙喻方子美❹，徒观更匪❺修竹倚❻。
亭亭戌削❼则不无，姗姗阎易❽非所拟。
率与易名曰介如，长言不足因成图。
正言辨物❾得揭揽❿，惠麓梁溪永静娱。

❶ 昂藏：仪表雄伟、气宇不凡的样子。
❷ 欤：语气助词，表示疑问语气。
❸ 设：假如。
❹ 子美：指杜甫，字子美。
❺ 匪：不是。
❻ 修竹倚：杜甫有诗《佳人》，其中有"天寒翠袖薄，日暮倚修竹。"之句。
❼ 戌削：形容衣服裁制合体。与下句"阎易"均出自《上林赋》："曳独茧之褕袣，眇阎易以恤削。"
❽ 阎易：指衣长的样子。
❾ 正言辨物：通过正确的言语来辨别事物的种类和情况，以达到名实相符的目的。
❿ 揭（qiè）揽：威武雄壮，有聚集勇武之气的意思。

元 倪瓒 《幽涧寒松图》 北京故宫博物院藏

参考文献

[1] 夏泉生，罗根兄. 无锡惠山祠堂群［M］. 长春：时代文艺出版社，2003：275.

[2] 孙志亮. 亲历者说：无锡山水城市建设［M］. 北京：清华大学出版社，2020：217.

[3] 无锡祠堂文化研究会. 祠堂博览［内部刊物］(2004—2021年). 无锡：无锡祠堂文化研究会.

[4] 傅德元. 无锡淮湘昭忠祠的修建与淮军历史遗迹新探：以无锡及全国4所淮军昭忠祠为中心的研究［J］. 白鹿塬论丛，2022,(00)：276-297.

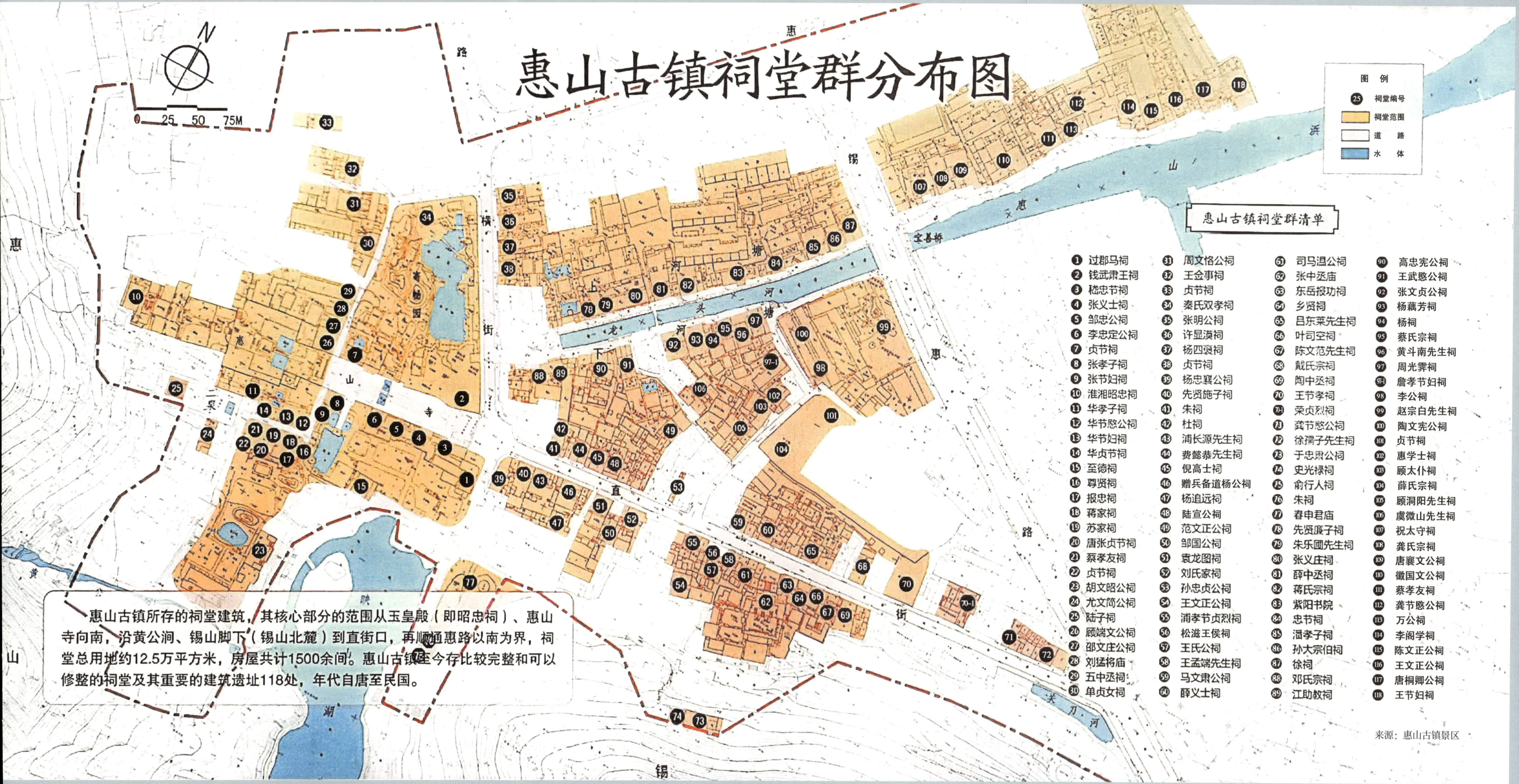

惠山古镇祠堂群分布图

图例
- ㉕ 祠堂编号
- 祠堂范围
- 道路
- 水体

惠山古镇所存的祠堂建筑，其核心部分的范围从玉皇殿（即昭忠祠）、惠山寺向南，沿黄公涧、锡山脚下（锡山北麓）到直街口，再顺通惠路以南为界，祠堂总用地约12.5万平方米，房屋共计1500余间。惠山古镇至今存比较完整和可以修整的祠堂及其重要的建筑遗址118处，年代自唐至民国。

惠山古镇祠堂群清单

❶ 过郡马祠	㉛ 周文恪公祠	61 司马温公祠	90 高忠宪公祠
❷ 钱武肃王祠	㉜ 王金事祠	62 张中丞庙	91 王武愍公祠
❸ 嵇忠节祠	㉝ 贞节祠	63 东岳报功祠	92 张文贞公祠
❹ 张义士祠	㉞ 秦氏双孝祠	64 乡贤祠	93 杨藕芳祠
❺ 邹忠公祠	㉟ 张明公祠	65 吕东莱先生祠	94 杨祠
❻ 李忠定公祠	㊱ 许显谟祠	66 叶司空祠	95 蔡氏宗祠
❼ 贞节祠	㊲ 杨四贤祠	67 陈文范先生祠	96 黄斗南先生祠
❽ 张孝子祠	㊳ 贞节祠	68 戴氏宗祠	97 周光霁祠
❾ 张节妇祠	㊴ 杨忠襄公祠	69 陶中丞祠	97-1 詹孝节妇祠
❿ 淮湘昭忠祠	㊵ 先贤施子祠	70 王节孝祠	98 李公祠
⓫ 华孝子祠	㊶ 朱祠	70-1 荣贞烈祠	99 赵宗白先生祠
⓬ 华节愍公祠	㊷ 杜祠	71 龚节愍公祠	100 陶文宪公祠
⓭ 华节妇祠	㊸ 浦长源先生祠	72 徐孺子先生祠	101 贞节祠
⓮ 华贞节祠	㊹ 费懿恭先生祠	73 于忠肃公祠	102 惠学士祠
⓯ 至德祠	㊺ 倪高士祠	74 史光禄祠	103 顾太仆祠
⓰ 尊贤祠	㊻ 赠兵备道杨公祠	75 俞行人祠	104 薛氏宗祠
⓱ 报忠祠	㊼ 杨追远祠	76 朱祠	105 顾洞阳先生祠
⓲ 蒋家祠	㊽ 陆宣公祠	77 春申君庙	106 虞微山先生祠
⓳ 苏家祠	㊾ 范文正公祠	78 先贤庳子祠	107 祝太守祠
⓴ 唐张贞节祠	50 邹国公祠	79 朱乐圃先生祠	108 龚氏宗祠
㉑ 蔡孝友祠	51 袁龙图祠	80 张义庄祠	109 唐襄文公祠
㉒ 贞节祠	52 刘氏家祠	81 薛中丞祠	110 徽国文公祠
㉓ 胡文昭公祠	53 孙忠贞公祠	82 蒋氏宗祠	111 蔡孝友祠
㉔ 尤文简公祠	54 王文正公祠	83 紫阳书院	112 龚节愍公祠
㉕ 陆子祠	55 浦孝节贞烈祠	84 忠节祠	113 万公祠
㉖ 顾端文公祠	56 松滋王侯祠	85 温孝子祠	114 李阁学祠
㉗ 邵文庄公祠	57 王氏公祠	86 孙大宗伯祠	115 陈文正公祠
㉘ 刘猛将庙	58 王孟端先生祠	87 徐祠	116 王文正公祠
㉙ 五中丞祠	59 马文肃公祠	88 邓氏宗祠	117 唐桐卿公祠
㉚ 单贞女祠	60 薛义士祠	89 江助教祠	118 王节妇祠

来源：惠山古镇景区